*Lex Orandi Series*

# The Sacrament of Reconciliation

*Lex Orandi* Series

John D. Laurance, S.J.
Editor

# The Sacrament of Reconciliation

David M. Coffey

**THE LITURGICAL PRESS**
Collegeville, Minnesota

www.litpress.org

Cover design by Greg Becker.

Cover illustration: Alberto Arnoldi (fl. 1351–64). Confession. Museo dell'Opera del Duomo, Florence, Italy. Scala/Art Resource, New York. Used with permission.

Excerpts from the English translation of *Rite of Penance* © 1974, International Committee on English in the Liturgy, Inc. (ICEL); excerpts from the English translation of *Pastoral Care of the Sick* © 1982, ICEL. All rights reserved.

Scripture quotations are from the Revised Standard Version of the Bible, © 1946, 1952, and 1971 by the Division of Christian Education of the National Council of the Churches of Christ in the U.S.A., and from the New Revised Standard Version of the Bible, copyright 1989 by the Division of Christian Education of the National Council of the Churches of Christ in the U.S.A. Used by permission. All rights reserved.

1     2     3     4     5     6     7     8

**Library of Congress Cataloging-in-Publication Data**

Coffey, David M.
 The Sacrament of reconciliation / David Coffey.
  p. cm.—(Lex orandi series)
 Includes bibliographical references and index.
 ISBN 0-8146-2519-3 (alk. paper)
  1. Confession—Catholic Church. 2. Catholic Church—Doctrines.
 3. Confession (Liturgy)—Catholic Church. 4. Catholic Church—Liturgy—
Theology. 5. Catholic Church. Ordo paenitentiae. I. Title. II. Series.

BX2265.3 .C64 2001
264'.02086—dc21

00-067166

To the memory of Fr. Paul Groh,
pastor of the parish of St. Hildegard, Munich-Pasing, 1961–1987

# Contents

# Preface to the *Lex Orandi* Series

The theology of the seven sacraments prevalent in the Catholic Church through most of the second millennium interpreted those rites more as sacred objects to be *passively* received than as *active* participations in Christ's paschal mystery. And their meaning was to be derived, not from the shape of their liturgical celebration, but from the Church's official teaching, teaching typically occasioned by historical challenges to her faith. Whereas in patristic times Church writers expounded the theology of the sacraments from the rites themselves, with the later expansion of Christianity into central Europe confidence waned that the form and enactment of the liturgy in any way *manifested* the Mystery it contained. As the *Adoro Te Devote,* a medieval hymn on the Church's use of bread in the Eucharistic liturgy, puts it, "Seeing, tasting, touching are in Thee deceived."

In recent times, however, there has been a kind of "Copernican revolution" in sacramental theology. Not only have sacraments come to be understood as actions of God *and* the Church, the truth of the ancient adage, *"lex orandi, lex credendi"* (how the Church prays expresses what she believes), has also been seen in a new light. Theologians have come to realize that, if all Church dogma is rooted ultimately in her faith-experience of God, so too must her understanding of the sacraments derive from her experience of their liturgical celebration. Sacraments, too, must *manifest* the Mystery they contain. Consequently, in the tradition of ancient mystagogies, "liturgical theology"—that is, God's word ("first theology") to the Church through her worship—has come to be understood, along with official Church teaching, as an indispensable source for sacramental theology. And sacramental theology itself has returned to its proper place within a larger "theology of liturgy." The works of theologians such as Guardini, Casel, Rahner, Schmemann, Kilmartin, and Chauvet mark various stages in this historical development.

Although much has been written on the role of the celebrating Church, up until now no set of studies on all seven sacraments that we know of has attempted to exegete their meaning primarily from their typical celebrations. The aim of this present series, then, is precisely to investigate the sacraments as liturgical events in order to discover in them the faith understanding of Christian life of which they are both the source and the summit (SC, 10).

However, since the theology of liturgy is but one part of the whole of systematic theology, liturgical events can be adequately interpreted as witnesses to the Church's faith only in light of the other ways she experiences God's word. Accordingly, individual volumes in this series analyze typical experiences of the rites they cover against the background of the rest of the Church's traditional life and teaching, and they do so guided by the unique synthesis of that tradition that each author as theologian brings to the work. To do anything less would be to fail in the task of theology. On occasion, then, authors will offer their own critique, whether of the rites themselves or of how they have experienced their celebration, doing so on the basis of other theological sources as well (including, for example, the official instructions introducing each rite).

Sacraments as liturgical *events* are not understood by most theologians today as they once were, that is, as so-called "moments of consecration" (the "This is my Body"; the pouring of water "in the name of the Father"; etc.). Rather, similar to how Aristotle's *Poetics* envisions Greek tragedies, sacraments are seen as events extended through time, having beginnings, middles, and ends. True, as protracted events they include indispensable high points, but separated off from the whole liturgical celebration those key moments, at least in the short run, lose much of their intelligibility and intensity and, therefore, of their efficacy as well (see SC, 14). Accordingly, volumes in this series attempt to study each sacrament as it unfolds through its total performance, discerning especially its basic structure and how various elements contribute to its overall faith meaning.

The motivating purpose of this new series on the sacraments is ultimately a pastoral one: to help foster the fuller liturgical participation called for by Vatican II, and not necessarily to "break new ground" in sacramental theology. The readership envisioned by the series, therefore, is a broad one, not confined just to liturgical experts. Individual volumes presuppose only a beginner's familiarity with Christian theology, such as that possessed by university upper-level undergraduate and master's level students.

Finally, the rites studied in this series are those of the Roman Rite of the Catholic Church in use today. As valuable as a comparison of various Christian liturgies would be, no one series can do everything. At the same time, it is hoped that efforts made here toward understanding the Roman Rite might help inspire other, more explicitly ecumenical studies of Christian liturgy.

John D. Laurance, S.J.
Marquette University

# Preface

In keeping with the general policy of the *Lex Orandi* series, of which this book forms part, this study of the sacrament of reconciliation is based on the current liturgy as laid down in *The Rite of Penance* (hereafter RP), published in English in 1975 at the behest of the National Conference of Catholic Bishops.[1] The previous year the Roman Congregation for Divine Worship had issued the *Ordo Paenitentiae* ("order of penance"), the "typical" Latin edition, which it amended just one month later.[2] RP is the official English translation of the amended text. By means of the *Ordo* and its various vernacular translations, including RP, there was carried out the directive of the Second Vatican Council that "the rite and formulas of Penance are to be revised so that they more clearly express both the nature and effect of the sacrament."[3] For the present book the *Lex Orandi* policy means that RP determines its subject matter and constitutes its first point of reference. But the book is intended as a theology, and not just as a commentary on RP. Where necessary, therefore, it will appeal to the original sources, Scripture and tradition, to the magisterium, and to other theology. It will also move beyond texts, and look to the practice of the Church, to the liturgy as it is regulated, celebrated, and experienced. In this way we hope to derive a theology of the sacrament of reconciliation truly based on, and inspired by, the liturgy. It will be molded by two contextual factors: the crisis that the sacrament is currently undergoing in the developed nations of the West, and the restrictions imposed by Rome on the "third rite," the most communal of the three forms of the sacrament approved by RP.

Since the sacrament exists for the forgiveness of postbaptismal sin, chapter 1 is devoted to a theology of sin. Here I identify what is in my view the main theological cause at the heart of the present crisis, namely a serious and widespread confusion about the nature of sin. Only partly is this explained by a lack of necessary education. The official doctrine of sin is also at fault. This is not to suggest that it is wrong, but it *is* to suggest that it is inadequate. It has not kept pace with developments that have taken place in theology and the social sciences, and until this situation is remedied little hope of overcoming the crisis can be entertained. Chapter 2 is about the Church's ministry of reconciliation, and specifically about the development of the sacrament. This chapter provides both essential knowledge and a response to the widely held view that one does not need to turn to the Church in order to obtain forgiveness from God for sin. Chapter 3 examines the four parts of the sacrament: contrition, confession, absolution, and the prescribed work of penance. The investigation here undertaken suggests theological limits to what might be possible in future reforms of the sacrament. In chapter 4 the three sacramental rites and the nonsacramental service set down by RP are examined in detail. Finally, in chapter 5, on the basis of the entire preceding study, some prognostications about the future of the sacrament are offered.

When the *Ordo* and RP were first published, the canon law in force was still the preconciliar one of 1917. As was to be expected, the *Ordo* (and RP) in many places reflected this body of law. But in 1983 there appeared the new Code of Canon Law, revised in accordance with the teachings of the Second Vatican Council. This meant that certain sections of RP itself now needed to be revised. The way in which this was done was by a "particular decree" *(decretum particulare)* of the Congregation for Divine Worship dated September 12, 1983.[4] This decree covered not just the sacrament of reconciliation but all liturgical changes to be made in the light of the new Code. Thus the other sacraments it dealt with were baptism, confirmation, anointing of the sick, and the Eucharist. Reconciliation is handled in section 8.[5] The method of the decree is simply to list the amendments to be incorporated "into new editions of the liturgical books." Strictly speaking, there is, however, no new "edition" of RP, but just a list of amendments to be made by publishers in printings undertaken after 1983. The articles of the main text of RP singled out by the decree for amendment are nos. 9, 12, 31–34, and 38–40, and in Appendix 1, no. 1. Further, the precise amendments to be made are spelled out. To my knowledge this directive has been carried out to date in English only in two publications, *The Rites of the Catholic Church*[6] and *Catholic Rites Today*,[7] neither of which makes any reference to the decree according to which the revisions are made.

When I discovered the existence of the "particular decree" (no mean feat in itself), I was faced with a decision. Should I take as my text of RP that contained in one or other of the publications mentioned above, or should I take the original RP, acknowledge the decree, and consider the canonical amendments separately? On reflection I opted for the latter course. First, the amended text does not claim to be, and should not be treated as, a second edition. It merely introduces the changes prescribed by the decree (and does so without comment). Secondly, it seemed sounder methodologically to deal with matters historically, that is, to treat the original RP as a legitimate text in its own right, and then the changes to be made to it in the light of the new canon law and the decree. Whether the reader approves of this procedure or not, I have at least given here an account and an explanation of what I have done in this book.

A feature of RP calling for comment is its use of noninclusive language. For this, perhaps, it can be excused, since at the time of its publication there existed little awareness of inclusiveness as an issue. Regrettably, the same cannot be said for the *Catechism of the Catholic Church*. While I have endeavored to use inclusive language when speaking in my own voice, I have made no such attempt when citing texts that do not use it. To do so I would regard as methodologically unacceptable.

An immediate question arises as to the name of the sacrament. Traditionally it has been called the sacrament of penance, a name that has never been withdrawn. It reflects the Greek word *metanoia*, which is translated "penance" and denotes "change of heart" or repentance and thus encapsulates a fundamental element of the preaching of Jesus: "Now after John was arrested, Jesus came into Galilee, preaching the gospel of God, and saying, 'The time is fulfilled, and the kingdom of God is at hand; repent *[metanoeite]*, and believe in the gospel'" (Mark 1:14-15). Here repentance is presented as an essential element of faith in Jesus, the faith that gives access to the kingdom that he preached. To give oneself in faith to him and so enter the kingdom of his Father, one must turn away from sin. This is one facet of the meaning of the sacrament of baptism, the other being the gift of the Holy Spirit, that is, the gift that is the Spirit himself, as we learn from Peter's Pentecost day address (see Acts 2:38). The repentance/faith that leads to baptism with its concomitant gift of the Spirit is itself the work of the Spirit (see Acts 10:44-48). The Holy Spirit inspires faith, leads to baptism, and is poured out in abundance in the sacrament. But *metanoia*, still the work of the Spirit, is called for also in the lives of those who are already Christians, people who have already entered the kingdom and the Church. Thus, Paul, having admonished the Corinthians in his first letter to them, consoles them in the second, with these words: "As it is, I rejoice, not because you were grieved, but because you were grieved into repenting *[metanoia]*; for you felt a godly grief, so that you suffered no loss through us. For godly grief produces a repentance that leads to salvation and brings no regret, but worldly grief produces death" (2 Cor 7:9-10; see 2 Pet 3:9). It is for such people that the sacrament of penance exists, the sins committed before baptism being forgiven in baptism itself. In chapter 4 we shall hear Franco Sottocornola say that "penance" was the name of the sacrament in the ancient Church because its main component was deemed to be the penitential works through which the sinner expiated their guilt before God. It is not in this sense that the word is used today to designate the sacrament. Now the "sacrament of penance" means the "sacrament of repentance." There remain sound reasons to maintain this name in the sense indicated.

However, since the council it has become usual to refer to this sacrament as the sacrament of reconciliation. The council itself opened the way to this when it said:

> Those who approach the sacrament of Penance obtain pardon through God's mercy for the offense committed against him, and are, at the same time, reconciled with the church which they have wounded by their sins and which by charity, by example and by prayer labors for their conversion.[8]

In RP, in both the introductory decree of the Worship Congregation and the introduction properly so called, this theme is developed as reconciliation with God and the Church, though the relationship between these two dimensions of reconciliation is left unexplored. It is a question that we shall take up in chapters 1 and 2. However, "reconciliation" does not in all circumstances appear the best name for the sacrament. RP, in no. 7 b, endorses the practice of "devotional confession," that is, the confession only of "venial" or non-grave sins when there are no grave sins to confess. As these do not disrupt one's relationship with God or the Church, devotional confession must be said to effect reconciliation only in an analogous sense. But as non-grave sins call for repentance (though not as urgently as grave ones do), "penance" is always an appropriate name. There can be no forgiveness of sin, either in or outside the sacrament, without repentance. Penance, on the other hand, is what the sinner does, a human work, even though it is inspired and borne by the grace of God, while reconciliation is the action of God (and of Christ and the Church). But to balance this it should be said that neither does any other sacrament express by its name the action of God. Each expresses only what the individual person or the Church does. Clearly, there are sound reasons supporting both names. RP opted for "penance," though "reconciliation" has become more common today, probably because it emphasizes the action of God, Christ, and the Church. One thinks of the text of Paul in which he speaks of God "who through Christ reconciled us to himself and gave us the ministry of reconciliation" (2 Cor 5:18). In this book I shall refer to the sacrament as either "penance" or "reconciliation," according as the context would suggest. In chapter 3 we shall encounter the work of Clement Tierney. He showed evenhandedness on this matter, titling his book *The Sacrament of Penance and Reconciliation.*[9]

I wish to acknowledge with gratitude the generous help of the Rev. John D. Laurance, S.J., of Marquette University, the editor of the series; and also of Scott Celsor, of the same university, who devoted many laborious hours to the project. With a single exception, which is taken from the New Revised Standard Version (NRSV), biblical quotations throughout the book are from the Revised Standard Version (RSV). Full references to *Vatican II: The Basic Sixteen Documents*, edited by Austin Flannery, and *The Christian Faith in the Doctrinal Documents of the Catholic Church*, edited by Jacques Dupuis, the two reference works constantly referred to in this book, are given on p. xviii, note 3, and p. 28, note 4, respectively. Otherwise they are referred to simply as Flannery, and Dupuis, respectively.

**Notes, Preface**

[1] The International Committee on English in the Liturgy, trans., *The Rite of Penance* (Collegeville: The Liturgical Press, 1975).

[2] Sacred Congregation for Divine Worship, *Ordo Paenitentiae* (Rome: Vatican Press, 1974). See the reverse side of the title page for the historical details given above.

[3] Vatican II's Constitution on the Sacred Liturgy *(Sacrosanctum concilium)* no. 72, in Austin Flannery, ed., *Vatican Council II: The Basic Sixteen Documents: Constitutions, Decrees, Declarations: A Completely Revised Translation in Inclusive Language* (Northport, N.Y.: Costello, 1996) 141. Hereafter this volume will be referred to as Flannery.

[4] "Decretum quo Variationes in novas editiones Librorum liturgicorum, ad normam Codicis iuris canonici nuper promulgati, introducendae statuuntur," in Xaverius Ochoa, ed., *Leges Ecclesiae post Codicem iuris canonici editae,* vol. 6, Leges annis 1979–1985 editae (Rome: Ediurcla, 1987) n. 4997, cols. 8669–76.

[5] See ibid., "Section VIII: In Ordinem Paenitentiae," cols. 8673–74.

[6] International Commission on English in the Liturgy, *The Rites of the Catholic Church,* 2 vols. (Collegeville: The Liturgical Press, 1990). See "Rite of Penance," vol. 1, 517–629. Though this publication has been updated and modified, it makes no claim to being a second edition.

[7] Allan Bouley, ed., *Catholic Rites Today: Abridged Text for Students* (Collegeville: The Liturgical Press, 1992). See "Part 4: Rite of Penance," 393–428.

[8] Vatican II's Dogmatic Constitution on the Church *(Lumen gentium)* no. 11, Flannery, 15.

[9] Clement Tierney, *The Sacrament of Penance and Reconciliation* (New York: Costello, 1983).

# Abbreviations

AAS     *Acta Apostolicae Sedis.* Rome, 1909–pres.

DS     H. Denzinger and A. Schönmetzer, eds. *Enchiridion Symbolorum Definitionum et Declarationum.* 36th ed. Freiburg (Germany), 1976.

LTK     J. Höfer and K. Rahner, eds. *Lexikon für Theologie und Kirche.* 2nd ed. Freiburg (Germany), 1957–1965.

       W. Kasper and K. Baumgartner (et al.), eds. *Lexikon für Theologie und Kirche.* 3rd ed. Freiburg (Germany), 1993–pres.

NRSV     New Revised Standard Version.

PG     J. P. Migne, ed. *Patrologiae cursus completus.* Series graeca. Paris, 1857–1866.

PL     J. P. Migne, ed. *Patrologiae cursus completus.* Series latina. Paris, 1844–1855.

RAC     Th. Klauser, ed. *Reallexikon für Antike und Christentum.* Stuttgart, 1950–pres.

RP     International Committee on English in the Liturgy. *The Rite of Penance.* Collegeville, Minn., 1975.

RSV     Revised Standard Version.

SM     K. Rahner (et al.), ed. *Sacramentum Mundi.* New York, 1968–1970.

ST     St. Thomas Aquinas. *Summa Theologiae.*

TI     K. Rahner. *Theological Investigations.* 23 vols. London, 1961–1992.

Chapter One

# A Theology of Sin

R P does not present a theology of sin, nor should we expect it to, given its nature as an official church document. But it does contain the essential elements of Catholic doctrine on sin. The distinction between doctrine and theology is important: doctrine is the official teaching of the Church, whereas theology is a systematic reflection, in the light of contemporary questions, not just on doctrine, but more fundamentally on Scripture and tradition (which includes liturgy). Though the Church has many doctrines, proposed with varying degrees of solemnity[1] and occupying different positions in the "hierarchy of truths,"[2] they constitute together a single homogeneous body. Theology on the other hand is pluralistic, limited only by the requirement that it conform to doctrine. In keeping with our overall method as outlined in the preface, in this chapter we shall report what RP has to say on the doctrine of sin, backing this up where necessary from earlier sources, and proceed from there to a discussion of contemporary theology of sin.

We begin this chapter by presenting sin as an offense against God, which is how RP itself sees the matter. This will be followed by an account of the various ways in which historically sins have been distinguished. Next, taking our cue from Karl Rahner, we investigate the "transcendental" factors affecting sin, that is, factors affecting the agent as such rather than the act as such. This will lead us into a study of charity insofar as this relates to the theology of sin, for if sin is an offense against God, it is above all an offense against God's covenantal love. From all this there will hopefully emerge a theology of sin suited

1

to the practice of the sacrament of reconciliation today. Let us move, then, into the first topic of our study.

## Sin as Offense against God

RP 5 describes sin as "an offense against God which disrupts our friendship with him." The fundamental idea in this description is that of friendship between God and us, yet at first sight it seems an inappropriate way of conceiving the relationship between such radically unequal parties. In our experience of human relations friendship either presupposes equality between the persons concerned or at least tends toward it. However, as our creator and redeemer, God is infinitely superior to us. This means that the difference between him and us could never be overcome, even by him. However, the Old Testament speaks of friendship between God and particular human beings, like Moses, Abraham, and Job, and also with the people of the covenant as a whole (see Exod 33:11; Isa 41:8; Job 29:4; Ps 25:14; Wis 7:14).

In the Gospel Jesus says explicitly that his disciples are his friends: "No longer do I call you servants, for the servant does not know what his master is doing; but I have called you friends, for all that I have heard from my Father I have made known to you" (John 15:15). Here Jesus highlights the intimacy existing between the disciples and himself, which is the relationship of true friends. By this intimacy they are admitted to the very intimacy obtaining between Jesus and the Father (which, interestingly, Jesus never presumes to call friendship), so that like Jesus though not in the same utterly radical way, they too become sons of God (see John 1:12). But note that their friendship with Jesus requires that they carry out his will in all things: "You are my friends if you do what I command you" (John 15:14). This is not a normal requirement of friendship, which tends to let the friend be, to live freely as he or she wants. In other words, friendship even with Jesus, let alone God, does not abolish the disciples' status as servants: rather it qualifies it in a unique way. Therefore, as people created and redeemed by God, people drawn into covenant with him, they, and we, remain forever subject to him. Therefore our relationship with him is undeniably that of servants to master. However, we are servants chosen to be friends, and if we keep his commands we find ourselves admitted to a relationship of mutual love and intimacy normally denied even the most faithful of servants (see John 14:21), so that in a sense that is truly unique we become his friends. It is in a similar sense that with Jesus too we are no longer servants but friends.

It is this relationship that sin disrupts. And it does so because it violates the commandments of God and of Jesus. All sin, then, is disobedience. This statement, however, should not be understood in a positivistic way, as though God decrees arbitrarily what human beings must or must not do. The commands of God are the positive revelation of how human beings, in their freedom, should live if they are fully to actualize their nature, which was founded by him and destined to a fulfillment beyond itself, a fulfillment, that is, in God "as he is in himself." In theory at least, the commands of God are discoverable by reason (which in fact will always be aided by grace) and thus able to inform the consciences even of unbelievers. The Second Vatican Council tells us that the law of God is inscribed on the hearts of all men and women.[3] Hence an alternative definition of sin would be: acting against conscience.

But not all sin disrupts our friendship with God. Only a serious offense will have this effect, just as only a serious offense will disrupt a friendship between mature humans. Lesser offenses may harm our friendship with God, but they will not disrupt it. A further possibility, also occurring in human relations, is that though an offense may be seriously harmful in its effect, the offended party may realize that it does not represent the true or the complete interior attitude of the offender, with the result that, while the relationship is put under strain, it is not disrupted. So it can be also with God. The offender may not be fully responsible before God for what he or she has done. God knows our responsibility exactly, for he sees our hearts better than we do ourselves. As our creator he sees them infallibly and perfectly, as it were "from within," whereas we see them only fallibly and imperfectly, through a process, that is, of introspection, reflection, and judgment: in a word, discernment (see 1 Chr 28:9; Rev 2:23; 1 Cor 4:4). While it may be accurate enough, this process has no absolute guarantee of accuracy.

## The Distinction of Sins

We have here introduced the idea of distinguishing among sins. Not all sins are the same; not all sins have the same effect. The Catholic tradition knows at least four ways of distinguishing sins.

## The Sin of Nature and Personal Sin

The first and most fundamental way is to distinguish between the sin of a person, that is, "personal" sin, and the sin of "nature," the sin in which all human beings (with the exception of Jesus and Mary) share by the very fact of possessing human nature, that is, "original" sin. This is not to say that human nature of itself is sinful. It was created good by God, but became tainted by sin through the sinful choice of human beings. For personal sin, but not for original sin, the sinner bears personal responsibility. Because of this difference, original sin is not called sin in exactly the same sense as personal sin: it is said to be sin only in an "analogous" sense. RP is concerned directly with personal sin, and only indirectly with original sin. The reason for this has been given already in the Preface, namely, that the concern of the sacrament of reconciliation is the forgiveness of personal sins committed after baptism.

Original sin, on the other hand, is overcome in each person through baptism itself. The indirect interest of RP in original sin arises from the fact that though this sin is forgiven already (in baptism), its effects remain. One of these effects, "concupiscence," can be overcome gradually, though never completely, through life. "Concupiscence," from the Latin *concupiscentia*, means "desire," and as a technical theological term denotes the inclination or attraction toward sin that is the experience of us all. The Council of Trent taught that though concupiscence is sometimes called sin by St. Paul, properly speaking it is not sin at all and is called so only because "it comes from sin and inclines to sin,"[4] that is to say, it derives from original sin and inclines all affected by it toward personal sins. These sins in turn have the effect of aggravating it. The act of penance that forms part of the sacrament of reconciliation is directed in part toward the healing of "our tainted nature"[5] not only from the harmful effects of our personal sins but from the concupiscence that remains in us from original sin and that comes to expression and is intensified through personal sins. RP says in this connection that the act of penance should be chosen so that by it the penitent "may restore the order which he disturbed and through the corresponding remedy be cured of the sickness from which he suffered."[6]

## Social Sin and Sin of the Individual Person

The second way of distinguishing sins is also based on the distinction of the individual and the group, but in this case the group is smaller, a long way short of being coextensive with the whole of the human race. In this case the sin of the group is called "social" sin, as distinct from the sin of the individual person. RP recognizes that "men frequently join together to commit injustice," and draws the conclusion that "it is thus only fitting that they should help each other in doing penance so that freed from sin by the grace of Christ they may work with all men of good will for justice and peace in the world."[7] The *Catechism of the Catholic Church* also speaks briefly about social sin, stating that:

> Sin makes men accomplices of one another and causes concupiscence, violence, and injustice to reign among them. Sin gives rise to social situations and institutions that are contrary to the divine goodness. "Structures of sin" are the expression and effect of personal sins. They lead their victims to do evil in their turn. In an analogous sense, they constitute a "social sin."[8]

Note the expression "structures of sin," which refers to legal or de facto power structures supportive of oppression or exploitation. Note too the assertion that social sin is sin only by analogy, that is, with personal sin, which always constitutes the primary analogue or point of reference. In another place the catechism applies to social sin the Johannine expression, "the sin of the world" (John 1:29), which Jesus, the Lamb of God, "takes away."[9]

Pope John Paul II has expressed the Church's teaching on social sin in greater detail in his post-synodal apostolic exhortation "Reconciliation and Penance" *(Reconciliatio et paenitentia)* of 1984. In the first place the Pope stresses the analogical character of social sin. This leads him to say that when the Church condemns "the collective behavior of certain social groups, big or small, or even of whole nations and blocs of nations, she knows and she proclaims that such cases of *social sin* are the result of the accumulation and concentration of many *personal sins*." He concludes that "the real responsibility, then, lies with individuals."[10]

The conclusion we can draw from this teaching is that the sacrament of reconciliation exists for the forgiveness of personal sins rather than social sin. Another way of putting this is to say that the sacrament exists for the forgiveness of persons as such rather than communities as such. It follows from this that, as with each of the other sacraments, reconciliation is administered to the individual person as such, notwithstanding that person's membership of the Church and the genuinely communitarian dimension of this and indeed every sacrament. This highlights the somewhat anomalous character of general absolution, a subject on which we shall have more to say later on. For the present we content ourselves with concluding that social sin becomes the subject matter of the sacrament of reconciliation only to the extent that individual persons judge themselves guilty of participating in it.

### Sins Distinguished According to the Virtue Violated

The third way of distinguishing sins is according to the virtue violated by the sin: thus for example there are sins of "imprudence," or sins of "injustice," to name offenses against just two of the four "cardinal" virtues.[11] The cardinal virtues are the chief Christian moral virtues. Taken over into Christianity from Plato and Aristotle, they are listed as prudence, justice, temperance, and fortitude.[12] The remaining moral virtues are subsumed under one or other of the cardinal virtues. The moral virtues as a category are distinguished from the "theological" virtues of faith, hope, and charity, called theological because they link us directly to God.

The greatest of all virtues and, as we shall argue later, the one in which all others participate, is charity, which is nothing other than love, love of God and love of neighbor. This is the teaching of Jesus himself:

> When the Pharisees heard that he [Jesus] had silenced the Sadducees, they came together. And one of them, a lawyer, asked him a question to test him. "Teacher, which is the greatest commandment in the law?" And he said to him, "You shall love the Lord your God with all your heart, and with all your soul, and with all your mind. This is the great and first commandment. And a second is like it, You shall love your neighbor as yourself. On these two commandments depend all the law and the prophets (Matt 22:34-40).

And in 1 Corinthians 13, St. Paul tells us that when all else has passed away, "faith, hope, love abide, these three; but the greatest of these is love" (v. 13). Scripture also tells us that love of God and love of neighbor are inseparable:

> If any one says, "I love God," and hates his brother, he is a liar; for he who does not love his brother whom he has seen, cannot love God whom he has not seen. And this commandment we have from him, that he who loves God should love his brother also (1 John 4:20-21).

We mentioned earlier that all sin is disobedience. It should now be clear that all sin is also against the love of God, against charity, a refusal to love God as we ought, which in the words of St. Thomas Aquinas is that we love him "above all else."[13] This expression means, as Aquinas explains, that we "refer our love of self and of all else to the love of God as its end." It does not therefore require that we experience a greater emotional attachment to God than to our loved ones on earth. Jesus says in the Gospel, "If you love me, you will keep my commandments" (John 14:15). Therefore not just offenses directly against charity, but any offense against a moral virtue or one of the remaining theological virtues will be a sin against charity. To put it another way, charity is lost not only by sins directly against it, but by any grave sin. This is a necessary conclusion from the teaching of the Council of Trent, the explicit relevant statements of which are on the one hand that grace and charity are inseparable,[14] and on the other that grace is lost by any grave sin.[15]

In two places RP bears witness to this teaching on charity. First, in RP 7, under the heading "The Necessity and Benefit of the Sacrament," it is stated that "those who by grave sin have withdrawn from the communion of love with God are called back in the sacrament of penance to the life they have lost." Here we find encapsulated the teaching of the inseparability of grace and charity and their loss through grave sin, but it is set in the positive context of their restoration through the sacrament of reconciliation. The other place is RP 5, which speaks of reconciliation with God and the Church, but here the connection with the teaching on charity needs to be spelled out.

RP 5 begins by presenting the sacrament as reconciliation with God in terms of the restoration of the relationship of mutual love between him and the sinner that previously obtained and that was disrupted through sin. Next it cites a statement from the apostolic constitution *Indulgentiarum doctrina* of Paul VI: "By the hidden and loving mystery of God's design men are joined together in the bonds of supernatural solidarity, so much so that the sin of one harms the others just as the holiness of one benefits the others."[16] For this passage the Pope acknowledges a reference to the following text from St. Augustine: "For thus, while the organic unity of the body remained, if it became ill in any of its members it would recover through their restoration to health rather than exclude all means of cure through being killed as a result of their amputation,"[17] where the reader is meant to draw an analogy between the human body and its members on the one hand and the Church and the individual faithful on the other. The text of Paul VI tacitly acknowledges an inseparable connection on the one hand between sin, which is an offense against God and against the whole human community, and on the other hand between a positive relationship to

God (holiness, which resides in charity) and an act of beneficence (which is a work of charity) toward the same human community. In other words the principle at the heart of the Pope's statement is the inseparable link between love of God and love of neighbor on the one hand and between an offense against God and an offense against the neighbor on the other, except that it goes further. For where the principle of love of God and neighbor applies to a neighbor in the singular or to a group of human beings, it does not necessarily embrace the entire human family, as the Pope's statement does.

We note that in this respect the Pope's statement goes beyond that of St. Augustine, as the latter embraces only the body or community of the Church. But the Pope is surely right in his broader formulation. The reason why the sin of one harms all human beings and the holiness of one is of benefit to all is that all are called to the one supernatural divine destiny, and are called, moreover, to help each other in its attainment. The Pope's statement therefore requires that a further element be added to the principle of love of God and neighbor, namely the spiritual solidarity of the whole human race. What is done to one, whether it be good or bad, is in a real sense done to all. When Vatican II speaks of reconciliation it does not go beyond St. Augustine's formulation, for it tells us that when the faithful are reconciled with God, they are reconciled also with the Church, "which they have wounded by their sins."[18] Here the council speaks of reconciliation with the Church rather than with the entire human race. But in the light of Paul VI's teaching, we can and indeed should understand this principle in the wider sense, thus: through the sacrament we are reconciled with God and the Church, and through the Church with the whole human family.

It follows from this that there is no such thing as an entirely private sin. While the law can speak of "victimless crime," and while we can commit sins that appear to us as affecting only ourselves, in fact every sin is a blow against the Church and the whole human race. It also follows that though we can commit serious sin by our individual decision, we cannot have it forgiven through our individual act of contrition: as we have harmed the human family through our sin, we need to bring it to the community of the Church, which here represents the whole of humanity, to have it forgiven. When this is for whatever reason impossible, God will accept our simple contrition, but according to his plan, founded as it is on the spiritual solidarity of human beings, we must also seek reconciliation from the Church, which we do when we approach the sacrament of reconciliation. When RP speaks of the necessity of the sacrament, as it does in no. 7a, it contents itself with repeating the obligation of the confession of serious sin to a priest as imposed by the Council of Trent. But in as much as the priest as leader of the community is here seen in his representative capacity, we need to understand that this obligation itself is rooted in the principle that our relationship with God, whether positive or negative, is inseparable from our relationship with the Church and the whole human family.

## Mortal and Venial Sin

The fourth way of distinguishing sins is according to their gravity, the so-called "theological" distinction of sins. RP does this by dividing sins into "grave"[19] (which is the same as "serious") and "venial."[20] The Council of Trent adopted the scholastic distinction of "mortal" (meaning "deadly") and "venial";[21] and though the 1983 Code of Canon Law retained the terminology of RP in 1984, in *Reconciliatio et paenitentia*, Pope John Paul II reverted to the Tridentine terminology of "mortal" and "venial," maintaining it in his 1993 encyclical *Veritatis splendor*. The most celebrated scholastic theologian to have used this terminology was St. Thomas Aquinas.[22]

Let us look now at some of the difficulties connected with this language. The traditional terminology of "mortal" and "venial" depends, as can be seen from Aquinas,[23] on "mortal" meaning "irreparable" and "venial" meaning "reparable." Aquinas's reasoning here was that mortal sin, being deadly in the sense that it kills the divine life in us, is like death itself, from which no one can recover, while venial sin, since it does not kill the divine life, is like sickness, from which one can recover. In this sense mortal sin is irreparable and venial sin reparable. Therefore the term "venial," coming from the Latin *venia*, meaning "pardon" or "forgiveness," denotes "forgivable" sin,[24] but "mortal," according to this line of thought, would denote unforgivable sin. This way of thinking about sin has to do with the presence or absence of charity, which links us to God, our ultimate end. As charity is lost by any mortal sin, and only in this way, mortal sin is irreparable (and hence unforgivable) in that charity, a gift of God, cannot be regained by anything we might do of ourselves (though it can be regained by God's grace, that is, by what we do in response to grace). We can lose charity by ourselves, but we cannot regain it by ourselves, just as we can fall into a well by ourselves, but not emerge from it by ourselves.[25] Asserting that mortal and venial sin are opposed as, respectively, irreparable and reparable, Aquinas hastens to add, however, "I say this in reference to any resource within [ourselves], but not in relation to the divine power, which can overcome any affliction, whether of body or of spirit."[26] In other words, even for Aquinas, the terminology of "mortal" and "venial" did not do justice to the actual situation of sin and its forgiveness. With him we should recognize that it omits the most important factor, namely, the love and mercy of God. Thus there is present in this language an ambiguity that, even if tolerated by Aquinas, can hardly be tolerated by us.

The basic reason for this is that speaking in this way suggests a somewhat Pelagian way of thinking about gaining God's forgiveness. Pelagianism, surely one of the most insidious of heresies, overemphasized the value of human effort before God, to the detriment or even denial of the necessity of grace. Without apology the Catholic faith teaches the necessity of human cooperation with grace, but in so doing it acknowledges the priority and infinite superiority of grace, nay more, the very sovereignty of grace, which means that, in a way we can never fully understand, grace that is effective *will include* actual human cooperation. The merciful love of God, who longs to forgive our sins, anticipates, rouses, and supports in us the repentance that is a necessary condition of forgiveness. The language of "mortal" and "venial," in the sense, respectively, of "irreparable" and "reparable," misplaces the emphasis that should fall on God as the one who alone forgives sin (see Mark 2:7; Isa 43:25).

Against this it can be objected that the New Testament speaks on at least three occasions of irreparable or unforgivable sin, namely the "sin against the Holy Spirit" (Mark 3:29 with parallels Matt 12:31f. and Luke 12:10), the sin of "apostasy" (Heb 6:4-6), and "mortal" sin (literally: "sin unto death," 1 John 5:16). Each of these, however, is an instance in which the impossibility of forgiveness stems not from God but from the sinner. In each case the circumstances are such that the sinner would be most unlikely to repent. The sin would therefore be unforgivable not in an absolute sense, but only in the relative sense that it is unlikely that the repentance essential for its forgiveness would be forthcoming. However, human beings cannot place any limit on the power of God, and sometimes even the apparently most hardened of sinners are converted.

If ultimately even mortal sin must be admitted to be forgivable, what is gained by continuing to call the other kind of sin "venial," given that this itself means "forgivable"? Usually, at this point ground is given and venial sin is redefined as "easily forgivable."[27] But this too is problematic. Is it harder for God to forgive mortal sin than venial sin? The only sense in which venial sin can be said to be more easily forgivable is that it is easier *for the sinner* to win forgiveness for it than for mortal sin. Mortal sin requires a more profound effort on the sinner's part, nothing short of reconversion to God, whereas such is God's love for us that venial sin is forgiven at the first sign of repentance. But while this is true, thus to put the emphasis on human effort is to enter once more upon a Pelagian mentality that is better avoided.

Perhaps, though, the term "venial" is a relic of the idea of "remissible" as opposed to "irremissible" sin, sin that is remissible or irremissible *by the Church*. A positive feature of this distinction would be that it recognizes the instrumental or mediatorial (sacramental) role of the Church in the forgiveness of sins by refraining from attributing to it the authority to forgive, leaving this to God to whom it ultimately belongs, and instead uses a general term more suitable to the subsidiary human role. In this connection it should be noted that in the sacrament the priest does not say, "I forgive you your sins," but rather, "I absolve you from your sins," where the word "absolve" recalls Jesus' word "loose" in his assurance to the Church, "Whatever you bind on earth shall be bound in heaven, and whatever you loose on earth shall be loosed in heaven" (Matt 18:18).[28] But we need to remember that the terms "remissible" and "irremissible" (that is, by the Church) were introduced by Tertullian in his Montanist (rigorist) polemic against the Catholic Church's penitential practice (in Carthage, early third century).[29] For him the sins of apostasy, murder and adultery, which he called "mortal," were so serious that the Church could not remit them. They had to be left to God alone, and even then they were remitted only after a period of penance culminating in the sinner's death. This, however, was never accepted as a Catholic distinction, though such was Tertullian's influence that in some places in the fourth and fifth centuries his triad of "mortal" sins were the only ones reserved to the institutional practice of penance.[30] It is possible, therefore, that the terminology of mortal and venial sin represents a lingering trace of this influence. But we must recognize that at least in this instance it was a baneful influence.

Grave or serious sin (I use the terms interchangeably) is correctly called mortal in the sense that by it grace and charity, the spiritual life of the person derived from God and establishing union with him, are lost. As long as the person continues in that condition they cannot be saved. Even so, there are problems with this terminology. First, it is not what Scripture meant when it spoke of "mortal sin" in 1 John 5:16. Commentators on this difficult text offer a variety of interpretations, but at least they agree that what is meant by this expression is not just *any* example of what in the present day might be considered mortal sin, but a particular kind of sin. Thus "sin which is not mortal" (see 1 John 5:16, 17) would comprehend many of the sins today held to be mortal.[31] Secondly, though mortal sin in the present sense of the term ends God's life in us, it does not completely sever our connection to God. For the Council of Trent teaches that only by a sin specifically against faith is faith itself lost; in all other mortal sins it remains, though not as "living."[32] The surviving connection with God is evident in the fact that the repentance to which the sinner is called is actuated by the appeal of God's grace to precisely this faith and also to hope, which remains in all sins not specifically against it. Thus is explained the relative impossibility of repentance in those scriptural passages that speak of unforgivable sin: such sins presume that the normal foundation of repentance, namely faith and hope, has also been lost (along with charity). Most likely, this is what is meant by the "mortal" sin of 1 John 5:16.[33] Hence to apply to all grave sins the term that Scripture reserves for one particular sin is to invite confusion.

Our conclusion must be that despite their long presence in the language of Catholic faith the terms "mortal" and "venial" as characterizing, respectively, grave and non-grave sin are far from ideal: they only complicate what is already a difficult situation in both doctrine and theology. "Grave" is certainly an apt term for the personal sin that destroys grace and charity in the sinner. This precise content supplies the basic meaning of the word "sin." Original sin, social sin, and personal sins that do not destroy grace and charity are all truly sin, but only by analogy with grave personal sin. Further, it is grave personal sins committed after baptism, and only these, that according to the Council of Trent must be submitted for forgiveness to the sacrament of penance (as Trent called it).[34] The other kind of personal sin, which does not destroy grace and charity and which does not have to be submitted to the sacrament, can without further ado be termed "non-grave." These terms, "grave" and "non-grave," have the advantage of being both accurate and clear.

A problem arises, however, when we try to find a suitable *positive* term for non-grave sins. If the gravity of a sin were determined purely by what was done by it, its "matter," there would be no problem: the sin would be either grave or "light." But in addition to matter and to "circumstances," which can also affect gravity (and kind), there is the level of the sinner's responsibility. If the matter is serious and the sinner fully responsible, the sin will be grave; but if the sinner is not fully responsible, the sin will not be grave, even though the matter is serious. RP, be it remembered, described sin as "an offense against God which disrupts our friendship with him." And friendship, even with fellow human beings, is not disrupted by adverse acts alone, but by fully responsible adverse acts. If we do something that could offend a friend, the friend will be appeased if they learn that we did not mean to offend. So it is with God, the best of friends, who dearly wants our friendship, and seeing our hearts as he does, understands them better than we do ourselves. For a sin to be grave, therefore, it must be so both objectively and subjectively. If subjective responsibility is lacking, or present but diminished, the sin is not grave. When the scribes and Pharisees complained that Jesus' disciples transgressed the tradition of the elders by not washing their hands when they ate, Jesus replied,

> Hear and understand: not what goes into the mouth defiles a man, but what comes out of the mouth, this defiles a man. . . . What comes out of the mouth proceeds from the heart, and this defiles a man. For out of the heart come evil thoughts, murder, adultery, fornication, theft, false witness, slander. These are what defile a man; but to eat with unwashed hands does not defile a man (Matt 15:10-11, 18-20. See Mark 7:14-15, 21-23).

In the matter of sin it will be rare that responsibility is entirely lacking. What is more usual, and what we shall take as our norm for sins with grave matter but anything less than full responsibility, is diminished responsibility. Bearing in mind the gravity of matter, the inappropriateness of calling such sins "light" or venial (in the sense of "light," which is how "venial" is normally understood) will now be obvious. Such terms are appropriate only if the matter itself is light. These are sins that *would* be grave if responsibility were complete. But something is lacking at the subjective level, and that which is lacking excuses the sin from being grave. Hence I have suggested elsewhere that such sins might be called "'mitigated,' 'attenuated,' or 'incomplete,' with a slight preference for the first."[35]

My suggestion, therefore, for distinguishing sins according to gravity is as follows. Sins are divided into grave and non-grave; and non-grave sins in turn are divided into mitigated and light. I trust that the case for so classifying them has been sufficiently argued. The terms are accurate and clear, and their advantages over the alternatives will now, I hope, be evident. In particular, there are pastoral advantages in calling sins with grave matter but diminished responsibility "mitigated." The sinner is consoled and encouraged at being assured that they are still friends with God. At the same time the term does not permit them complacency about their spiritual situation. It urges them to accept the struggle of the spiritual warfare that confronts all without exception and to develop both humanly and spiritually into fully responsible persons in the service of God and neighbor. The suggested terms do not contradict the traditional terminology of "mortal" and "venial." Rather, while affirming the same content, they do it in a way that is theologically more precise and pastorally more helpful. In the rest of this book, therefore, I shall use them when speaking in my own voice on this matter.

## Transcendental Factors Affecting Sin

For most of the remainder of this chapter we shall be pursuing the reflection that we began earlier on the virtue of charity, that is, insofar as it affects the theology of sin. Charity operates within the covenant between God and human beings, the covenant between Christ and the Church. Marriage also is a covenant, indeed a reflection of this very covenant (see Eph 5:21-33). In the traditional marriage vow the bride promised to "love, honor, and obey" the bridegroom. If, in respect to the promise to obey, this formula has now become dated and generally unsuitable, the same cannot be said in regard to the covenant relationship of the Christian to God: we are still (and always) called to love, honor, and obey him, obedience and honor reaching their completion in love. Sin is in the first instance a refusal to obey God, and therefore at the same time a refusal to honor, and above all to love him. Hence there exists an all-important connection between charity and the theology of sin.

We shall now be presenting some important features of the theology of Karl Rahner, and these call for an explanation of two key terms that he uses, namely "categorial" and "transcendental."[36] An act, for example, will be "categorial" if it fits into the constitutive categories of the world. This means that its content can be described in such categories. If "justice" means to give the neighbor their due, then clearly an act of justice is to be characterized as a categorial act. This will mean in turn that the agent will be engaged in the act only in regard to those categories and not with their entire being. A "transcendental" act, on the other hand, will be one that escapes these categories, which means that it will be directed toward God, and indeed God "as he is in himself." Since our concepts and words arise from our interaction with this world, when we address a mental or conceptual act toward God we approach him categorially, even though we may be aware that we are using concepts and words differently from the way we normally do. A "transcendental" approach to God can hardly be described as an act at all; it will be more like a disposition of the human person toward God, a disposition made possible only by the spiritual nature of human beings in relation to God who is "spirit" (see John 4:24). Words can be found to describe this disposition, but they are totally inadequate to what they describe, and are felt to be such. In truth, a transcendental experience cannot properly be described in words at all. And because the one experienced is God, creator and lord of the human person, the human agent will be involved in and with their entire being in this disposition toward God. Another question is whether a transcendental act is possible in regard to the neighbor. We shall see that this is a disputed question. My own position on it will emerge in the course of our treatment.

In the pages ahead we shall devote quite some space to showing that charity is a transcendental virtue, indeed *the* transcendental virtue, as in my view this insight of Karl Rahner is crucial to the development of a sound theology of sin. This makes charity the most important transcendental factor in the question of sin. But it is not the only one. The starting point for our consideration here will therefore be a general treatment of the transcendental factors affecting the theology of sin, from which we shall proceed to our treatment of charity.

### Rahner's Negative General Factor: "Imposed Necessity"

We begin by examining how a sin that would otherwise be grave (as it involves serious matter) can become "mitigated" (to invoke the terminology that I set up earlier). We mentioned in the last section that the reason for this is a diminution of personal responsibility. Traditionally, such diminution has been understood to come about through the influence of an inhibiting factor on the freedom of the act whereby it is rendered less than fully human. Examples of such factors would be error or ignorance (of the immorality, or the seriousness of the immorality, of what one is doing), or passion such as anger or lust in circumstances where the strength of the passion is excusable. Such factors bear on the act. But in addition to them there are factors that affect the person *antecedently* to their acts. These factors are called personal. They are also called transcendental, in that they transcend, and are antecedent to, particular acts. The *Catechism of the Catholic Church* lists some of these as "affective immaturity, force of acquired habit, conditions of anxiety, or other psychological or social factors that can lessen moral culpability, perhaps even reducing it to a minimum."[37] The consideration of such factors is a relatively modern development in moral theology, and it represents a swing away from an act-centered morality toward a person-centered one. But by no means does it abolish act-centered morality. This development simply means that a consideration of the morality of the act as such needs to be complemented by a consideration of such relevant personal factors as may be operative, as these could have the effect of changing a judgment of grave sin into one of mitigated sin. According to the moralist James Keenan the shift from an act-centered to a person-centered morality is characteristic of contemporary moral thinking.[38]

For Karl Rahner the transcendental factors mitigating the gravity of sin are included under a heading that he terms "imposed necessity":

> With regard to individual free actions in his life, the subject never has an absolute certainty about the subjective and therefore moral quality of these individual actions because, as real and as objectified in knowledge, these actions are always a synthesis of original freedom and imposed necessity, a synthesis which cannot be resolved completely in reflection.[39]

There are two things to note here. First, because "original freedom" and imposed necessity are synthesized in the person's action and because both are transcendental and a priori, the person cannot by reflective analysis get "behind" or "underneath" them in order to be able to judge with certainty in the case of any given action to what extent it is free or to what extent necessitated. As Rahner goes on to observe, "We can never know with ultimate certainty whether we really are sinners."[40] As was said earlier, only God can see directly into the human heart. But the person can listen to what others, guides, counselors, and confessors, have to say, and he or she can in quiet prayer ask the Holy Spirit for enlightenment so that on the basis of such advice and their own reflection a sound prudential judgment as to their responsibility can be reached. This is supported by the Council of Trent, which taught that "no one can know with a certitude of faith which cannot be subject to error, that one has obtained God's grace."[41] And it is why RP, in no. 7a, urges an "examination of conscience" before confession. This is not simply the drawing up of a list of sins, but a prayerful act of discernment in which one comes to a practical judgment as to one's relationship with God and determines what is to be confessed in the sacrament. It is not something that can be done "on the run," but rather an exercise of reflective prayer requiring a period of peace and quiet before going to confession.

### Rahner's Positive Factor: "Original Freedom"

The second thing we need to note has already been mentioned, but it now needs to be made the direct object of our consideration. It is that of the two realities declared by Rahner to be synthesized in the person's action, not only the second, imposed necessity, but also the first, original freedom, is transcendental. And this is so despite the fact that each comes to expression in a merely categorial way in the concrete action. The transcendental character of the first is indicated by Rahner through his choice of the adjective "original" to qualify the substantive, "freedom." We now need to identify this transcendental reality. It is more than freedom of choice, for that is only the categorial freedom immediately evident in the act. I shall now argue, from Rahner, that it is nothing other than charity: love of God and neighbor. It presupposes that the person has reached the point in their personal and spiritual development where, in response to the prompting of grace, they are able to give themselves unconditionally to God (to love God "above all else") and have in fact done so. They now possess "original" freedom, in that, despite temptations stemming from concupiscence, they are no longer slaves to any power (especially they are not slaves to passion or sin) but truly, even if paradoxically, "possess" themselves. I say "paradoxically," because their self-possession comes about precisely through their radical giving-away of themselves to God. This assertion is supported in the theology of Rahner by his statement that "human reality . . . consists of the fact that man *is* in so far as he gives up himself."[42] And, speaking at the level of nature, he said that "when we reflect upon the real transcendental relationship between God and a creature, then it is clear that here genuine reality and radical dependence are simply just two sides of one and the same reality, *and therefore they vary in direct and not in inverse proportion* [emphasis added]."[43] This general principle is verified also at the level of human self-realization in the order of grace, in which self-realization is nothing other than response. In this context, for "genuine reality" we read "self-possession," and for "radical dependence" we read "radical giving-away of oneself to God."

In light of these two observations and the Rahnerian text on which they serve as comments, we can conclude that the question of gravity of sin is decided not just by a judgment of serious matter along with full knowledge and consent, but also, and ultimately, by a judgment as to whether some imposed necessity is present and operative, such that despite the presence of the aforesaid factors personal responsibility is impaired, with the result that the final judgment is one of mitigated rather than grave sin. To the objection that the imposed necessity can be judged to impair full knowledge and consent directly, and that therefore all consideration of original freedom is irrelevant,[44] the following answer can be given. In a sense the objection is valid (I shall return to it later), but it presumes that some qualified guide or confessor has pointed out the existence of the imposed necessity to the counselee or penitent and convinced them of its relevance to their case. Otherwise they could not know it. An imposed necessity cannot be known by its bearer just by introspection, as is known the presence of a mitigating factor bearing simply on an *act*, like, for example, anger or intoxication. Hence from an unaided examination of conscience apart from such advice they would probably in all sincerity have judged themselves guilty of grave sin, that is, of embracing serious matter with full knowledge and consent. The point is that the operation of the imposed necessity has prevented their subjectively and objectively gravely sinful act from overturning their original freedom. Their friendship with God, therefore, has not been disrupted.

## Charity

I realize that much remains to be shown, but unfortunately this cannot be done in detail in the few pages to which we are here restricted. Therefore what I propose to do is to present, in the context of our reflection on charity, on which we now embark, a succession of theses in logical order, most of them either drawn directly from Rahner or inspired by him, with indications, where necessary, of where they can be found argued in a more thorough way.[45] In cases where such argumentation is lacking, I shall offer it in the text. This explains why some of the thesis presentations are longer than others. These theses, if accepted, should provide the necessary framework within which the value of my assertions on mitigated sin can be judged.

## First Thesis: Love of God and Love of Neighbor

Love of God and love of neighbor are two inseparable though distinguishable aspects of one and the same human love, with neighbor love as the primary act of the love of God. Rahner's essay, "Reflections on the Unity of the Love of Neighbor and the Love of God,"[46] is devoted to establishing this basic thesis of his theological system. It is founded not just on Scripture's insistence that the two loves belong inseparably together, but on the insight that only loving encounter with fellow human beings can activate one's transcendental orientation to God, the "Thou" as such.

## Second Thesis: The Relation of the Moral Virtues to Charity

The moral virtues must be understood as partial realizations of neighbor love. This is the thesis of Rahner's essay "The 'Commandment' of Love in Relation to the Other Commandments."[47] It results from the insight that the moral virtues are based on moral values, which are recognized as residing in the person as such (that is, the "other" person), and that ultimately the only adequate and therefore appropriate response to the person is love. Each moral virtue, therefore, must be some partial aspect of neighbor love.

## Third Thesis: Categorial and Specific Acts of Charity

This thesis comes only indirectly from Rahner. It is this: Any good act in which the good of the neighbor is intended is a categorial act of neighbor love, but this does not suffice to make it a specific act of neighbor love. For that, this would have to be its last and most precise classification. But a good act in which the good of the neighbor is intended is, on the contrary, the first and most general classification of the act. Every exercise of a moral virtue is a categorial act of neighbor love, not just in intention, but also objectively, in that the moral virtue itself is a partial realization of neighbor love. Thus, specific acts of justice and mercy, respectively, being motivated by and participating in charity, are categorial but not specific acts of charity. I should add that this explicit distinction of "categorial" and "specific" is my own;[48] it is only implicit in Rahner.

### Fourth Thesis: Charity Has no Specific Act

The question arises: Does charity, as love of God and love of neighbor, have specific acts? The question needs to be made more precise, since it is obvious that, whether as love of God or love of neighbor, charity has specific *internal* acts, that is, interior, spiritual acts by which we affirm our love of God or the neighbor. As to external acts, it is obvious that the only external specific act of love of God as distinct from love of neighbor (though Rahner rightly observes that the intrinsic dependence of the former on the latter remains in force even here[49]) is nothing more than the external expression of the internal act in prayer, whether private or public. Our question must therefore be: Does charity precisely as neighbor love have specific external acts? Jean Porter, contrasting Rahner with her reading of Aquinas on neighbor love, correctly observes:

> What Rahner emphasizes are precisely the transcendental aspects of [neighbor] love. The act of love is not seen by him as being tied to any specific kinds of actions; rather, it consists in an absolute openness to the Other, which in its embrace of created finitude, is simultaneously an act of openness to God.[50]

With Rahner I give a negative answer to the question asked: as the transcendental virtue, charity, even in neighbor love, lacks specific external acts. In other words, in regard to the disputed question announced at the beginning of this section, I argue that a transcendental act in regard to the neighbor is possible, and identify this act as neighbor love. It will therefore lack its own specific act. This, therefore, constitutes our fourth thesis.

It is necessary now to clarify further the distinction between categorial and specific acts, for the following objection can be raised immediately against our thesis. If charity has no specific act, it must be transcendental, and this in turn means that it cannot have categorial acts. How, then, can it be granted that charity *has* categorial acts? In the third thesis (above) I presented the reasons for the categoriality of acts of neighbor love: first, they are motivated by charity, and second, the moral virtues exercised in them are in themselves participations in charity. But now the point must be made: it is not insofar as they are acts of charity that these acts are categorial; they are categorial in that *specifically* they are acts of some moral virtue. When this point is joined to the reasons repeated above, it will be appreciated that acts of neighbor love are rightly designated categorial, though in a sense unique to themselves. But this is not surprising. Charity, being transcendental, *is* unique.

At this stage it is necessary to mention an exchange that I, in some dependence on James Keenan, had with Jean Porter.[51] The point at issue was whether neighbor love has its own specific acts. It is clear that for Rahner it does not. What Keenan, Porter, and I all wanted to do was to ascertain the position of St. Thomas on this. Keenan argued that St. Thomas's answer was that neighbor love does not have its own acts, while Porter argued that the opposite was the case, that is, that St. Thomas held that neighbor love does have its own acts. What I propose to do now is to conduct my own inquiry into St. Thomas, bearing in mind the views expressed by both Keenan and Porter.[52] What will emerge from this will be a conclusion that shows that Keenan and Porter are each only partly correct in their interpretation of St. Thomas, though Keenan more so than Porter. I shall also show that St. Thomas can be invoked in support of Rahner. Given the authority of St. Thomas, to pursue his opinion will be a worthwhile exercise in itself, and it will become more so if his position can be correlated with Rahner's.

Here, then, is the first relevant text from St. Thomas:

> A virtue or an art to which pertains an ultimate end commands the virtues or arts to which pertain secondary ends, as military art commands the art of using cavalry, as is said in *I Ethics*. And so, because charity has as its object the ultimate end of human life, namely eternal beatitude, it extends itself to all the acts of human life by way of command [that is, in this case, motivation], but not by way of eliciting all the acts of the [other] virtues.[53]

On the basis of this text, and also *De caritate*, a. 5 ad 3, which is similar to it, it would appear that for Aquinas charity has no specific acts of its own. However, there are three places in which it is agreed by both Keenan and Porter that he asserts the opposite, namely, that charity does have its own specific acts, Keenan claiming that these are exceptions in St. Thomas's thought, and Porter that there is nothing exceptional about them at all. I shall now examine each of these texts in turn, saving my own comments until I have completed my presentation.

The first text is ST II-II, q. 32, a. 1, which has to do with almsgiving. It is true that Aquinas here says that "to give alms is an act of charity," but he adds immediately, "through the mediation of mercy." And he also says in the same place, "It is clear that to give alms is properly speaking an act of mercy." The second text is ST II-II, q. 33, a. 1, concerning fraternal correction. Aquinas treats it from two points of view, first when it is a remedy for sin for the sinners themselves, and second when it is a remedy for sin in as much as its consequences affect others. The second case he relates to justice rather than charity. The first he says to be charity in the *corpus articuli* (the body of the article), but in the response to the second objection he clarifies this statement by relating charity to prudence, thus: "It is clear that such an admonition is principally an act of charity in that charity commands it, but secondarily an act of prudence, in that prudence carries it out and directs it." The third and last text is ST II-II, q. 31, a. 1, which treats beneficence ("doing good"). In another text, ST II-II, q. 31, a. 4, Aquinas says clearly that an act of beneficence is an act of charity, because beneficence has the same formal object (the objective aim of the act, in this case "doing good") as charity. However, in ST II-II, q. 31, a. 1, he approaches the matter from two points of view, the first a general understanding of good, and the second a particular understanding of it. In regard to the first he says that it is an act of charity, because it includes benevolence, by which one intends to promote the other's good in a general way. But in regard to the second viewpoint, this is what he says: "But if the good one does to another be taken in the sense of a particular good, beneficence will take on a particular character and belong to some particular [other] virtue."[54]

Now for my comments. In the second text on beneficence referred to above, and in regard to the first sense of the word itself in the second text, special comment is required. (The same sense of the word is present in both places.) I have already pointed out that the word itself means "doing good." Particularly as in the third text it is combined with benevolence, it is clear that it is used as a non-specific term covering all good neighbor-related actions in the abstract. But in the concrete, as Aquinas himself admits in the very next sentence (the one quoted above), it will be an act of whichever moral virtue is indicated by the nature of the good done. In my terms, the connection just mentioned between charity and the subordinate virtue will render the act a categorial act of charity and a specific act of the subordinate virtue. An apparent complication is caused by the fact that in one text, ST III, q. 85, a. 2, ad 1, Aquinas speaks of *two* ways in which acts are derived from charity, one "as elicited by it," the other "as commanded" by it. The main subject of this text is the virtue of penance. Accordingly, the text proceeds to relate penance to charity, that is, to the two kinds of act of charity to which I have referred. But note how Aquinas does this:

> If in the act of a penitent only sorrow for past sin is considered, this pertains immediately to charity, as does also joy concerning past goods. But the intention of doing something to obtain forgiveness for past sin requires some particular virtue subordinate to charity [namely penance].[55]

The basic distinction between these two acts is, in my terminology, that the first is a specific act of charity, while the second is only a categorial act (of charity). But there is a further difference, of the highest importance: the first act remains purely interior to the agent, while the second passes over into external action. I have already granted the possibility and the actuality of a purely interior specific act of charity, in regard to both God and neighbor. This is not the point at issue. At issue is only whether the external act of neighbor love is necessarily categorial as distinct from specific.

It is clear that in each of the texts allowed by Keenan and Porter as showing that Aquinas was willing to nominate particular acts as specific acts of charity, a more thorough examination has revealed that he meant no more than that these were acts "commanded" by charity. They were acts of charity in the sense of being motivated by it, but were acts of some other virtue in as much as they reached their completion in that virtue. Here Aquinas was saying something quite close to what Rahner said and what I wish to endorse. The difference, nevertheless, is not insignificant. Whereas Aquinas saw only an external connection between charity and the other virtues, Rahner saw an internal connection that renders the latter partial realizations of the former. This is the essential reason why I have taken the position that uniquely in the case of charity a categorial act is not a specific act of that virtue.

In this study we have not encountered a single text from St. Thomas that tells against the position of Rahner and myself (and Keenan, if we discount his "exceptions"). In fact, on the evidence we can claim St. Thomas as supporting our position. His position is accurately stated by saying that in its external acts neighbor love, being concerned with the neighbor's ultimate good, orders the other virtues practiced in his or her regard as intermediate ends toward this ultimate good. However, this does not mean that neighbor love thereby becomes abstract or removed from real life. It means, rather, that its task is to direct the acts of other virtues exercised in the world. It lacks its own specific act because it is concerned directly not with particular goods, but with the disposition of the entire loving subject desiring and effecting as far as they can the ultimate and entire good of the "thou," the neighbor encountered in the world. It does this through many acts of the moral virtues, each of which is as it were a "fragment" of neighbor love directed to a partial and intermediate good pertaining to the neighbor.

Rather than being *a* transcendental virtue, therefore, neighbor love must be acknowledged to pertain to *the* transcendental virtue, charity pure and simple. For the love of God is also transcendental. Even if expressed in categorial acts of prayer, in its deepest essence it is transcendental, because it consists in the *self*-gift of the entire person to God, and to God as the ultimate and transcendent end of their life. Therefore as love of both God and neighbor, charity is correctly characterized as *the* transcendental virtue. In the light of these comments we can discern the foundations of Rahner's position in St. Thomas.

## *Fifth Thesis: Fundamental Option*

At this point we can and should say something about the importance of the last (that is, the fourth) thesis in our overall presentation. It is this: having acquired the position that charity is the transcendental virtue, we can now proceed to identify it with what modern theologians call the fundamental option for God. To do so will illuminate both charity and the fundamental option. Our fifth thesis, then, is the assertion of this identity.

As Josef Fuchs recognizes, the theology of fundamental option was largely worked out by Karl Rahner, though in preference to this term Rahner usually spoke of "the human person's disposition of his self as a whole."[56] Rahner himself makes the identification of the fundamental option with charity and states that the means by which it is achieved is categorial acts of neighbor love.[57] A theory of fundamental option is necessary because the spiritual nature of human beings requires that, underlying particular choices and formed through such of them as are morally significant, there must be a spiritual disposition of the person as such. There is a true reciprocity between fundamental option and particular actions. If there were only particular choices without a fundamental option there would be little to distinguish a human being from an animal, which is also capable of choices (albeit within a limited sphere). Though Rahner has been able to give the theory a new level of sophistication through his transcendental philosophy and theology, it did not begin with him. Rather, it is to be found, in simpler form, in Aquinas with his doctrine of the graced spirit in relation to outer action;[58] prior to that it is found in Augustine with his doctrine of *libertas,* true freedom (the disposition), and *liberum arbitrium,* free will (particular acts);[59] and its ultimate roots are in the gospel itself, particularly in the teaching of Jesus on the relation of the "heart" of the human being to that person's external actions (Mark 7:14-23 and parallels).

Though up to the present Pope John Paul II has spoken only negatively of fundamental option, it should be noted that this is in regard not to the theory as such, but only to formulations of it that minimize the category of mortal or grave sin.[60] The broad church tradition on fundamental option can be found in the 1982 report of the International Theological Commission, "Penance and Reconciliation," which states:

> The fundamental option determines in the last analysis the moral condition of man. But the concept of fundamental option is not a criterion which allows one to distinguish concretely between grave and venial sins. The concept, rather, is a help to make the nature of grave sin theologically clear. Although basically man can express his option or change it in a single act, viz. in those cases in which this act is done with full awareness and complete freedom, it is not necessary that this fundamental option enter in its entirety into each individual act, so that each sin does not have to be, *eo ipso,* a revision of an (explicit or implicit) fundamental option.[61]

It is at this point that I wish to return to Timothy O'Connell's objection partly dealt with earlier.[62] The Commission has here said exactly what I would want to say to him: I concede that fundamental option does not supply a direct criterion for distinguishing between grave and non-grave sins, but I emphasize that it supplies an indirect criterion, insofar as it makes the nature of grave sin clear.

A point calling for explanation here is *how* the fundamental option can be changed in a single act. We might be tempted to think that because of its depth in the human person it would require more than one act to change it. The identification of the option with charity is the key to this question. For charity is not just the love of God, but the love of God "above all else." This expression indicates that through charity God as he is in himself is constituted the ultimate end of a human being's life. The implication of this is that the human person places their total good or salvation in God. The rejection of God by which charity is lost does not have to be an act of hatred of God; it is sufficient that it be an act by which God is demoted from his unique position as ultimate end. And this is done whenever God is disobeyed in a serious matter through a fully free act. In this case the person has deliberately chosen their own will over that of God, which means that they no longer accept God as the ultimate end of their life. This is what grave sin is.

But the question arises: How often in practice does this happen? Certainly, grave sin is not only possible; it actually occurs. But it is most unlikely to occur as often as has been thought in the past. For even though at the conscious level the sinner may have believed themselves to have acted with full knowledge and consent, at the deeper level where transcendental factors operate an imposed necessity might well have blocked the full operation of their freedom, with the result that their fundamental option for God has been left intact. The fundamental option can be overturned, but only with difficulty. This was known by Aquinas, for in answering the objection that grace is lost easily, that is, through a single act of mortal sin, his reply was:

> Though grace is lost through a single act of mortal sin, grace is not lost easily. For it is not easy for a person possessing grace to perform such an act, the reason being their inclination to the contrary. As Aristotle said in 5 *Ethics* (ch. 6), it is difficult for a good person to do things that are not good.[63]

Only a theology of fundamental option can adequately ground this profound insight of Aquinas and his mentor Aristotle. The mistaken idea, sadly still widely prevalent, that a person serious about living a Christian life can easily fall in and out of grave sin, is thus properly answered. At the level of persons, therefore, and insofar as the sacrament of reconciliation is concerned, many sins previously thought to be grave would need to be reclassified as mitigated. This is not to suggest that a serious Christian cannot commit grave sin. Such is the power of evil that this danger always remains a possibility.

There is one final point to be considered. Aquinas had the curious doctrine that though charity can increase in a person, and also be lost, it cannot be diminished.[64] According to him, venial sin does not diminish charity. His reason for this was that charity is a virtue infused by God, poured into our hearts by the Holy Spirit (see Rom 5:5). Human beings have no part to play in it. In this opinion he was generally followed by theologians until recent times. But the reason he gives is not valid. While charity is certainly an infused virtue, once infused it is exercised by human beings, in dependence, of course, on God's help. It is significant that in his discussion of the issue Aquinas actually uses the telltale expression "the quantity of charity." But charity is not a measurable quantity, which after infusion human beings cannot touch (except to expel altogether). Rather, it is a *quality* and a relationship, which, being fluid, can wane as well as wax. I can only account for this lapse in Aquinas's thought by suggesting that it might represent a lingering relic of Peter Lombard's teaching on charity (which Aquinas otherwise opposed), namely that there is no created habit of charity, but that the love by which we love God (and the neighbor) is none other than the Holy Spirit in person.[65] It is of great interest to note that the new *Catechism of the Catholic Church* has quietly overturned the teaching of Aquinas on this point by simply saying, "Venial sin weakens charity."[66]

## Conclusion

Let us draw this chapter to a conclusion by reaffirming the understanding of sin that has emerged from it. The sins that must be brought to the sacrament of reconciliation are our grave personal sins committed after baptism, though we may bring lesser sins as well, and indeed are encouraged to do so. As offenses against God, our grave sins will all be sins of disobedience, dishonor, and rejection of his love, with the result that by them grace and the love of God "above all else" are lost. Because of the inseparable connection of love of neighbor and love of God, our sins against the neighbor, though specifically sins against one or other of the moral virtues, will also be sins against the love of neighbor, and hence also against the love of God. Grave sins, however, are not as common as once thought, as in addition to mitigating factors that might apply to particular acts as such, there may well be some imposed necessity operating at the more basic level of person, preventing the sin from being a withdrawal of that person's love of God. This love of God, grounded in the love of neighbor, is the fundamental option of the mature Christian person, and though it can be changed, it cannot be changed easily. Sincere Christian people do not tumble in and out of the state of grace.

## Notes, Chapter One

[1] See Vatican II's Dogmatic Constitution on the Church *(Lumen gentium)* no. 25, Flannery, 34–36. See also the 1989 Profession of Faith, *Origins* 18, no. 40 (March 16, 1989) 663.

[2] See Vatican II's Decree on Ecumenism *(Unitatis redintegratio)* no. 11, Flannery, 511.

[3] See Vatican II's Constitution on the Church in the Modern World *(Gaudium et spes)* no. 16, Flannery, 178.

[4] The Decree on Original Sin of the Council of Trent, in Jacques Dupuis, ed., *The Christian Faith in the Doctrinal Documents of the Catholic Church*, 6th ed. (New York: Alba House, 1996) (hereafter Dupuis) no. 512.

[5] To quote William Wordsworth's sonnet, "The Virgin" (1821).

[6] RP 6c.

[7] Ibid., 5.

[8] *Catechism of the Catholic Church* (St. Paul: Wanderer Press, 1994) no. 1869, 457.

[9] See ibid., no. 408, 103.

[10] Pope John Paul II, Post-Synodal Apostolic Exhortation "Reconciliation and Penance" *(Reconciliatio et paenitentia)* no. 16 (Washington, D.C.: United States Catholic Conference, 1984) 50–56, at 54, 55.

[11] See Josef Pieper, *The Four Cardinal Virtues: Prudence, Justice, Fortitude, Temperance*, trans. Richard and Clara Winton and others (New York: Harcourt, Brace & World, 1965).

[12] Observe the order in which St. Thomas Aquinas lists them in ST I-II, q. 61, a. 2.

[13] See ST I-II, q. 109, a. 3.

[14] The council rejects the proposition that "people are justified either by the imputation of Christ's justice alone, or by the remission of sins alone, excluding grace and charity, which is poured into their hearts by the Holy Spirit and inheres in them." See Trent's Decree on Justification, Dupuis 1961. Note that grace and charity are so conceived as a unity that they are assigned a singular verb, "is poured" (Latin: *diffundatur*), when they constitute its subject.

[15] See ch. 15 of Trent's Decree on Justification, Dupuis 1945, from which it will suffice to quote just the heading: "By every mortal sin grace is lost, but not faith."

[16] Paul VI, Apostolic Constitution on Indulgences *(Indulgentiarum doctrina)* (Washington, D.C.: United States Catholic Conference, 1967) no. 4, which has a different trans. from that found in RP.

[17] St. Augustine, *On Baptism, Against the Donatists* 1, 28 (PL 43, 124) my trans.

[18] Vatican II's Dogmatic Constitution on the Church *(Lumen gentium)* no. 11, Flannery, 15.

[19] RP 7a.

[20] RP 7b.

²¹ See DS 1544, 1577, 1669, 1679, 1680, 1707, 1710.

²² See ST I-II, q. 88, a. 1.

²³ Ibid. Also ST I-II, q. 72, a. 5.

²⁴ J. F. Niemeyer, *venialis*, in his *Mediae Latinitatis Lexicon Minus*, has "pardonable." E. Forcellini, *venialis*, in *Totius latinitatis lexicon*, has as the strictly etymological meaning *veniam pertinens*, that is, "pertaining to pardon." Since the relation to pardon is here indicated as positive but not further specified, the transition to "pardonable" or "forgivable" is understandable.

²⁵ This is the example given by John Fearon, editor of vol. 25 of the Blackfriars edition of the *Summa Theologiae* (New York: McGraw Hill, 1969) 45, note j.

²⁶ ST I-II, q. 88, a. 1; my trans.

²⁷ This is what John Fearon wrongly claims the etymological meaning of "venial" to be. See Blackfriars *Summa Theologiae*, vol. 25, 42, n. f.

²⁸ However, etymologically the word "absolution" means nothing more than the "conclusion," the drawing-to-an-end of the ritual.

²⁹ See ch. 2 of Tertullian's *De pudicitia* (On Purity) (PL 2, 985). See William Le Saint's translation of this passage in *Tertullian: Treatises on Penance*, vol. 28 of *Ancient Christian Writers* (New York: Newman Press, 1959) 59–60.

³⁰ See James Dallen, *The Reconciling Community: The Rite of Penance* (New York: Pueblo, 1986) 59.

³¹ See Bruce Vawter on 1 John 5:16f. in "The Johannine Epistles," *The Jerome Biblical Commentary*, ed. R. Brown, J. Fitzmyer, and R. Murphy (Englewood Cliffs, N.J.: Prentice-Hall, 1968) no. 62:29, 412 a. See also Raymond Brown's exhaustive discussion of this text in *The Epistles of John* (Garden City, N.Y.: Doubleday, 1982) 610–19.

³² See ch. 15 and can. 28 of the Council of Trent's Decree on Justification, Dupuis 1945, 1978.

³³ See the explanation offered by Raymond Brown in *The Epistles of John*, 617–19.

³⁴ See ch. 5 of the Council of Trent's Doctrine on the Sacrament of Penance, Dupuis 1625, 1626; see also canons 1 and 7, DS 1701, 1707.

³⁵ David Coffey, "Rahner's Theology of Fundamental Option," *Philosophy and Theology* 10, no. 1 (1997) 255–84, at 280.

³⁶ Rahner has coined the word "categorial" (German: *kategorial*) in order to avoid "categorical" (German: *kategorisch*), as the latter, having its own distinct meaning, would be misleading in this context.

³⁷ In preference to the official English translation, I have here translated the Latin text of *Catechismus Catholicae Ecclesiae* (Vatican City: Libreria Editrice Vaticana, 1997) no. 2352. Note that the relevance of such factors is here recognized in regard to a sexual sin (masturbation), but is not mentioned when the catechism speaks of the requirements for "mortal" sin in general (no. 1857), where it is content to quote Pope John Paul II's statement in *Reconciliatio et paenitentia*, no. 17, that "it [the Synod] . . . recalled that *mortal sin* is sin whose object is grave matter and which is also committed with full knowledge and deliberate consent."

³⁸ See James Keenan, "The Problem with Thomas Aquinas's Concept of Sin," *Heythrop Journal* 35 (1994) 401–20, at 411.

[39] Karl Rahner, *Foundations of Christian Faith: An Introduction to the Idea of Christianity*, trans. William Dych (New York: Seabury, 1978) 97.

[40] Ibid., 104.

[41] The Council of Trent's Decree on Justification, ch. 9, Dupuis 1936 (DS 1534).

[42] Karl Rahner, "On the Theology of the Incarnation," in *Theological Investigations*, vol. 4, trans. Kevin Smyth (Baltimore: Helicon Press, 1966) 110.

[43] Rahner, *Foundations of Christian Faith*, 79.

[44] This objection is that of Timothy O'Connell, in "The Question of Grundentscheidung," *Philosophy and Theology* 10, no. 1 (1997) 143–68, at 164–67.

[45] See Coffey, "Rahner's Theology of Fundamental Option," in which I argue in more detail much of the case presented here. Here, though, I also take the opportunity to respond to criticisms on some matters of importance occurring in the article.

[46] Karl Rahner, "Reflections on the Unity of the Love of Neighbor and the Love of God," in *Theological Investigations*, vol. 6, trans. Karl-H. and Boniface Kruger (Baltimore: Helicon, 1969) 231–49.

[47] Karl Rahner, "The 'Commandment' of Love in Relation to the Other Commandments," in *Theological Investigations*, vol. 5, trans. Karl-H. Kruger (Baltimore: Helicon, 1966) 439–59.

[48] See Coffey, "Rahner's Theology of Fundamental Option," 264–65.

[49] See Rahner, "Reflections on the Unity of the Love of Neighbor and the Love of God," 247.

[50] Jean Porter, "Moral Language and the Language of Grace: The Fundamental Option and the Virtue of Charity," *Philosophy and Theology* 10, no. 1 (1997) 169–98, at 181–82.

[51] See my article, "Rahner's Theology of Fundamental Option"; Keenan, "The Problem with Thomas Aquinas's Concept of Sin"; and Porter's reply, "A Response to Brian Linnane and David Coffey," *Philosophy and Theology* 10, no. 1 (1997) 285–92.

[52] See Keenan, "The Problem with Thomas Aquinas's Concept of Sin," 406–7, 409; and Jean Porter, "A Response," 288–91.

[53] ST II-II, q. 23, a. 4 ad 2 (my trans.).

[54] All trans. in this paragraph are my own.

[55] My trans.

[56] Josef Fuchs, "Good Acts and Good Persons," in *Understanding Veritatis Splendor*, ed. John Wilkins (London: SPCK, 1994) 21–26, at 21–22.

[57] See Rahner, "Theology of Freedom," *Theological Investigations*, vol. 6, 178–96, at 189–90.

[58] See Stephen Duffy, *The Dynamics of Grace: Perspectives in Theological Anthropology* (Collegeville: The Liturgical Press, 1993) 159–60.

[59] See ibid., 99.

[60] See Pope John Paul II, "Reconciliation and Penance" *(Reconciliatio et paenitentia)*, no. 17, at 63–64, and Encyclical Letter on Certain Fundamental Questions of the Church's Moral Teaching, "The Splendor of Truth" *(Veritatis splendor)* nos. 65–70 (Boston: St. Paul Books & Media, 1993) 82–90.

⁶¹ Report of the International Theological Commission, "Penance and Reconciliation," *Origins* 13, no. 31 (Jan. 12, 1984) 513–24, at 523, col. 3.

⁶² See n. 44.

⁶³ *De veritate,* q. 27, a. 1 ad 9; my trans.

⁶⁴ ST II-II, q. 24, a. 10 and 2, and *De malo,* q. 7, a. 2.

⁶⁵ See *I Sent,* dist. 17, chs. 1 and 2.

⁶⁶ *Catechism,* no. 1863, 456.

Chapter Two

# The Church's Ministry of Reconciliation

I n this chapter we shall investigate the emergence of an official ministry of reconciliation in the Church and the subsequent history of this ministry. On the basis of this we shall offer a theological reflection on the sacrament of reconciliation. While we refrain in this chapter from speculation as to how the sacrament will continue to develop in the future, we shall point out that its trajectory shaped over the centuries does rule out certain forms one hears advocated today. The object of the exercise is to attain a deeper appreciation of what constitutes the essence of the sacrament and what it actually does or is intended to do. Because baptism, anointing of the sick, and Eucharist are also, in their own ways, sacraments of reconciliation, we shall then examine how the four of them relate to each other, and we shall conclude with a brief section on the necessity of the sacrament of reconciliation, an aspect of it much challenged today.

## Reconciliation in Salvation History

In its introduction RP sets out to situate the sacrament of reconciliation in its proper context of the history of salvation. It devotes the first section of the introduction, RP 1 and 2, to this purpose under the heading "The Mystery of Reconciliation in the History of Salvation." In fact, though, it treats here not salvation history in itself, but only its consummation in Christ and his ministry. It does, however, briefly *refer* to salvation history, by alluding to the fact that the summons to repentance had often been "sounded by the prophets" of Israel and had been central to the message of Christ's precursor, John the Baptist, who had come "preaching a baptism of repentance for the forgiveness of sins" (Mark 1:4). It could have provided a sketch of the entire history of God's dealings with his people, starting with his election of them to be his own and his entering into covenant with them, so that on behalf of all creation they might offer him fitting worship and become the means whereby the other peoples of the world might be drawn to the worship of the true God. It would then have been necessary to show that this purpose was constantly threatened through the infidelity of human beings, so that time and again it became necessary to recall them to it through repentance and renewal. This was done not only through the ministry of prophets, but through the rituals of established religion, principally the annual observance of the Day of Atonement (see Lev 16:23, 27-32 and Num 29:7-11), with which Jesus' atonement on the cross is dramatically contrasted in the Letter to the Hebrews. Reconciliation was not primary in God's plan of leading human beings to fulfillment, but given the sinfulness of the people it became an indispensable secondary element of it. God's whole purpose, including reconciliation, was superabundantly realized in the person of Christ, in his life, death, and resurrection.

Christ's community, the Church, whose work was nothing other than to perpetuate that of Christ, accordingly became the new people of God, bearer of the new covenant foretold by the prophet Jeremiah (31:31). After this there could be no further covenant, for this one was perfect, made so through the perfect obedience of Christ (see Hebrews 8, 9). Never again could God's purpose be threatened by his covenanted people. However, because of their personal infidelities, they, taken individually, like their counterparts of Israel, stood in constant need of reconciliation and forgiveness, and this was so from the beginning of their history. Hence the provision in the Church of the sacrament of reconciliation, comparable to the rituals and prophetic ministry of old. But where the sacrament differed from former ways was that it restored the baptismal union of Christians with Christ, and this included participation in his perfect covenant holiness and obedience. For whereas the dealings of the Israelites with God were situated in a history in progress toward the fulfillment (technically the "eschaton"), a progress that was not always positive and that was constantly exposed to threat, the dealings of Christians with him are always and inevitably referred to the perfect once-for-all eschatological fulfillment of salvation history that has already been attained in principle in Christ. Hopefully, these personal observations fill out what is at best implicit in the treatment provided by RP.

## Reconciliation in the Ministry of Jesus

RP 1 is devoted to a summary presentation of the importance of reconciliation in the earthly ministry of Jesus. As is proper, it begins with a firm statement that in Christ it was the Father who principally accomplished the work of reconciliation; further, he was reconciling the world to himself, and in so doing was revealing his mercy. The scriptural references given are 2 Cor 5:18ff. and Col 1:20. RP 1 continues, again with scriptural backing, to assert that the life of Jesus should be seen as the fulfillment of this charge laid upon him by the Father. It then goes on to list the various activities or actions of Jesus that bear out the truth of this assertion.

The first of these is preaching. Mark 1:14-15 tells us: "(14) Now after John was arrested, Jesus came into Galilee, preaching the gospel of God, (15) and saying, 'The time is fulfilled, and the kingdom of God is at hand; repent [*metanoeite*], and believe in the gospel.'" RP quotes only v. 15b, but the whole text is necessary if we are to understand that Jesus' words here encapsulate "the gospel of God," and that repentance and faith are the two requirements for entering the kingdom (reign, dominion) of God, on which the Gospel, the "good news" from God, is centered. *Metanoia* (repentance, change of heart) and faith are the two sides of the one coin. To give oneself in faith to Jesus on the basis of his preached word and so to enter the kingdom of his Father, one must heed his injunction to turn away from sin. A good understanding of this text enables us to appreciate how basic penance was to the Gospel that he preached.

The second activity of Jesus that bears witness to the centrality of reconciliation in his ministry is the fact that he "welcomed sinners and reconciled them with the Father," the scriptural references being Luke 5:20, 27-32, and 7:48. The first and the third of these texts refer to instances where Jesus declared the sins of a particular person forgiven. The second is an instance of his eating and drinking, his "table-fellowship," with sinners, which the Gospels inform us gave great offense to his critics. The very fact of extending table-fellowship to sinners was an offer of reconciliation and salvation on the part of Jesus and therefore of his Father also. Commenting on this practice of Jesus, Joachim Jeremias wrote, "The inclusion of sinners in the community of salvation, achieved in table-fellowship, is the most meaningful expression of the message of the redeeming love of God."[1] As we shall see, this theme was prominent in the accounts of the Last Supper, and it remains so in the sacrament of the Eucharist today.

The third activity of Jesus mentioned by RP in connection with reconciliation is the healing of the sick. In the text referred to, Matt 9:2-8, a link between healing and reconciliation is emphasized. For the purposes of the narrative a purely external, apologetical link would have sufficed, but in fact the link is intrinsic. For the Jewish people thought of the human person as a unified whole; and accordingly, the healing of the visible dimension of the person, the body, became a sign of the healing of the invisible dimension, the soul, and of the person as a whole. I shall quote from the Marcan version, 2:1-12, to which the Matthean text along with Luke 5:17-26 is a parallel. Like the parallels, it has Jesus speak first to the bystanders and then to the paralytic whose sins he has just declared forgiven. Verses 10-11 read, "(10) 'But that you may know that the Son of man has authority on earth to forgive sins'—he said to the paralytic—(11) 'I say to you, rise, take up your pallet and go home.'" The intrinsic link here affirmed between bodily and spiritual healing is implicit in all the gospel accounts of Jesus' healings.

Before we move on, there is a point in regard to the last two activities of Jesus that needs to be clarified. It is this: nowhere in the gospels does Jesus claim to be able to forgive sins directly. In each place where he speaks of this power in relation to his ministry (Mark 2:1-12 and parallels and Luke 7:36-50) he claims no more than the power authoritatively to declare sins forgiven by God on the basis of the perceived disposition, the ardor, of the recipient. In the first instance the disposition is the faith of the paralytic and his friends evident in the successful accomplishment of their difficult maneuver, and in the second it is the love of the sinful woman manifested in her tears and her kissing and anointing of Jesus' feet. Admittedly, in the Marcan passage just quoted, as in the parallels, Jesus does appear to claim direct power to forgive sins. But there is wide agreement among commentators, based on sound arguments, that the entire verse in which he does this (v. 10 in Mark) is a statement stemming from the evangelist rather than from Jesus.[2] It reflects a post-resurrection faith on the part of Mark in Jesus' messiah-ship and divinity. Admittedly, too, Jesus appears, in John 20:21-23, to hand on to his disciples the power to forgive sins, a power, so the argument goes, which he must have had himself. But here too it is the risen Jesus who speaks, which is to say that the evangelist and his community came to recognize this power in him on the basis of his resurrection.

In any case, later in the chapter we shall need to consider the precise application of this injunction, which is open to various interpretations. This does not mean that Jesus did not possess a ministry of forgiveness of sins. He did possess this ministry, but it is evident from what he was remembered to have said in his earthly life that he understood it as a ministry of authoritative declaration of forgiveness by God rather than of forgiveness stemming directly from himself. It is important here to understand that the New Testament, written as it was from the stand-point of the resurrection, has the last word in judging the saving effec-tiveness of Jesus. In doing this, it goes beyond its memory of Jesus' actual claim, which insofar as it had to do with himself was only an implicit claim in any case. There is nothing shocking or even surprising in this: it bears witness to what we should expect, the presence of a truly human consciousness in Jesus, that is, a developing consciousness. The rele-vance and importance of Jesus' remembered claim will become clear when we come to consider the attitude of the early Church to its own ministry of reconciliation.

The fourth action of Jesus is his endowing the Last Supper with a sacrificial and saving character in constituting it a ritual anticipation of his death. The Scripture text to which RP refers in this connection is Matt 26:28: "This is my blood of the covenant, which is poured out for many for the forgiveness of sins." Of the four Last Supper accounts this is the only one containing the phrase "for the forgiveness of sins." The Old Testament text on which this verse draws is Exod 24:8, in which Moses is said to sprinkle the people with the blood of sacrifice. It has been pointed out that Jewish tradition interpreted this act as ex-piatory and that it is evident from Heb 9:19-22 that this view was still current in the first century.[3] It follows from this that just as Moses' rit-ual act participated in the expiatory character of the sacrifice offered by the "young men of the people of Israel," so does Jesus' ritual act at the Last Supper share in the expiatory character of his forthcoming death. As Paul tells us, this death was "for our trespasses" (Rom 4:25).

The fifth action of Jesus is the deliberate laying down of his life for our sins. RP, in echoing Rom 4:25 by saying that "he himself died for our sins and rose again for our justification," goes beyond Jesus' historical life in the second part of the statement, but in the first part, that "he died for our sins," remains within the bounds of demonstrable history. First, we can point to the interpretation of his forthcoming death that he had just given at the Last Supper. Of this, Hans Kessler wrote that "in the face of the non-acceptance of salvation (with the consequence of judgment), Jesus learned that the salvation that is God's lordship was to come no longer just in his existence for others, but through his death for sinners. . . . At the Last Supper he expressed this in unfamiliar gestures and with rather indirect words (Isaiah 53 or 2 Maccabees 7, and elsewhere)."[4] Secondly, we can invoke the fact that in undergoing the death of a sinner under the Law, a manner of death he could have avoided, Jesus did no more than affirm in an ultimate way the identification of himself with sinners (in order that they might be saved) that we have seen him make constantly and undeviatingly throughout the course of his life in obedience to the Father's charge.

## The Grounding of the Sacrament in the Ministry of Jesus

The five activities or actions of Jesus discussed in the last section are presented by RP in order to establish the centrality of penance and reconciliation in his earthly mission. It comes as no surprise, therefore, when it says, "Our Savior Jesus Christ, when he gave his apostles and their successors power to forgive sins, instituted in his Church the sacrament of penance." No scriptural reference is given at this point, but earlier it had said, "After his resurrection he sent the Holy Spirit upon the apostles, empowering them to forgive or retain sins [reference: John 20:19-23] and sending them forth to all peoples to preach repentance and the forgiveness of sins in his name [reference: Luke 24:47]." Note that the "forgiveness of sins in his name" to which RP and the Lucan text refer is the *preaching* of this forgiveness, the proclamation of the Gospel, and not the sacrament of reconciliation, even in rudimentary form.[5] Is RP, therefore, attaching the whole burden of supplying a scriptural basis for the sacrament to the Johannine passage? Let us look into this question.

The key verses of this passage, 21-23, read as follows:

> (21) Jesus said to them again, "Peace be with you. As the Father has sent me, even so I send you." (22) And when he had said this, he

breathed on them and said to them, "Receive the Holy Spirit. (23) If
you forgive the sins of any, they are forgiven; if you retain the sins of
any, they are retained."

On any reckoning, RP is making a minimal explicit claim for this passage. The Council of Trent was much more forthright when it said,
"The Lord instituted the sacrament of penance, principally when after
his resurrection he breathed upon his disciples and said: 'Receive the
Holy Spirit. If you forgive the sins of any, they are forgiven them; if you
retain the sins of any, they are retained'" [John 20:22-23].[6] Moreover, it
went on to condemn those who related these words to the proclamation of the Gospel rather than the sacrament of penance, as well as those
who either denied that priests in the state of sin could absolve, or as-
serted that this power belonged to each of the faithful.[7]

Raymond Brown reports an opinion of Catholic exegetes that what
was defined here is only that the Church's penitential discipline is a legitimate application of this text, not that this was the meaning in the
evangelist's mind when he wrote it.[8] This allows Catholic scholars to
propose alternative interpretations, which many do, including varia-
tions of the opinions rejected by Trent, mentioned above.[9] Brown's own
view is that the purely exegetical evidence is not strong enough to establish any particular position.[10] For him it is not clear whether v. 23
refers to all the disciples or just to "the twelve" mentioned in the following verse; it *is* clear that, like the "binding" and "loosing" of Matt
16:19 and 18:18, this verse refers to the exercise of discriminatory judgment, but whether this is confined to the decision as to who is to be admitted to baptism or is extended to judgments about whose sins are to
be forgiven in the postbaptismal community of the Church is not clear.

It is clear, however, that as a post-resurrection saying of Jesus this
can be presumed to reflect no less a conviction of Jesus' divinity and
hence his direct power to forgive sins than we already saw present in
Mark 2:10. But the memory of Jesus' actual practice in his ministry
was, as we saw, also accurately remembered and faithfully recorded in
the gospels, and this amounted to no more than an authoritative declaration of sins forgiven by God. Further, when we look at what the New
Testament tells us of the actual practice of the Church of that time, as
we soon shall (and admittedly there is not much to go by), we see that
in this regard it dared do more than Jesus was remembered to have done
in his lifetime. But this is true not only of New Testament times but for
many centuries of the later history of the Church. This makes it more

likely that John 20:23, which emerged out of precisely this milieu, refers to the forgiveness of sins stemming from the preaching of the gospel and the administration of baptism rather than from a postbaptismal institution for the forgiveness of sins. This view, as we saw, is in any case that espoused by some Catholic, as well as non-Catholic, commentators. The alternative, not so plausible, would be to attribute to this passage from the end of the first century a consciousness that did not surface again in the Church until the thirteenth century.

The reticence of RP on this matter is therefore understandable, but this does not mean that the Church is left without firm scriptural foundation for the sacrament of reconciliation. We have already seen on the basis of Scripture the centrality of penance in the mission of Jesus, the continuation of which is the mission, that is, the entire mission, of the Church. Modern scriptural studies have rendered it impossible for us to accept the institution of the sacraments by Christ, or even the institution of the Church itself, in the simple and direct manner taken for granted by Trent. Karl Rahner admits that "at least prescinding from the institution of the Lord's Supper, the same problem exists for all the sacraments with regard to their 'institution' by Jesus (and this includes the sacraments which are recognized in non-Catholic churches)."[11] It is necessary, therefore, to acquire a more nuanced and sophisticated understanding of the expression "instituted by Christ" in regard to the sacraments. Rahner offers just such an understanding with these words:

> The sacramentality of the church's basic activity is implied by the very essence of the church as the irreversible presence of God's salvific offer in Christ. This sacramentality is interpreted by the church in the seven sacraments, just as the church developed its own essence in its constitution.[12]

This means that every element central to Christ's mission will be inherited by the Church as central to *its* mission. And the principal way in which the Church discharges this mission is through word and sacrament. If, therefore, historically, such an element has appeared as one of the Church's seven sacraments, no further proof to establish its authenticity from Scripture is needed beyond a demonstration that this element was in fact central to Christ's mission. This we have already shown in the case of penance. But in this instance Scripture tells us more. For it says that Christ handed on to his disciples his own ministry of the forgiveness of sins, as we saw in quoting John 20:21-23. Whether or not such a handing-on included specific instructions regarding the sacrament of reconciliation is immaterial. Trent was therefore acting correctly when it claimed that its interpretation of John 20:22-23 was a legitimate application of the text. Had it so wished, RP could have appealed to other texts as well. Thus in two places in the Pauline literature witness is borne to the fact that within thirty years of the death and resurrection of Jesus the apostle was showing confidence in dealing constructively with the problem of sin among his converts. Thus in 1 Cor 5:1-5 and 9-13 he revealed his way of handling a case of "incest" (living with one's father's wife) that occurred in the Corinthian community. Following the lead of Deuteronomy (17:7; 19:19; and 22:24), he imposed punishment by exclusion on the guilty person. In part this meant not sharing meals, which presumably would also include the Eucharist, with the sinner (see 1 Cor 5:11), the aim being to bring him to his senses so that he could be saved (see 1 Cor 5:5). The text is silent as to when or how this discipline was to be brought to an end. In the second place, 2 Cor 2:5-11, Paul deals with another case of sin at Corinth, namely someone who has given serious, unidentified offense to him and the community. This person has already suffered punishment by exclusion at the hands of the majority (2 Cor 2:6), and now Paul declares that this punishment has been enough and should be ended through forgiveness on the part of the community, a forgiveness to which Paul will add his own (2 Cor 2:10-11), lest the guilty person be overwhelmed with sorrow (2 Cor 2:7-8). This forgiveness is expressed through readmission to fellowship, sharing of meals including presumably the Eucharist, and perhaps "a holy kiss" such as is commended in Rom 16:16.

But what exactly is this forgiveness extended by Paul and the community? Surely it is nothing more than the readmission of the excluded person to their fellowship on the grounds that through suffering he has expiated his sin before God. This does not amount to a direct forgiveness of the sin in the name of Christ and God on the part of Paul and the community. It surpasses the remembered practice of Jesus himself only in its insistence on what we might call the "Deuteronomic norm," that is, expiation of sin through penance by temporary exclusion from the community. When we look at the later history of the sacrament, as we soon shall, we shall see that it took many centuries for the consciousness to emerge that the Church itself, through its office-bearers, possessed the power to do what, as a result of the resurrection, Jesus, despite his more modest practice, was perceived already in the gospels as able to do.

This position on the meaning of the expression "instituted by Christ" in regard to the sacraments is supported by the *Catechism of the Catho-*

*lic Church.* Immediately after asserting with the Council of Trent that "the sacraments of the new law were . . . all instituted by Jesus Christ our Lord," it continues:

> Jesus' words and actions during his hidden life and public ministry were already salvific, for they anticipated the power of his Paschal mystery. They announced and prepared what he was going to give the Church when all was accomplished. The mysteries of Christ's life are the foundations of what he would henceforth dispense in the sacraments, through the ministers of his Church, for "what was visible in our Savior has passed over into his mysteries" [St. Leo the Great]. Sacraments are "powers that come forth" from the Body of Christ, which is ever-living and life-giving. They are actions of the Holy Spirit at work in his Body, the Church.[13]

We are now in a better position to answer the question put earlier, namely whether RP places the whole burden of providing scriptural justification for the sacrament of reconciliation on John 20:23. Our answer must be that it does not. This text merely takes its place with others in establishing the centrality of reconciliation in the mission of Jesus, his handing-on of that ministry to the Church that succeeded him, and the fact that within a few years of his death the Church had begun, at least through the apostle Paul, to exercise that ministry with confidence, though not with the full consciousness that it later attained. It was a ministry that was to remain in the Church up to the present time and beyond, though undergoing major transformations in the course of its rather checkered history. To that history we now turn, though only in the briefest summary way, in order to throw into relief the theological principles operative in its development.

## The History of the Sacrament

The three main divisions of the history of the sacrament are, with some overlapping, the ancient period (the first six centuries), the medieval period (seventh through fifteenth centuries), and the modern period (from the sixteenth century on).[14] In the early stage of the ancient period, immediately following the New Testament, the reconciliation of sinners was conducted along the lines laid down by Paul. This procedure, however, was followed only in cases of sin experienced as most scandalous by the community. Ordinary sinners expiated their sin through prayer, fasting, and almsgiving, practices that were already traditional in Judaism and would become so in Christianity as well. The early centuries saw a growing institutionalization of the procedures for dealing with the gravest cases of sin, with authority becoming centered on the person of the bishop.

Thanks to the writings of Tertullian, a lay observer (probably), we can observe an early stage of this process at Carthage at the beginning of the third century. Tertullian speaks of the *exomologesis* or "confession" of those seeking reconciliation. He used this word, however, in a broader sense than is usual today. For him it denoted primarily a confession of faith, then the praise of God, especially of his mercy, and only then a confession of sinfulness. Furthermore, it was to be expressed in deeds more than words. When the penitents were deemed to have established through works of penance the genuineness and depth of their reconversion to God, and the Church, led by its presbyters, had prayed earnestly for them, they were readmitted to full fellowship, which was understood to signalize reconciliation with God.

In the mid-third century there was further development, brought about by Cyprian, bishop of Carthage, in his response to the challenge of what to do about those who had defected from the faith during the Decian persecution and now sought reconciliation. His decision was to reconcile all who so petitioned, no matter how serious their sin, but it was necessary for them to submit to the reconciliation process. For Cyprian *exomologesis* stood for the entire participation of the penitent in the process, which was marked by one laying-on of hands at the beginning and another at the end. It seems that the first imposition of hands was an exorcism, namely the signification of the expulsion of the spirit of evil, an expulsion that would be accomplished and made manifest through the performance of the prescribed works of penance. When all had been done to Cyprian's satisfaction, there would follow the second imposition of hands, which signified peace with the Church and readmission to its life, which was life in the Spirit. This was the sense in which it indicated a giving of the Holy Spirit. The penitential works did not of themselves expiate sin, nor was Cyprian conscious of granting direct forgiveness in the name of God; rather, on the basis of the manifestation of the operation of grace in the changed life of the penitents, he felt enabled to bring them back into the fellowship of the Church, which was also a fellowship with God in the Holy Spirit.

In the fourth century the reconciliation process began to be encumbered with detailed regional canonical and liturgical legislation. Hence the name by which it is identified: canonical penance. It resulted in the West in a rigid separation of those undertaking it from the rest of the community and the imposition on them, for the rest of their lives, of an exacting discipline. Further, it could be undergone only once after baptism. This represented the hardening into law of a principle and practice that had been operative since the second century, that is, since "The Shepherd" of Hermas. Not surprisingly, those bound to canonical penance tended to postpone it to late in life, even to their deathbed. This trend reached its peak in the fifth century, but by the end of that century the Church's official penitential discipline had become so unpopular and neglected that change became inevitable.

The East had a somewhat milder experience. Developments parallel to those in the West took place there too, but with this difference: side by side with the public process a more private official means of overcoming sin was developed. The public process was still required for the most serious cases. But penitents not bound to it were encouraged to approach presbyters or holy non-ordained people to seek both encouragement toward a more profound inner repentance and counsel as to appropriate works of penance. The doubtful were urged to follow the same route in order to learn whether their offense was such that these gentler remedies would suffice in their case, or alternatively, whether it was such that it would be necessary for them to enroll in the public process. In these circumstances it appears that the private process had a mitigating effect on the public one. Significantly, some Eastern churches never adopted the Western practice of unrepeatable public penance.

In the West the time was ripe for change, and so began what we have called the medieval period. In the sixth century there began a period of evangelization of western Europe by Irish monks, who brought with them their own religious system, which had been developed through the contacts of Irish monasticism with the East. This was essentially spiritual direction, concerned mainly with growth in the spiritual life, but secondarily with the overcoming of sin through counsel and works of penance. In the secular (non-monastic) European and Gallic setting this emphasis was reversed. As a penitential system it achieved instant popularity, which inevitably brought it into conflict with the moribund public penance still officially in place, particularly as many of the missionaries were not ordained.

Its popularity can be accounted for on several scores. First, it was private; second, it was repeatable; and third, the monks accepted all comers, even those legally bound to canonical penance. After an initially hostile reception on the part of the authorities, a compromise with the official system was gradually reached over the next few centuries through various local councils. According to this "Carolingian" compromise, for grave sins publicly known the canonical public penance remained prescribed, but for grave sins not publicly known the new private form was declared sufficient. However, even though there was as yet no priestly absolution, the confessors had to be priests, though it took centuries for this requirement to be accepted universally. But insofar as the legislation continued to prescribe canonical penance, it was a dead letter. Private confession to a priest eventually won the day. However, readmission to the Eucharist lost its place in the process of reconciliation with the Church, and now merely meant the restoration of the right to receive Holy Communion, a right only rarely exercised in any case.

At this point something needs to be said about the season of Lent. Originally a time of preparation for baptism, by the fifth century it had become a recurring period of penance. A penitential discipline culminating in reconciliation on Holy Thursday was developed for it, and thus it became the earliest form of repeatable penance in the Church. I mention it now because of its relevance to the question of absolution. According to the Carolingian compromise, those who had confessed privately to a priest were expected to present themselves to the bishop for "absolution" at the solemn Lenten penitential service. What was this absolution? Certainly not what it is today. The term goes back to the time of canonical penance, and in itself means no more than the official termination of the penitential process. That is exactly what it was originally, and in practice it took the form of a blessing given by the bishop. At that time there was no suggestion that it played a causal role in the forgiveness of sin. (As we shall see, that idea first arose, in the course of discussion, in the middle of the thirteenth century.) In fact, the requirement of recourse to the bishop proved impractical, so much so that absolution (in its original sense) came to be given by the priest-confessor immediately after the confession. Penitents were trusted to perform the prescribed works of penance in a satisfactory manner on their own, as they still are.

Initially, the same expiatory value and importance as ever was assigned to these works, but by the twelfth century they had decreased, as their penitential, expiatory value came to be transferred to the confession itself, and this because of the difficulty and humiliation perceived as involved in confessing one's sins to another. Here there is a point of considerable theological interest. At different times in the history of penance divine forgiveness was thought to be attached to different elements of the penance process. That it was attached to repentance goes without saying, but it was also attached, successively, to the works of penance, to confession, and finally, as we shall see, to absolution. At the end of this brief historical summary, I shall offer a theological comment on this fascinating phenomenon. In any case, by the thirteenth century penance had become private and was accomplished through confession to a priest and priestly absolution with the subsequent performance of a prescribed token penitential work. In this form it was laid down for the whole Church by the Fourth Lateran Council in 1215.[15]

The next step was the acquisition of the conviction that absolution actually imparted divine forgiveness. This came around the middle of the thirteenth century in the work of several theologians, William of Auvergne, Hugh of St. Cher, and William of Middleton, and was taken up by St. Bonaventure and St. Thomas Aquinas. However, each of these theologians in his own way protected the transcendence of God (God alone gives grace, God alone forgives sin) by seeing absolution as dispositive, that is to say, having the function of bringing the penitent's repentance to the perfection that calls down God's grace and forgiveness. St. Thomas's way of conceiving this was truly ingenious. He saw the acts of the penitent, repentance ("contrition"), confession, and work of penance ("satisfaction"), as the "matter" of the sacrament, and absolution as its "form." This was a modification and application of an element of Aristotle's philosophy. According to Aristotle, matter and form are the constitutive principles of all material being, matter being the principle to be determined, and form the determining principle. With Aristotle, Thomas held that matter has to be prepared ("disposed") by a form in order to receive this form (for example, a log of wood must first be heated in order to receive the form of fire).

Thomas went on to say that the "ultimate" disposition, the very last disposition *before* the communication of the form, is also the very *first* element of the communication of the form itself. Applied to the sacrament, this meant that the ultimate disposition of the penitent for God's grace and forgiveness, namely "perfect contrition," was actually given by God as the first element pertaining strictly to grace and forgiveness itself. In this way Thomas was able to raise the status of priestly absolution from being purely dispositive to being the instrumental cause, that is the means, by which God himself imparts grace and forgiveness. This was Thomas's way of explaining the direct instrumental role played by priestly absolution in the forgiveness of sins in the sacrament, at the same time safeguarding the transcendence of God.

A few decades later, Duns Scotus taught that absolution constituted the essence of the sacrament, with the acts of the penitent being merely necessary conditions for forgiveness. But though his influence was widespread, the ecclesiastical magisterium did not endorse this view. Nevertheless, because of his authority his doctrine on this matter served to put an end at last to the practice of confession to non-ordained confessors. But note that St. Thomas's doctrine would have had this effect in any case, for while he did not hold that absolution *constituted* the essence of the sacrament, he did teach that it *pertained* to the essence, along with the acts of the penitent.

The final act of the medieval period was the canonization of the greater part of the Thomistic doctrine at the Council of Florence in 1439. The council taught that the "quasi-matter" ("quasi" because only *like* matter, not actually matter) of the sacrament consists of the three acts of the penitent, contrition, confession, and satisfaction, while "the form of the sacrament is the words of absolution spoken by the priest," and "the effect of this sacrament is absolution from sins."[16] Note that missing from this statement is St. Thomas's explanation of *how* absolution brings about this effect. Quite properly, the council did not want to get involved in theological matters still open to debate.

With the sixteenth century there began the modern period in the history of the sacrament. This history is centered on two principal events, the Council of Trent (1545–63), the Catholic Church's answer to the Protestant Reformation, and the Second Vatican Council (1962–65), the council of Catholic "aggiornamento" or renewal. We shall not here summarize the teachings of Trent on the sacrament, contained in its Decree on Justification (1547)[17] and its Doctrine on the Sacrament of Penance (1551),[18] as they are retained in RP and we shall have the opportunity to study them there at the appropriate time. Suffice it to say that there is no significant change from the doctrine that emerged at the end of the medieval period. Enshrined in the Tridentine doctrine is the scholastic distinction of "perfect" and "imperfect" contrition, with the latter declared as sufficient for the sacrament.[19] Also it enjoins the so-called "integral" confession, that is, the confession of all mortal sins "of which penitents after a diligent self-examination are conscious."[20] The Tridentine ritual of Pope Paul V, published in 1614, presents a streamlined and private liturgy focused on confession and absolution, with little sense of the ecclesial dimension rightly belonging to this as to every sacrament, and scarcely any "confession" *(exomologesis)* in the broad sense that we found in Tertullian.

Nor will it be necessary for us to say much here about Vatican II, since RP is intended as precisely the embodiment of its directives. Just two things will suffice. First, in the Dogmatic Constitution on the Church *(Lumen gentium)* there is a single sentence of high importance, in art. 11:

> Those who approach the sacrament of Penance obtain pardon through God's mercy for the offense committed against him, and are, at the same time, reconciled with the church which they have wounded by their sins and which by charity, by example and by prayer labors for their conversion.[21]

This statement about reconciliation with the Church represents a recovery from early times of a significant aspect almost entirely missing from Trent. Secondly, Vatican II's Constitution on the Sacred Liturgy *(Sacrosanctum concilium)* showed its determination to reintroduce this idea into the liturgy of penance when it decreed that "the rite and formulas of Penance are to be revised so that they more clearly express both the nature and the effect of the sacrament,"[22] particularly when it is realized that according to the council's own official interpretation "nature" in this context denotes precisely the sacrament's "social and ecclesial character."[23] The extent to which RP has done this successfully we shall have to judge for ourselves as we proceed. Thus we draw to a conclusion this brief but necessary history of the sacrament of reconciliation, which doubtless will come as a surprise to those not already familiar with it. They will appreciate the quip I once heard Rahner make in a lecture, when he remarked that "St. Joseph did not build the first confessional."

## Theological Reflection on the History

Let us move on now to a theological reflection arising out of this history. And as I have a good number of comments to make, it will be necessary to keep them brief. The first is that from the beginning the Church had different ways of dealing with grave and non-grave sin. The former was handled through an official process, while the latter could safely be left to penitents themselves. This remained a constant principle, despite the fact that there were changes (developments) in the thinking about what actually constituted grave sin, and the fact that in the modern period it became acceptable, indeed recommended, to approach the sacrament even when the only sins were non-grave (the so-called confession of devotion, hereafter devotional confession).

Next it needs to be pointed out that the sacrament has a genuine history, and, as I said earlier, a rather checkered one at that. Clearly it did not come to us from Christ in anything like the form that it has today. However, its scriptural foundations are clear. From Scripture we learn that reconciliation was central to the ministry of Christ. More-over, on the basis of his resurrection the gospels saw him as possessing the direct power of forgiving sins. It is also clear that he passed on this power to the Church, though for many centuries it interpreted its man-date only in an indirect way. Originally it carried it out through pre-senting the forgiveness of sins as an essential element of the Gospel that it preached. Then it had to deal with the occurrence of sin in the evangelized Christian community, and hence there began the development of penance as a distinct sacrament. What we observe in the Church, therefore, is the sacrament's gradual formation, such that it attained what now appears as its full essence only in the late Middle Ages. From the beginning, though, it was evident that God alone for-gives sins, and that he readily (but only) forgives those who are truly re-pentant. The Church entered the process through the inescapable fact that sin was more than merely a private matter between the sinner and God: it was social and had a damaging effect on the community; furthermore, the community needed to have care for its erring mem-bers. It was necessary, therefore, that a public and official way of deal-ing with the problem of sin be developed.

## Development of the Sacrament

According to the Deuteronomic norm, the first social elements to appear were exclusion from, and eventual reconciliation with, the com-munity. Exclusion from the community involved exclusion from the Eucharist, an effect of grave sin that remains to this day. The purpose of exclusion was to bring sinners to their senses. Soon the time of ex-clusion was filled with works of penance, the purpose being the same: to authenticate and establish the inner repentance in a changed way of life and to expiate the sin before God. Initially, therefore, this element, later known as satisfaction, marked the beginning of the penitential process; later, as we shall see, it was transferred to the end.

Reconciliation, signified by the laying-on of hands and readmission to the Eucharist, was an official act of the Church performed originally on the order of the apostle, later by the bishop, and later still by priests. The point to note is that *as* an official act, it had to be performed by officials and could not be performed by a layperson, though in the early medieval period the phenomenon of lay confession did appear, and lasted some centuries. Further, an important aspect of the Eucharist comes to light here: it is not just communion with Christ and God, but is also communion (fellowship) with the Church. This dimension of the Eucharist needs to be remembered as an important principle for procedure in our own day when questions of "eucharistic sharing" (intercommunion) arise, as they frequently do. (Unfortunately, however, as a result of the individualism of the age, it is often overlooked.) This reconciliation was not yet seen as direct reconciliation with God, though it *was* an application of the Matthean principle that what was bound or loosed by the Church on earth was bound or loosed in heaven. However, even in this perspective, it was not seen as anything more than the final seal put on a reconciliation with God already secured and manifested through faithful adherence to the prescribed works of penance. After the Carolingian compromise, however, reconciliation with the Church became, in Rahner's phrase, one of the "forgotten truths concerning the sacrament of penance,"[24] to be recovered only at Vatican II.

The next element to appear was confession, though it had been there from the beginning in the sense that the penitent's sins were publicly known. It became explicit, however, in the phenomenon of the Irish penance imported to the continent at the start of the Middle Ages. As mentioned above, it brought with it the practice of confession to nonordained ministers, which survived until the fourteenth century. However, as absolution in the modern sense did not yet exist, this practice was understandable. Moreover, the official reaction to it was never friendly: it was resisted, and after the Carolingian compromise it was supposed to go out of existence. As we know, it survived, but this was because at that time the act of confession itself was credited with gaining God's forgiveness. However, like Jas 5:16, which is not concerned with the sacrament or indeed any official process, it cannot be appealed to today as a precedent for the possibility of reintroducing lay confession.

The priest-confessors who increasingly gained the ascendancy after the Carolingian compromise came to give absolution to penitents immediately after making their confession, but it was absolution only in the sense of officially terminating the penance ritual, and reconciliation only in the sense of granting permission to receive Communion again. This practice was facilitated by the perception that expiation occurred as a result of the confession itself, and that therefore the subsequent prescribed work of penance was a mere token. To the extent that this absolution can be called reconciliation (which it can, in a sense), we have here a change of order of acts which remains to this day: satisfaction-reconciliation became reconciliation-satisfaction. However, it is possible to invest satisfaction with real (and not just token) significance (as indeed we should today) without changing the present order, which is demanded by sheer practicality.

The Church can, however, if it sees fit, change the order of the acts without disturbing the substance of the sacrament. Thus—and this is a point appreciated by all too few people—all that has been changed in the requirements for the absolution of grave sins in the new so-called "third rite" ("general absolution") is the order confession-reconciliation to reconciliation-confession, or, to express the latter more exactly, general confession-reconciliation-specific confession. It is decidedly *not* a feature of the new rite that grave sins forgiven in this way do not have to be specifically confessed. This is a point we shall return to. Note that we have *not* here said that the third rite differs from the previous discipline only by a cosmetic change in the order of the acts. It is much more than that: it is an experience, *the* experience, of the fully communal celebration of penance and reconciliation, and it has other positive features as well. But my point remains true: the third rite does not dispense with the obligation to confess grave sins not already confessed.

The last arrival on the scene was absolution in the modern sense, an event that occurred in the mid-thirteenth century. This was forgiveness in the name of Christ and God, in which the priest-minister was seen to play an instrumental role. Thus finally was settled the question of precisely where in the penance process reconciliation with God occurred. Demanded of the penitent was true contrition manifested in sincere confession and willingness to amend their life, this willingness being signified and established in the subsequent performance of a prescribed work of penance. From this it is clear that the two most important elements of the sacrament were contrition and absolution.

What we have here is a power given by Christ, a power exercised in the Church from the beginning, but a power that took twelve and a half centuries to develop its full realization (translation into historical reality). This realization was expressed officially by the Councils of Florence and Trent in their doctrine of the "parts" of penance, namely the three acts of the penitent (contrition, confession, and satisfaction) and the absolution of the priest-minister. It would be naive to expect the sacrament to have existed from the beginning in the form in which it is found today, as any such expectation would founder on the rocks of historical research. It is only in relatively modern times that people have evinced a marked historical consciousness, and so we have inherited from the past expressions, like "instituted by Christ," that are innocent of any such awareness. We can retain these expressions, but we need to interpret them according to modern criteria. For "instituted by Christ" I trust I have done just that in the first sentence of this paragraph.

## *Reconciliation:* Iure Divino

Thus is raised a further question, which needs to be considered here, and which has a bearing on the possible ways in which the sacrament could develop in the future. (For we have no warrant for thinking that the development process which began at the dawn of the Christian era and has continued to the present is going to stop now.) The question is that of the exact meaning of the expression *ius divinum.* There is no problem about how this expression should be *translated:* it means "divine right." Something is *de iure divino,* or simply *iure divino,* "of divine right," if it is of divine foundation, that is, founded or instituted by God or by Christ. The importance of the question will now be evident. For when we say that the sacraments, and reconciliation in particular, are *iure divino,* technically we are saying that they were instituted by Christ. Granted that to be *iure divino* a thing does not have to come to us *directly* by the command of God or from the hands of Christ, the problem, and the question, then, is: What are the indispensable requirements for a thing in order that it be rightly characterized in this way? In modern theology the answer that has emerged is that, with the Church's teaching of tradition as well as Scripture as the source of divine revelation, that is, of God's revealed will for the Church, it is enough that there be something positively enjoined by God or founded by Christ, something evidenced in the New Testament, and evidenced, moreover, as central to God's plan, that in the course of history has developed in the Church into the reality thus characterized. Moreover, this process will have taken place through a series of historically contingent authoritative decisions, decisions, that is, that theoretically could have been different from what they actually were. This is the minimum that is both necessary and sufficient.

Let me give an example: the Roman primacy (the primacy of the pope). In reporting to Rome on its response to the Final Report of ARCIC (the Anglican-Roman Catholic International Commission), the Australian Episcopal Conference first summarized the ARCIC position on the *iure divino* character of the Roman primacy in this way:

> The documents state that the Roman primacy is necessary if God's will for the unity in love and truth of the whole Christian community is to be fulfilled and suggest that the acknowledgement of its emergence by divine providence is the equivalent of recognizing its status as *iure divino*.

But it added immediately:

> To us, however, it does not seem that these statements sufficiently assure the *iure divino* character of the primacy. For this it would be necessary to add that the primacy flows from the nature of the Church as intended by Our Lord and evidenced in the New Testament.[25]

I wish to endorse this statement. It is not enough to say that something emerged in the Church "by divine providence." This statement could be made, for example, about the Society of Jesus (the Jesuits), but no one would claim that the Society is *iure divino*. What I am suggesting here is that the sacrament of reconciliation is *iure divino* in the same way that the Roman primacy is *iure divino*. (Note that the Roman primacy is not just a matter of jurisdiction; it is an essential element of the sacrament of Order, which itself as a totality is *iure divino*.)

The application of this to the sacrament of reconciliation is that the teaching of the Council of Trent and RP about its constitutive parts must be respected both now and in the future. I say "respected," as I do not wish to say that this teaching cannot change. It can, but only in the sense of further development. No one can predict positively what such development would be, but a theologian might make an educated guess or even a recommendation. But what is held as *iure divino* cannot be changed in the sense of abolished, reversed, or rescinded, even in order to be replaced by something claimed to be better.[26] Hence now that they have been acquired, and even though their total acquisition took centuries to accomplish, none of the four parts of the sacrament, contrition, confession, priestly absolution, and satisfaction, can be dispensed with, now or in the future.

We shall return to this principle in detail in the next chapter. But one point should be clarified immediately. We mentioned earlier that grave sins forgiven in the third rite need to be confessed subsequently. But if a person has no grave sins, they are not bound to subsequent confession. There is nothing strange or new about this, for no one is ever bound to confess non-grave sins. They do not require the sacrament for their forgiveness, though one may confess them if one wishes, and indeed is encouraged by RP to do so, in what is called a devotional confession.[27]

A question sometimes asked is that, if the four parts of the sacrament constitute its essence, must we admit that before these were fully in place there existed no sacrament for the forgiveness of postbaptismal sins, but only non-sacramental forms? I offer two brief comments before responding to this question: first, the question betrays an ahistorical mentality; and second, it would in any case be impossible for a sacrament of the Church suddenly to appear from nowhere at some point of its existence. The answer to the question is that the sacrament was not present fully formed at the beginning of the Church's history, but from its roots in the ministry of Christ was formed gradually over a long period. The important point is that the Church was never without an official way of handling positively the problem of postbaptismal sin. Early Christians were not disadvantaged, though the forms of official penance were admittedly more severe then than they are today. From the beginning the Church distinguished between grave and non-grave sin, and was content, as it remains today, to leave the latter to penitents themselves to handle by means of penitential practices that were already traditional, coming as they did from the Old Testament. Through its official discipline it has always concentrated on exercising an effective pastoral ministry to those guilty of grave sin.

## *The* Res et Sacramentum *of Reconciliation*

As the final point in our theological reflection on our brief history of the sacrament, I now wish to consider a matter the importance of which has emerged only since Vatican II, namely the question of the *res et sacramentum* of this sacrament. In the case of each of the sacraments scholasticism had distinguished between the *sacramentum* or *sacramentum tantum* ("the sign only") and the *res* or *res sacramenti* (literally, "the thing of the sign," that is, the ultimate spiritual effect produced by the ritual performance of the sign). For convenience, in what follows let us refer to the *sacramentum* as the "symbol," and to the *res* as the "reality." The symbol was the ritual of the sacrament, including the material elements it involved. For example, in the Eucharist the symbol was the eucharistic ritual, which included the priest's taking the bread and wine, saying Christ's words over them, and giving them to the faithful to eat and drink, while the reality was fellowship by grace with Christ and God. Further, for each sacrament the scholastics placed between the symbol and the reality a mid term, which they called the *res et sacramentum* (reality and symbol), and which we shall call the "symbolic reality."

This entity served a double role: in relation to the symbol it was a "reality," but in relation to the reality it was a symbol. In our example, the Eucharist, it was identified as the real presence of Christ in the elements. Thus the real presence was what was directly signified and brought about by the rite. But it was not an end in itself, for it was oriented beyond itself. As food and drink for the soul it in turn signified and brought about the ultimate reality of the Eucharist, namely fellowship by grace with Christ and God. Hence it was both *sacramentum* and *res,* that is, *res et sacramentum,* in English, symbol and reality, or symbolic reality.

By both earlier and later standards, however, the actual identifications of the symbolic reality made in the Middle Ages were rather impoverished, as we can see from our chosen example, the Eucharist. In this case the understanding of the symbolic reality was restricted to what happened to the bread and wine; there was no mention of the community, the Church. But, speaking of the symbolic reality, Rahner has pointed out that on the basis of research into the early centuries "a more precise analysis of those sacraments in which such an intermediate factor between sign and effect is most clearly perceptible shows that this factor *always has an ecclesiological character*" [emphasis mine]. For the Eucharist he identifies this factor as "deeper incorporation into the Mystical Body of Christ [the Church] through communal reception of his Body."[28] In our brief history we were able to see for ourselves the truth of these statements in regard to the Eucharist. Since Vatican II, theology has set itself the task of rediscovering the symbolic reality of all the sacraments in terms of the ecclesial dimension of each, and of modifying catechesis accordingly.[29] Recall that restructuring the sacrament of penance according to this insight was precisely the mandate that Vatican II gave in its constitution on the liturgy to the prospective revisers of the rite, and that the result of their work is what we have in RP.

The identification of the symbolic reality of penance followed a similar pattern. St. Thomas had identified it in the *Summa* as "interior repentance," with the symbol as the three acts of the penitent plus the absolution of the priest, and the reality as the remission of sin.[30] However, it is interesting to note that, though others might have forgotten about reconciliation with the Church, he did not, though it did not occur to him to suggest that it might constitute the symbolic reality of the sacrament.[31] At the time of Vatican II, however, so James Dallen informs us, "almost all Catholic theologians who held that reconciliation with the Church is an effect of penance regarded it as the *res et sacramentum.*"[32] Considering that Vatican II, as we have seen, taught that reconciliation with the Church *is* an effect of penance, we can safely claim that the position that reconciliation with the Church is the symbolic reality of penance is for all practical purposes now held universally among Catholic theologians. The truth of this position we have also been able to see from our brief history. For we saw that the penitent was reconciled with God *because* the Church reconciled them to itself, and that what the Church bound or loosed on earth was considered bound or loosed in heaven.

It is rather surprising, therefore, that in the two formulas of absolution offered by RP there is no mention of reconciliation with the Church.[33] However, it is implied in the direction to the priest to extend his hands, or at least his right hand, over the head of the penitent, or, in the case of general absolution, to extend his hands over the penitents.[34] While not exactly an imposition of hands, this is clearly an approximation to it, and the significance is the same. We saw in our brief history how Cyprian reconciled penitents to the Church by a ritual the highpoint of which was his imposing hands on their heads.[35] As this meaning is not expressed verbally in the new liturgy, care should be taken to explain it in instructions given periodically on the sacrament.

We conclude this reflection on the *res et sacramentum,* and also on the history of penance, by drawing attention to the importance of the former. First, it highlights the "social and ecclesial character" of the sacrament according to the expressed wish of Vatican II. Second, it exemplifies the role of the priest as acting *in persona Ecclesiae,* "in the person of the Church," that is, as representative of the Church, as well as *in persona Christi,* "in the person of Christ," representative of Christ. It is clear that in the first instance the priest acts on behalf of the Church, whose official representative he is, and so reconciles the penitent with the Church, mystical body of Christ, readmitting them to full fellowship with it, which is signified through subsequent reception of the Eucharist, Christ's sacramental body. Understood as operative throughout this process is the principle that what the Church looses on earth is thereby loosed in heaven. The penitent is therefore at the same time reconciled with God. This bears out my position, argued elsewhere, that, as the head and directive principle of the Church is Christ, in representing the Church the priest also represents Christ.[36] Edward Kilmartin has well explained the relationship between these two representations as follows: "The first [*in persona Ecclesiae*] begins with what is more accessible and progresses toward what is ultimately signified; the second [*in persona Christi*] analyzes the actual process in which what is ultimately signified directs the whole process of symbolization."[37] Finally, our reflection on the *res et sacramentum* of penance has shown from yet another perspective, and by a simple argument, the impossibility of the Church's ever resuming lay confession as a future form of the sacrament: in order to represent the Church a person must have the requisite authority of office, and office implies ordination. Priestly absolution is an essential element of the sacrament.

## The Relation of Reconciliation to Baptism, Anointing, and Eucharist

This chapter continues with a treatment of the relation of this sacrament to baptism, anointing, and Eucharist. RP 2 states that both baptism and Eucharist have to do with the forgiveness of sin. Further, it states that reconciliation is the sacramental means given us by Christ for the forgiveness of postbaptismal sin. In this connection RP quotes St. Ambrose: the Church "possesses both water and tears: the water of baptism, the tears of penance."[38] But on the relation of baptism and reconciliation to the Eucharist, and the need for reconciliation given the existence of the Eucharist, it is silent. Also, as we shall see, the postconciliar revision of the sacrament of anointing of the sick states that it too, if necessary, brings about forgiveness. Let us then take up the inter-relationships of these four sacraments as our next question.

### Reconciliation and Baptism

We begin with the relation of reconciliation to baptism. Baptism is the sacrament of first conversion and reconciliation, of turning away from sin, embracing Christ in faith, and being incorporated into his community, the Church. It implies such a dedication to Christ that in principle further sin is ruled out, so that the question of what to do about postbaptismal sin should not even arise. From the start, however, experience showed that such was the weakness of human nature that this problem did occur, and the Church was faced with the question of how to deal with it in the best interests of both the sinner and the community. Hence the sacrament of reconciliation, which gave Christians the ability to make a fresh start, to regain the dedication and purity of their baptism.

That reconciliation repeats part of the function of baptism is here obvious. The connection was first expressed by Tertullian, who linked them as "these two planks, as it were, of human salvation,"[39] a first offer of salvation, followed by a second, to an otherwise doomed person. The image here is that of an unconverted person floundering around shipwrecked in a sea of faithlessness and sin. They can be saved only if God offers them the plank of baptism, which will carry them to the shore of salvation. But what if through further sin they lose their grip on the plank? God is so good that he will send them another plank, that of penance. The first time Tertullian used this image had been a little earlier in the same work. In this instance he had urged the sinner to "seize and embrace" penance "as a shipwrecked person grasps hold of faith by means of some plank."[40] The image was rounded off some two hundred years later by St. Jerome when he referred to penance as "the second plank after shipwreck."[41]

The idea of shipwreck in this connection had been first suggested to Tertullian by a verse from 1 Timothy in which Timothy was urged to hold on to faith and a good conscience. The text continues: "By rejecting conscience, certain persons have made shipwreck of their faith" (1.19). As faith and repentance belong together, so do faith and good conscience. Hence a person who rejects conscience also rejects faith, "makes shipwreck" of it. Here the ship is the ship of faith, reminiscent of Noah's ark, which bore a group of righteous people to salvation (see 1 Pet 3:20-21; Gen 7:1). But obviously, in Tertullian and Jerome the image of shipwreck is applied in a different way from that employed by the 1 Timothy text. In the latter there is no mention of a "plank," though the pious hope is expressed that through exclusion from the community the offenders may be brought to repentance (see 1.20). Tertullian and Jerome's penance-oriented version of the image, complete with plank, was taken up and applied to penance by the Council of Trent.[42]

### The Eucharist

Let us move on now to the Eucharist. Of it St. Thomas wrote, "In this sacrament the entire mystery of our salvation is comprehended."[43] This is because, as he wrote elsewhere,

> Since this is the sacrament of the Lord's passion, it contains in itself the
> suffering Christ. Hence whatever is the effect of the Lord's passion, this
> in its entirety is also the effect of this sacrament. For this sacrament is
> nothing other than the application of the Lord's passion to us.[44]

The suffering Christ, as Christ offering his entire life and death to the
Father, represents all that Christ accomplished and will accomplish, all
that he was, is, and will be. And in the Eucharist all this is made available to us. Essentially this content consists in reconciliation with God,
which in turn consists of the double gift of forgiveness of sins and communion with God, each in and through the suffering Christ. However,
the comprehensiveness of the Eucharist goes beyond meeting all the
spiritual needs of particular persons: it also embraces all the spiritual
needs of the human race as such. That is to say, it is extensively universal in its scope. St. Thomas expressed the matter thus:

> This sacrament is universal, because the life it confers is not just life
> for this person, but in itself it is life for the whole world, and for this
> the death of Christ is sufficient, according to 1 John 2:2: "He is the
> expiation for our sins, and not for ours only but also for the sins of
> the whole world."[45]

We cannot, however, proceed with this reflection without introducing a distinction which lay at the heart of the doctrine of the Council
of Trent on the Eucharist, namely, that it was there considered under
two aspects: sacrament and sacrifice. Such was the separation of these
that the first, sacrament, was the subject of one document, issued at
Trent in 1551,[46] and the second, sacrifice, the subject of another, issued
at Bologna (whither the council had moved), in 1562.[47] At the council
this separation was dictated by the fact that the Reformers had principally attacked the Catholic doctrine of the Mass as a sacrifice rather
than the Eucharist as the sacrament of Holy Communion.[48] Today
sacramental theology closely combines these two aspects, insisting that it
is precisely as a sacrament, that is, the sacrament of the death of Christ,
that the Eucharist is a sacrifice. Nevertheless the two concepts remain
distinct and admit of valid distinctions that still need to be made.

Speaking of the Eucharist as a sacrifice, the council said:

> Therefore the holy Synod teaches that this sacrifice is truly propitiatory [for the forgiveness of sins], and that through this same sacrifice
> it comes to pass that, provided we draw near to God with a sincere
> heart and true faith, with fear and reverence, in contrition and repen-

tance, "we obtain mercy, and find the grace which helps us in our time of need" [Heb 4:16]. For by this sacrificial offering the Lord is indeed appeased, concedes the grace and gift of repentance, forgives great faults and even heinous sins.[49]

There are two points to be made from this quotation. The first is that, when the Eucharist is considered as a sacrifice, its extensively universal aspect comes to the fore. The offerer and beneficiary of the sacrifice is not just the individual priest or the individual member of the faithful with him, but the eucharistic community, which in turn represents the universal Church and, at least as beneficiary, the whole human race. While grace is given in the first instance to the individuals comprising the community, no personalized sacramental word is addressed to them. The second point is that, in as much as the Eucharist makes present the saving death of Christ in all its effectiveness, it overcomes the grave sins of those in the community who have been moved to contrition by its grace. But it does this only indirectly, by moving them to the sorrow and love that comprise the necessary condition of divine forgiveness. Addressing no saving word to them personally (as does the sacrament of reconciliation), it offers them no assurance that they have been so moved. They may discern that such is the case, but they lack any external guarantee to this effect.

By contrast, when speaking of the Eucharist as a sacrament, the council said, in the second chapter of the relevant document, that it was "a remedy to free us from our daily faults and to preserve us from mortal sin."[50] This statement, however, stands in second place to the assertion of a positive fruit of the Eucharist, namely that it is "the soul's spiritual food." In these statements it is the *particular* aspect of the Eucharist that comes to the fore. Here also there are two points to be made. First, it is significant that there is now no mention of the forgiveness of grave sin. The grace of the Eucharist as Holy Communion extends only as far as is implied by spiritual nourishment. All that the council has to say about sin now is that venial sins are forgiven (as they would be in the placing of any devotional deed), and that the communicant is strengthened against mortal sin in the future. Second, the Eucharist is particular in that it is addressed to the communicants individually, with its effect limited to them. Each is addressed by the sacramental word, which now is "The body [or blood] of Christ,"[51] this being a pledge of union with the suffering Lord.[52] In these statements of the council we discern not only a focusing of eucharistic grace on the individual person, but a limitation of its content. As we shall see, this leaves room for each of the other sacraments to channel eucharistic grace in its own way.

There is no inconsistency in the different positions that the council takes in these two documents on the power of the Eucharist to remit sin. As a sacrifice, the Eucharist is declared to have the power of remitting grave sin, but it has it only indirectly, and then without being able to give assurance in regard to the sins of any particular person. And when the Eucharist is considered as a sacrament, which reaches into the hearts of the recipients, no such assurance is given. In the chapter referred to in the last paragraph, the title of which is "The reason for the institution of this most holy sacrament," the only reference to sin is the one which I quoted in that place. It is of interest to note, however, that the corresponding canon (canon 5) reads, "If anyone says that the principal fruit of the most holy Eucharist is the forgiveness of sins, or that no other effects come from it, *anathema sit* [let him be condemned]."[53] This should be interpreted in line with the council's positive teaching, which I have just adduced. We can confidently assert that the canon refers to the Eucharist only as sacrament, not as sacrifice, and this for two reasons. First, the doctrine on sacrifice was not yet formulated, but still lay eleven years into the future. Second, the document in which the canon occurs is only about the Eucharist as sacrament.

Since the teaching of chapter two of this document is that the Eucharist remits only venial sin (and even that only indirectly), it is clear that the council would reject the doctrine condemned in the canon. But if we *were* to extend the scope of the canon to the Eucharist as sacrifice (which, I stress, would be illegitimate from a methodological point of view), the force of the canon would still hold, for the traditional doctrine of the "four ends" of the eucharistic sacrifice, restated by Pius XII in the encyclical *Mediator Dei*, are there listed (in descending order of importance) as praise, thanksgiving, propitiation, and impetration (effective petition).[54]

In other words, even when the Eucharist is considered as sacrifice, effecting the forgiveness of sins (including now mortal sins), far from being its only end or its principal end, appears among its four ends only in third place. One would not think this from reading the relevant chapter (chapter two) in the document on the Eucharist as sacrifice. There one would gain the impression that it was the most important end of the sacrifice, if not the only one. But this would only be because propitiation was the end under attack from the Reformers, and therefore the one singled out for strong affirmation by the council. A more realistic perspective, however, is to be discovered from the accompanying canon, canon 3. There one can discern that the eucharistic sacrifice has other values in addition to propitiation, namely praise, thanksgiving, and impetration (and satisfaction as well), though no attempt is made to grade them in importance.[55]

## Baptism and Eucharist

Let us now resume our argument. We have shown that as sacrifice the Eucharist is universal in the double sense of meeting every spiritual need of the particular person, and of embracing the entire human race in its scope. On the other hand, each of the other sacraments (and this includes the Eucharist as sacrament), is particular, in the first instance in that it offers us a particular aspect of this total mystery, corresponding to a particular need that we have, and in the way best suited pastorally toward meeting that need. (We shall treat soon the second sense in which the sacraments are particular.) Here we restrict ourselves to a consideration of the relationship of just one of the sacraments, baptism, to the Eucharist. St. Thomas said, on this relation:

> Both baptism and Eucharist represent the Lord's passion and death, but in different ways. For in baptism the death of Christ is commemorated in so far as this person dies with Christ in order to be reborn into new life. But in the sacrament of the Eucharist the death of Christ is commemorated in so far as the suffering Christ himself is presented to us as a paschal meal, according to the text of St. Paul, "Christ, our paschal lamb has been sacrificed: let us therefore celebrate the festival" (1 Cor 5:7-8).[56]

And elsewhere:

> Baptism is a sacrament of the passion and death of Christ in so far as this person is reborn in Christ by virtue of his passion. But the Eucharist is a sacrament of the passion of Christ in so far as this person is made perfect in being united to the suffering Christ.[57]

In these two quotations it is evident that St. Thomas is considering the Eucharist primarily as a sacrament, a sacrament that mediates the effects of the sacrifice. It is also clear, however, that it does not mediate that dimension of the sacrifice mediated by baptism. Rather, it completes and perfects what is mediated by baptism. In baptism this person dies and is reborn in Christ, but in the Eucharist he or she, sharing in the paschal meal, is advanced on the way to perfection through union with the all-perfect suffering Christ and Savior. Even as a sacrament, therefore, the Eucharist is more than just one of the seven sacraments. Just as it completes the work of baptism, it also completes that of the other sacraments. And as sacrifice it contains and offers the entire mystery of Christ. Hence as sacrifice and sacrament combined, it is truly the great and "blessed" sacrament.

## Universality and Particularity of the Sacraments

We have seen that the universality of the Eucharist as sacrifice embraces both the totality of salvation and the totality of humankind to whom it is offered. This implies that the particularity of the sacraments has to do not only with the singularity of the aspect of salvation that each signifies and contains, but also with the singularity of the person to whom it is offered. Thus every one of the sacraments, with the apparent exception of the third rite of reconciliation ("general absolution"), is addressed not to a group but to a particular person. The saving word of each sacrament is addressed to a single hearer, who receives it in faith and thus appropriates the gift that it signifies and contains. In this way, according to God's plan, salvation reaches into the heart of each individual person as the object of his providence.

The third rite of reconciliation is only an apparent exception to this rule, as in principle it is not the entire congregation that is absolved, but only those persons who designate themselves as recipients by some clear sign, such as kneeling or bowing the head.[58] Hence even here the sacramental word is addressed to individuals, though perhaps not in the unmistakably clear way found in the other sacraments and even in the other two rites of reconciliation. To this extent the third rite remains something of a theological and liturgical anomaly, requiring justification for its use, as we shall see. The eucharistic sacrifice brings forgiveness and life for all people; baptism and reconciliation, as indispensable specifications of this sacrifice, bring the same forgiveness and life to each particular person who desires these gifts. Christ died for all; but who is actually saved by his death? Only those who *appropriate* his saving death through the personal decision of faith (or, in the case of infant baptism through a decision of faith made on their behalf). St. Paul never tires of reminding us that we are justified, changed from sinners to sons and daughters of God, through *faith*. And *this* faith achieves its social and ecclesial dimension in the first instance in the reception of the sacraments of baptism and reconciliation, the two so-called "sacraments of the dead," the sacraments directed to the spiritually dead, that is, to those in grave sin, though not exclusively to them.

Because each of the other sacraments represents a pastoral outreach by Christ and the Church to a particular spiritual need of a particular person, they are not rendered superfluous by the Eucharist, whether considered as sacrifice or as sacrament. As sacrifice, it does not address the individual person as such. As sacrament, it does, but there its grace has a specific quality that requires the other sacraments for its mediation as sacrifice in the other particular ways necessary from a pastoral point of view. Simply put, the Eucharist cannot do precisely what they do. With regard to baptism, this is manifest in the revealed will of Christ in that the efficacy of the Eucharist depends on the prior reception of baptism. Baptism is necessary for the valid and fruitful reception of the Eucharist, as it is for all the other sacraments as well. We can put it this way (and I shall be invoking this again soon in modified form in the case of reconciliation): the prior reception of baptism is *iure divino* necessary for the reception of the Eucharist.

### Reconciliation and Eucharist

By analogy with baptism, we can make the following statements about the relation of reconciliation (the "second plank") and the Eucharist. Clearly, penance is *the* sacrament of reconciliation, in the sense that it is revealed in its whole structure, with review of life, confession, spiritual counsel, giving of penance, and personalized word of forgiveness, as the sacrament specifically designed to meet our particular needs in regard to postbaptismal reconciliation. Only reconciliation addresses the divine word of forgiveness to the individual contrite sinner. Like baptism, it draws its efficacy from, and points ahead to, the Eucharist. This was most clearly evident in the ancient Church, where the Eucharist concluded and cemented the whole process of reconciliation. There is, of course, this difference: baptism can be celebrated only once, since only once can an absolute beginning be made; but reconciliation can be repeated as often as one lapses into postbaptismal sin. The Eucharist remains the great sacrament of reconciliation, but not in the sense of ever rendering penance unnecessary or superfluous. Just as the Eucharist never replaces baptism, though it fulfills it, so it never replaces reconciliation, though it fulfills it also.

A view sometimes proposed is that, as Jesus in his ministry ate with sinners, thus inviting them to participation in the kingdom and reconciliation with God, so we today should not exclude sinners from the Eucharist. Rather, we should welcome them just as Jesus did. This view overlooks the fact that the ministry of Jesus predated the Church with its seven sacraments. Undoubtedly there exists a certain correspondence between the meals to which Jesus invited sinners and the later Eucharist, but the correspondence is not exact, and there is no identity. Perhaps we can say that if today we had no sacrament of reconciliation, the present-day Eucharist would have the same effect as did the meals of Jesus: it would reconcile sinners. This would be because they would be rightly disposed, and because in drawing them into communion with Christ, the Father, and the Church, the "fellowship of the Holy Spirit," Holy Communion would first have to overcome their sins. But this would be only an indirect effect of the sacrament.

Pastorally it would do nothing to overcome the problem of sin in their lives, to bring them to accept responsibility for what they had done, to confess their sins, and to experience the mercy of God as he, the Father of prodigal sons and daughters, pronounces through his minister the loving word of forgiveness over them. This is the reason for the distinct existence of the sacrament of reconciliation. It is not of human, but of divine, institution, founded by Christ in obedience to the Father, as his and the Church's way of dealing with postbaptismal sin. Thus the forgiveness of grave sin, the direct effect of reconciliation, cannot now be an effect of Holy Communion, which is a "sacrament of the living."

As was pointed out earlier, the first statement of the Council of Trent was that the Eucharist as Holy Communion is "the soul's spiritual food." Food is of no use to a person who is dead. It nourishes only the living. Ordinary food does two things for us, the first insofar as our nature is animal, the second insofar as it is rational. It nourishes the body, and it fosters connectedness with other human beings. By analogy, spiritual food nourishes the graced soul, and strengthens fellowship, communion, with God in Christ, and with our fellow members of the Church. Forgiveness is not included here as an effect, even for someone who may believe his or her grave sins forgiven, *ex opere operantis,* through the Eucharist as sacrifice, for Holy Communion, like any of the sacraments, effects only what it signifies, and given the actual existence of the sacrament of reconciliation, it does not signify reconciliation, even indirectly.

From what has been said it will be clear that a person conscious of grave sin should receive the sacrament of reconciliation before receiving Holy Communion. This was enjoined by Trent in the document on the Eucharist as sacrament, in chapter 7, "The preparation to be made to receive the holy Eucharist worthily," and in the appended canon 11.[59] However, no claim for an *iure divino* status for this obligation was made, and indeed the council was content to call it an "ecclesiastical custom," though one with the force of law.[60] And to the canon condemning propagation of the contrary view was attached not the *anathema sit* (let him be condemned) that befitted heresy (or denial of faith) as with the other ten canons of the series, but automatic excommunication for defiance of authority. Nor was the obligation claimed as absolute. In this regard the council said:

> This sacred synod has decreed that this [the obligation to confess] is to be observed in perpetuity by all Christians, even by priests obliged to celebrate [Mass], provided a confessor is available. But if a priest celebrates because obliged by necessity, he must confess as soon as possible.[61]

The ground of this injunction as stated by the council was respect for the Eucharist, and this was backed up by reference to 1 Cor 11:

> "Those who eat and drink unworthily, without discerning the body of the Lord, eat and drink judgement upon themselves" [1 Cor 11:29 Vulg.]. Therefore, whoever desires to communicate must be reminded of the precept: "But let a man examine himself" [1 Cor 11:28].[62]

The discipline of the contemporary Church allows a slightly more lenient practice, which is formulated thus in canon 916 of the 1983 Code of Canon Law:

> Anyone who is conscious of grave sin may not celebrate Mass or receive the Body of the Lord without previously having been to sacramental confession, unless there is a grave reason and there is no opportunity to confess; in this case the person is to remember the obligation to make an act of perfect contrition, which includes the resolve to go to confession as soon as possible.[63]

I now wish to offer some observations on what I have here recorded on the obligation of confession before Holy Communion when it is a matter of grave sin. Most contemporary theologians accept without question the assertion of Trent that this is a stipulation of ecclesiastical "custom" and law and that it is not *iure divino*. An examination of the acts of the council, however, reveals that Trent seriously considered whether this was a matter of divine or ecclesiastical law, and only concluded in favor of the second alternative because it found no convincing evidence for the first. Trent did not definitively decide this issue, but fell back to the safer position while leaving the issue an open question. We are therefore entitled to ask: What kind of evidence would Trent have accepted as probative in this matter? And it is clear that nothing short of a text from Scripture stating the necessity of confession before Holy Communion would have sufficed. We have to remember that the Fathers and theologians of the council lacked the historical knowledge that we have today concerning this sacrament. They believed that auricular confession existed from the beginning, and that therefore the possibility of a text to this effect was not ruled out in advance. The only text they could find that came anywhere near what they were looking for was 1 Cor 11:28, but it only said, "Let a man examine himself," not "Let this man go to confession," which, so they thought, Paul could have said had he wanted to.

Several speeches at the council could be cited in support of this contention. Let me quote a typical one, from Francis de Villalba, theologian, delivered on September 16, 1551:

> There is no divine precept concerning sacramental confession before receiving the Eucharist. This is proved by the fact that, if there were such a precept, it would certainly have come from Paul, who said, "But let a man examine himself, etc. [1 Cor 11:28]" But Paul speaks here not about confession, but about contrition. Ergo. I prove the minor, first from the fact that, when theologians dispute, treat, or diligently search, none has ever indicated this place in Paul for proving that sacramental confession is *iure divino*. Certainly, if Paul were here speaking about confession, some theologian would have understood him so. Moreover, Paul was speaking to the Corinthians, who hardly ever went to confession. For how can you have confession when "one is hungry and another is drunk [1 Cor 11:21]"?[64]

Villalba then refers to the Acts of the Apostles: "Moreover it is established that in the ancient Church people at first communicated *daily*, according to church precept, for which see Acts 2:46," then to St. Augustine, and to two ancient church councils, Agde and Tours, both in Gaul, and continues:

> Yet nowhere in these places is there any mention of confession. Therefore the Fathers understood the precept of Paul as being about contrition only. Otherwise, they would have advised the people accordingly. Moreover it is certain that a person is bound to examine himself but not bound to confess, even when a confessor is available. Therefore

Paul is not speaking about confession. This is proved thus: If someone did not celebrate [Mass] for a month or two, and yet was not
conscious of mortal sin, and if he then wanted to celebrate, he would
be bound to examine himself, and he would sin if he did not do so,
but he would not be bound to confess. This is certain. Ergo.[65]

We know today that there was no possibility of finding a scriptural
text like the one Villalba and others were searching for, for the simple
reason that auricular confession did not exist in New Testament times
or in the ancient Church. The essence of the sacrament took many centuries to develop, and it was not until the establishment of the Carolingian compromise that confession was recognized and required as an
essential element of reconciliation. But this does not rule out the possibility that the obligation of reconciliation before Holy Communion in
the case of grave sin may be *iure divino,* though demonstrating this
would require some other route than the adducing of scriptural texts
demanded by Trent. This is precisely what I shall now undertake to do.

The argument depends on the fact that we are here dealing with two
*sacraments,* reconciliation and Eucharist, two ecclesial institutions each
of which possesses *iure divino* status. The first of these, reconciliation,
is immediately and intrinsically related to a third sacrament, baptism,
which is also *iure divino:* baptism is the first, reconciliation the second,
plank of salvation. Between baptism and Eucharist, as we have already
shown, there exists an order which is itself *iure divino:* baptism, the first
plank, is *iure divino* necessary for the valid, let alone the fruitful, participation in, and reception of, the Eucharist. It follows that, when it is required at all (that is, in the case of grave sin), reconciliation, the second
plank, is also required *iure divino* for the Eucharist. Just as the order,
baptism-Eucharist, is divinely willed, so the order, reconciliation-
Eucharist, is divinely willed, that is, when reconciliation is necessary at all.

But there is this difference: whereas in the case of baptism the order
is absolute (exceptionless), in the case of reconciliation it is not absolute
(it admits of exception). Why is this so? The reason for the invariabil-
ity of the order, baptism-Eucharist, is that only baptism admits a person to the visible reality of the Church, to which order the Eucharist
belongs. Baptism confers the power to receive the other sacraments,
Eucharist included. The baptized sinner, on the other hand, already belongs to the Church. Under normal circumstances they should, as we
said, receive the sacrament of reconciliation before approaching the Eucharist. The normal, divinely willed order is reconciliation-Eucharist.

But as they already belong to the Church, and already, in the case under discussion, have regained the innermost reality of reconciliation through contrition, they may, provided they have a sufficiently strong reason, receive the Eucharist before receiving the sacrament of reconciliation. But only such a reason can justify a reversal of the logical, appropriate, and divinely willed order of these two sacraments. This, as we saw, is the present discipline of the Church, and it cannot simply be surrendered, as it directly reflects divine law. A person violating it for a trivial reason would stand convicted of the sin of sacrilege.

It should also be borne in mind that, although the state of grace, lost by sin, is regained through perfect contrition, this cannot happen without the desire of the sacrament of reconciliation.[66] Another, perhaps better, way of putting this is to say that contrition (or attrition) is the indispensable personal beginning of the process that issues in the social and ecclesial domain of the celebration of the sacrament of reconciliation. At the personal level, with contrition, communion with Christ and God is already reestablished, but this too needs to be drawn into the social and ecclesial domain through the celebration of the Eucharist. As there is a divinely given, absolute order of reconciliation and communion at the private and personal level, there is likewise a divinely given, though not absolute, order of reconciliation and communion at the social and ecclesial level as well, manifest in the order of the sacraments of reconciliation and Eucharist.

Against the possibility of *iure divino* status for the obligation of the confession of grave sin before receiving Holy Communion, the objection has been raised that the obligation is not absolute. If the obligation came from God, so the argument goes, it would admit of no exception. The very fact that it does admit of exception shows that it is a human, not a divine law. This objection was raised at Trent,[67] and it was raised again recently by James Dallen.[68] However, it is not valid. In the next chapter we shall see Carl Peter refuting it in a different context, that of the obligation of integral confession, which also admits of exceptions. I shall now attempt something similar here.

We need to distinguish two different kinds of context in which the concept of *iure divino* applies. The first has to do with nature, the natural law, and here there are no exceptions. The whole of nature, including human nature, was founded by God. Once we understand what human nature is and what it requires, we must *never* act against it. To do so would be to commit sin. The laws of human nature are *iure divino,* and they admit of no exception. Purely human laws regulating civil society, on the other hand, admit of all sorts of exceptions. The other context in which *iure divino* applies is that of grace. Beyond the order of nature, God has freely acted in establishing the order of grace. This order is in accord with nature, and it perfects it, but it carries it to a higher end than it could aspire to of itself, namely to God as he is in himself. The freedom, the personal quality, the lack of determination of this order gives rise to the possibility that God may establish certain institutions of this order, like the sacraments, for which he has clearly indicated his will, which will always be in accord with the best and highest interests of the human nature which he has created, but which will exhibit a flexibility unknown in the order of nature.

The flexibility of this personal order allows for the further possibility that there be exceptions, which of course would have to be justified, to the order that he has established. Thus, in the case in point, the order of confession before Holy Communion may be the general dispensation willed by God, but there may be the possibility that in the best interests of a particular person at a particular time this order may be changed for as long as the exceptional situation lasts. The judge of the circumstances in which this can be done is the Church, to which God has said, through his Son, "whatever you bind on earth shall be bound in heaven, and whatever you loose on earth shall be loosed in heaven" (Matt 16:19). This is exactly what the Church has done in the matter of confession before Holy Communion, and in no way does it militate against the possibility of *iure divino* status for the dispensation concerned.

The question arises: Is the person who is justified in the course of the celebration of the Eucharist justified by the Eucharist (as sacrifice), by the desire of reconciliation, or in some other way? We know that this person is justified through their contrition, but we also know that if contrition is sincere it will include the desire of reconciliation. We have already given the answer that the Eucharist as sacrifice can justify the sinner indirectly. However, when this occurs, it will always be on the basis of his or her contrition in any case. As we saw, it is not easy to say if this happens in a particular case, but when it does, it does not of itself confer the right immediately to receive Holy Communion. There still has to be some necessity, some serious reason, to justify receiving Communion before the sacrament of reconciliation. And even when such a reason is present, the person remains bound to submit their grave sin subsequently to the "power of the keys" in the sacrament of reconciliation.

With these preliminaries stated, we can proceed to answer the question. When Trent, speaking of contrition, recognized that through it grave sins are forgiven even *before* receiving the sacrament of reconciliation (but only if it includes the "desire" of the sacrament), it was invoking, in regard to the sacraments, the typically Western construct of a physical or "naturalistic" concept of time. A better approach might be to say that one and the same forgiving grace of God seeks the sinner out, moves him or her to repentance, leads him or her to the sacrament, is effective in the sentence of absolution, and is translated into life through the work of penance. When and how is the sin forgiven? According to the sacramental concept of time, forgiveness begins when grace begins its work and is consummated at the end of the process. This enables us to see that when we assert, with Trent, that forgiveness is granted because of a contrition that includes the desire of the sacrament, we are effectively saying that God grants forgiveness not just through contrition, nor through the Eucharist even as sacrifice (except as the source of the sacrament of reconciliation), but precisely through this last named sacrament. That the process can be interrupted, by death or through some other circumstance, does not overturn the validity of what I am here suggesting.

It is not within the purview of this book to discuss in general what would, and what would not, constitute a sufficiently serious reason to justify receiving Holy Communion before receiving the sacrament of reconciliation when it is a question of grave sin. That is a question pertaining to moral theology and canon law. But there is one opinion that I shall discuss, and it is that suggested by Franco Sottocornola, secretary of the committee responsible for RP and author of an important commentary on it.[69] This opinion has been endorsed by James Dallen.[70]

Sottocornola's commentary appeared before the current Code of Canon Law. He refers, therefore, not to canon 916 of the current Code (1983), but to the relevant canon of the previous one, canon 856 of the 1917 Code. The two canons are almost identical, but whereas canon 916 speaks of a "serious reason" needed to justify Holy Communion before confession, canon 856 speaks of a "necessity." This difference is purely verbal. The only real difference between the two canons is that canon 916 "makes it explicit that a perfect act of contrition [which both canons affirm as necessary] includes the intention to confess as soon as possible."[71] Here, then, is Sottocornola's opinion in his own words:

> Now that the reform of the liturgy and the life of the Church renewed by the Council demand that we take part actively and fully in the sacraments, it seems important to emphasize that the necessity to participate in the Eucharist is always verified—objectively, at least—

when we are present at the Lord's Supper. In this case, if one is in a situation where it is impossible to go to confession, the *sincere desire* to receive Communion can be deemed sufficient reason to participate in the Eucharist, if at least one sincerely regrets one's sin. Communion becomes, therefore, for the penitent as well, the effective sacrament of reconciliation, that is, the sign of reconciliation with God and one's brethren.[72]

Sottocornola's claim, therefore, is that mere presence at the Eucharist, combined with sincere regret for sin and a sincere desire to communicate, constitutes the necessity that justifies reception of the Eucharist by a person with grave sin who has not yet received sacramental reconciliation.

The stages along the way to the formulation of this opinion are the statement of Trent about the power of the Eucharist as sacrifice to remit grave sin, the presentation of this as a direct power of remission, the invocation of the common opinion that the obligation to confess before communicating is only an ecclesiastical law, and the expression of the opinion that it would be well nigh impossible for a believing Catholic to assist sincerely at Mass without being moved to contrition for their sins.[73] The last of these can be happily conceded as it stands. The first and second, however, do not do justice to the Tridentine teaching. They overlook Trent's statements about the Eucharist as sacrament, and so do not at all face up to the apparent contradiction between its two sets of statements about the power of the Eucharist over sin. As I was at pains to show, the reasonable supposition that the council does not contradict itself requires us to interpret these statements in the sense that this power over sin is indirect rather than direct. In any case, if it were direct, the Eucharist would render the sacrament of reconciliation superfluous. It should be noted, however, that Sottocornola upholds the obligation of subsequent confession, but only as a matter of positive ecclesiastical law.[74]

The third stage represents a position that I have criticized in this chapter. If I am correct, the obligation to confess grave sin, whether before or after Communion, is one of divine law *(iure divino),* not merely ecclesiastical law. The ultimate basis of Sottocornola's opinion is not his ascription of a direct power of remitting sin to the Eucharist, but his judgment that, in the light of Vatican II's teaching about the liturgy and particularly the sacraments, mere presence at the Eucharist constitutes a sufficiently serious reason for communicating before confessing grave sin. I say this because, whether the Eucharist's power over sin is direct or indirect, either way Sottocornola's opinion would permit, indeed encourage, communicating without first confessing, and would still endorse the obligation to confess subsequently.

What, then, is our judgment on this central point on which Sottocornola's opinion rests? It seems to me that the serious justifying reason envisaged by canon (and I would add divine) law must be sought outside the liturgy, not inside it. In principle the reason would have to be something like an obligation to celebrate Mass in the case of a priest, or a close relationship to the deceased in the case of a relative present at a funeral Mass. In both these examples (and that is all they are) the reason is external to the liturgy itself. Sottocornola's reason, however, is internal to the liturgy. According to him, a heightened appreciation of the Eucharist permits its reception even if one's grave sin has not been confessed. In my opinion, one can argue more convincingly the opposite way: a heightened appreciation of the Eucharist should deter such a person from receiving it. Their very abstention would be a means of honoring it, of showing it the reverence enjoined by Paul when he said that it was necessary to "discern the body [of the Lord]" (1 Cor 11:29). In this perspective Sottocornola's justifying reason is no reason at all. Readers can marshall for themselves additional arguments against Sottocornola's opinion from earlier sections of this chapter. A final word is a reminder: all we are talking about here is certainly grave sin, a commodity I have strongly suggested in this book to be not as common as was previously thought.

## The Sacrament of Anointing of the Sick

At this point we introduce into our discussion the sacrament of anointing of the sick (before Vatican II known as "extreme unction"). It merits consideration among the sacraments of reconciliation, since its principal scriptural foundation is the following passage from Jas 5:14-15, which includes forgiveness in the effect of the rite performed:

> (14) Is any among you sick? Let him call for the elders of the church, and let them pray over him, anointing him with oil in the name of the Lord; (15) and the prayer of faith will save the sick man, and the Lord will raise him up; and if he has committed sins, he will be forgiven.

There is no reason to restrict the word "sins" in v. 15 to light sins. As no limitation is implied, the term must be taken to include grave sins. Indeed in Scripture the word "sin" normally denotes grave sin.

The postconciliar revision of the sacrament of anointing states the following:

> This sacrament gives the grace of the Holy Spirit to those who are sick: by this grace the whole person is helped and saved, sustained by trust in God, and strengthened against the temptations of the Evil One and against anxiety over death. Thus the sick person is able not only to bear suffering bravely, but also to fight against it. A return to physical health may follow the reception of this sacrament if it will be beneficial to the sick person's salvation. If necessary, the sacrament also provides the sick person with the forgiveness of sins and the completion of Christian penance.[75]

From this it is clear that the effect of the sacrament is the restoration of the well-being of the whole person seen primarily in terms of their relationship to the creating and life-giving God. This relationship is threatened by their illness in as much as it is a temptation to spiritual torpor or even despair. The restoration effected by the sacrament will in the first instance be spiritual, and therefore, if need be, will include the forgiveness of sins. But it does not replace the sacrament of reconciliation, since forgiveness of sins is not its primary object and it does not include confession. Physical healing, should it occur, is also to be understood in terms of the holistic orientation of the sacrament. The statement, "the sacrament also provides the sick person with . . . the completion of Christian penance," should be understood as referring to the sacrament, and not just the virtue, of penance.[76] The purpose of reconciliation is simply spiritual, that is, the forgiveness of sins, but the purpose of anointing is holistic. In that sense, therefore, anointing is the completion of reconciliation.

It follows from this that anointing forgives sin indirectly. The fact that forgiveness is explicitly mentioned in the James text does not imply that it is a direct effect of the sacrament. Indeed the conditional form of the statement about forgiveness supports my assertion of an indirect character, which is explained by the sacrament's holistic orientation. As a sacrament of the living, it should not be received by a person with grave sin until they have been reconciled through absolution. A person in grave sin receiving anointing in good faith would have their sin forgiven, but would still be obliged to receive reconciliation, and, further, to do so before again receiving Holy Communion. The postconciliar revision has inverted the order of reception of anointing and Eucharist. The latter is now placed last in the series reconciliation-anointing-Eucharist, because as Viaticum (food for the journey), the Eucharist is understood as the true "last" sacrament, the sacrament of the dying.

It is reported that some recipients of anointing are confused by the apparent contradiction involved in, on the one hand, the assertion of the Letter of James, that anointing forgives even grave sin, and, on the other, the Church's prior requirement of the sacrament of reconciliation, if it be possible, for grave sin. Here I respond by analogy to the response given earlier to the problem of the requirement of reconciliation prior to Holy Communion in a case of grave sin. Only the sacrament of reconciliation, or at least the desire of it, is, according to the will of Christ, the appointed means for the forgiveness of grave post-baptismal sin. Given the existence of the sacrament of reconciliation, it is sometimes said that anointing will forgive only such grave sins as cannot be forgiven through reconciliation. However, what these might be, it is impossible to say.[77] In the community of James the situation would most likely have been different from that which obtains with us. We do not know whether his community had an institutional way of dealing with scandalous sin, as did at least Paul's community at Corinth. If it did, this institution would not have been available to a person in the urgent situation of serious illness. But it is more likely that the community's only means of dealing with postbaptismal sin was communal acknowledgment of guilt and mutual prayer, as commended in the three verses (16 to 18) that follow the James text already quoted. In any case we can readily understand why James would have given the assurance that he did regarding sin and forgiveness.

Given the problem just addressed, to those who question the pastoral prudence of reading the text of James to a person about to be anointed, as the revised ritual suggests, the following can be said. Most people would have no difficulty with the prior requirement of reconciliation for a case of grave sin. To those who did have a difficulty, the answer suggested above could be given. It should be borne in mind, however, that reading the text of James is not obligatory, and that the references to it in the sacramental formula should not of themselves raise the problem of the necessity of confession in the minds of prospective recipients.

If anointing strengthens or restores the sick person's relationship to God, it will do the same for their relationship to the community of the Church, which relationship is also threatened by their illness, in as much as illness tends to marginalize and isolate them, even alienate them. Indeed we might suggest that strengthening or restoring the sick person's relationship to the Church is the *res et sacramentum* of the sacrament.[78] Especially if the sacrament is celebrated with the participation and on-going support of the local community, family, friends, and neighbors, it can be a powerful means whereby the community reclaims a member whose illness was threatening to separate him or her from it. If the sick person is not destined to recover, the sacrament will still restore them to the Church, which then commits them to the loving mercy of God in death. This "second face" of the sacrament results from the Church's essential orientation to the eschaton.

From this the relationship of anointing to the Eucharist is clearly evident. The restoration to God and the community effected by anointing is celebrated and deepened by the Eucharist, the great sacrament of communion with God and the Church. Even if it not be God's will that the sick person should recover, the relationship to the Eucharist, a relationship of beginning to end, will still hold. As Viaticum, the Eucharist will complete and perfect the sick person's restoration to God and the Church as they prepare to set out for the final stage of the Kingdom of God, the messianic banquet of Isa 25:6, which the Eucharist as Viaticum signifies and anticipates. We have said that anointing is the completion of reconciliation. But have we not said earlier that *the Eucharist* is the completion of reconciliation? Yes, but each is a completion in a different way. The Eucharist completes reconciliation in that it seals and celebrates it, but anointing completes it in the line of restoration. Something similar can be said about confirmation: both confirmation and the Eucharist complete baptism, but confirmation completes it as a sacrament of initiation, while the Eucharist completes it in an ultimate sense, as a sacrament of communion.

## The Necessity of the Sacrament of Reconciliation

Finally, we consider the necessity of this sacrament. RP devotes a section, no. 7, to its "necessity and benefit." There are three possible senses in which it might be said to be necessary. The strongest is that in which it would be necessary with a necessity of means, which is to say that in the nature of things there would be no other way in which sins could be forgiven. But if this were so, there would be no forgiveness of sins for those outside those churches, principally the Catholic Church, that actually have the sacrament, which clearly is not the case. In any event no such claim is made for the necessity of the sacrament in Catholic doctrine or theology.

The second sense is that in which it would be necessary because it constituted an element of God's actual plan of salvation, this particular divine ordinance, like all others, not being arbitrary but corresponding to and engaging an aspect of human nature as created by him. This is what is normally meant by the necessity of the sacrament, and is the sense on which I shall comment, though it is not the one taken up by RP.

The third, the least strong sense, is that in which it would be necessary merely with a necessity of fact, that is to say, it was a way in which forgiveness was in fact obtained and which exhibited some advantage in this regard. As this is the only sense which RP mentions, let us say a brief word about it now before passing on.

The advantage to which RP draws attention is that, as the sacrament handles all sin, whether grave or non-grave, it is suited to all people in the Church. But RP cautions that the sacrament will not attain its full effect unless it takes root in the lives of the people. It does not say how this is to be achieved, but surely the answer is that reception of the sacrament must be grounded in a deep appreciation of the *virtue* of penance. The interior virtue will then be translated into the practice of penance in everyday life, and will reach its highpoint in the fruitful celebration of the sacrament. The final sentence of RP 7 resumes certain features of *exomologesis* that we observed in our brief history: in the celebration of the sacrament "the Church proclaims its faith, gives thanks to God for the freedom with which Christ has made us free, and offers its life as a spiritual sacrifice in praise of God's glory, as it hastens to meet the Lord Jesus."

The sacrament is necessary in the second and third of the senses distinguished, with the second as the one obviously calling for comment. In this sense the sacrament is necessary with the same necessity that the Church itself possesses. The Church is necessary in the sense that God sent his Son Jesus Christ into the world so that through his life, death, and resurrection he might be the means of saving humankind. Jesus founded the Church as the divinely appointed mode of his continued presence and activity so that his salvation would continually be offered to succeeding generations of human beings. This way of executing the divine plan engages an aspect of our nature as created by God, namely its social dimension. A human being is not meant to be an isolated individual, but is destined to come to fulfillment in society and at the same time to contribute to society's welfare. This is true at all levels, including and especially the spiritual. We do not encounter God *only* as individual persons, though we do encounter him that way, and it is an indispensable way of encountering him. But we also encounter him as members of the human family and of the Church. The sacrament of reconciliation—and more clearly since Vatican II—expresses and engages this social dimension of our relationship with God, both in its negative side, sin, and in its positive side, reconciliation. Just as sin is not only (though it is primarily) sin against God, but sin against Christ and the Church, so reconciliation is reconciliation with the Church and Christ as well as with God.

As we have pointed out, however, the most basic and important act of the penitent is repentance, without which there can be no forgiveness of sins. For that repentance to be sincere and complete, and for it to move beyond being merely private and attain social reality and expression, it needs to be expressed in confession and satisfaction. But if these latter for any reason cannot be done, God will not insist on them. He does not ask the impossible, and he will forgive the penitent person even so. But all things being equal, or if the impossibility is overcome, the full expression of repentance in confession, satisfaction, and the reception of absolution again becomes necessary. Thus is explained the necessity of the sacrament of reconciliation. It is not absolutely necessary like repentance, but it is necessary in the sense that it is required by God, given that he has sent Christ into the world for its salvation, and that he created human nature with an essential social dimension.[79]

I conclude this section with a comment on a defective attitude to the sacrament that surfaces frequently enough at the present time. People will say that they do not "need" the sacrament of reconciliation, for they can turn to God in their hearts and ask pardon from him in that way. This is "enough" for them. But against this it must be said that they are in no position to determine what is enough for them. The one offended by sin is ultimately *God*, and therefore it is for him to say what is enough for forgiveness. God has done this, by sending his beloved Son to give his life for our sins. In seeking forgiveness, then, how can a person who professes to be Christian bypass Christ and his ministry? Even if such a person approaches Christ in private prayer, if this is all they do they are still laying down their own terms for forgiveness, for Christ has given us the Church and the sacrament of reconciliation for this very purpose. It is a different matter if this person, for whatever reason, does not know these things. As I said before, God does not ask the impossible, and he will be merciful to such a person. But the life of a Christian should be fundamentally oriented to discovering God's will for them and putting it into practice. As sons and daughters of God, they should seek to live in no other way than did the beloved Son, who said, "Not my will, but thine be done."

# Conclusion

This has been a pivotal chapter of our book on penance and reconciliation. The first chapter, on sin, showed that sin is not just a private matter between the sinner and God. Rather, it has a social dimension, inevitably involving, and harming in some way, our fellow human beings and particularly our fellow members of the Church. It follows that reconciliation, coming as it does from the "God, the Father of mercies" (as the prayer of absolution puts it), will likewise have a social dimension. It will be reconciliation not only with him, but with the Church. Indeed, we were able to show that reconciliation with the Church was the sacrament's "symbolic reality," its immediate spiritual effect, which in turn symbolized and brought about its ultimate effect, reconciliation with God.

We found it necessary to speak of reconciliation not in isolation but in its relation to the Eucharist, the great sacrament of reconciliation, and in so doing we found its immediate point of reference to be baptism, some of the effects of which, lost by sin, are restored through it. Very important to our study was the realization, brought about this century through historical research, of the gradual development of the sacrament over the centuries from its beginnings in the ministry of Christ. This showed us that, along with the absolution of the priest, the three acts of the penitent, contrition, confession, and satisfaction, constitute the non-negotiable essential elements of the sacrament. But it has also shown us that we have no reason to think that the process of development is complete in our own day. If the sacrament developed to its present form, it will continue to develop in the future in ways we cannot predict, so as to meet the ever-changing pastoral needs of the Church. In the next chapter we analyze the four just named essential parts of the sacrament, and in the fourth chapter we examine the concrete forms assigned to reconciliation as a result of the Vatican II reform.

# Notes, Chapter 2

[1] Joachim Jeremias, *New Testament Theology*, vol. 1, *The Proclamation of Jesus*, trans. John Bowden, The New Testament Library, ed. Alan Richardson, C.F.D. Moule, C.F. Evans, and Floyd V. Filson (London: SCM Press, 1971) 116.

[2] See, for example, C.E.B. Cranfield, *The Gospel According to Saint Mark*, Cambridge Greek Testament Commentary, ed. C.F.D. Moule (Cambridge: Cambridge University Press, 1977) 100; and William L. Lane, *The Gospel According to Mark*, New International Commentary on the New Testament, ed. F.F. Bruce (Grand Rapids, Mich.: Eerdmans, 1974) 97.

[3] See W. D. Davies and Dale C. Allison, *The Gospel According to Saint Matthew*, vol. 3, International Critical Commentary (Edinburgh: T & T Clark, 1997) 475.

[4] Hans Kessler, "Erlösung/Soteriologie," *Neues Handbuch theologischer Grundbegriffe*, vol. 1, ed. Peter Eicher (Munich: Kösel Verlag, 1984) 244; my trans.

[5] Luke Timothy Johnson makes the point that in this verse Luke reveals part of his program for his second volume, the Acts of the Apostles. Every constitutive element of the verse can be backed up with numerous references to Acts; and every reference concerning the forgiveness of sins has to do with the proclamation of the gospel and baptism rather than an institutional form of reconciliation for those already baptized. See Johnson's *The Gospel of Luke*, Sacra Pagina, vol. 3 (Collegeville: The Liturgical Press, 1991) 403.

[6] Dupuis 1617.

[7] See Dupuis 1643 and 1650.

[8] See Raymond Brown, *The Gospel According to John*, vol. 2, The Anchor Bible (Garden City, N.Y.: Doubleday, 1970) 1041.

[9] For example, Francis Moloney in *The Gospel of John*, Sacra Pagina, vol. 4 (Collegeville: The Liturgical Press, 1998). Moloney writes, on p. 535, "There are not two 'gifts of the Spirit.' The one Spirit is given in the one 'hour of Jesus' to the members of the Christian community (19:30) so that they might be witnesses to Jesus (20:22)." He has just written, on p. 533, "They will bring God's forgiveness for all sin that is to be forgiven, and lay bare all sinfulness (v. 23)."

[10] See Brown, *The Gospel According to John*, vol. 2, 1044.

[11] Karl Rahner, *Foundations of Christian Faith: An Introduction to the Idea of Christianity*, trans. W. Dych (New York: Seabury Press, 1978) 413.

[12] Ibid., 413.

[13] *Catechism*, nos. 1114–16, 289.

[14] The main work on the history of the sacrament was done by Bernhard Poschmann, *Penance and Anointing of the Sick*, trans. Francis Courtney (New York: Herder and Herder, 1964) (German original 1951), and Karl Rahner, *Penance in the Early Church*, vol. 15 of *Theological Investigations*, trans. Lionel Swain (New York: Crossroad, 1982) (German original 1973). Here I depend principally on: James Dallen, *The Reconciling Community: The Rite of Penance*, vol. 3 of Studies in the Reformed Rites of the Catholic Church (New York: Pueblo, 1986); Dallen,

"History and the Reform of Penance," in *Reconciling Embrace: Foundations for the Future of Sacramental Reconciliation,* ed. Robert Kennedy (Chicago: Liturgy Training Publications, 1998) 79–90, 120–23; Herbert Vorgrimler, *Sacramental Theology,* trans. Linda Maloney (Collegeville: The Liturgical Press, 1992) 200–25; and Vorgrimler, *Busse und Krankensalbung,* vol. 4, pt. 3 of Handbuch der Dogmengeschichte (Freiburg [Germany]: Herder, 1978).

[15] See Dupuis 1608.

[16] See ibid., 1612.

[17] Ibid., 1924–83, at 1943–44, 1979–80.

[18] Ibid., 1615–34, 1641–55.

[19] See ibid., 1622–24.

[20] Ibid., 1626. See also nos. 1647–48.

[21] Flannery, 15.

[22] *Sacrosanctum Concilium* no. 72, Flannery, 141.

[23] See the *relatio* (official interpretation) given by Archbishop Paul Hallinan, *Acta Synodalia Sacrosancti Concilii Vaticani II,* vol. 2, part 2 (Rome: Typis Polyglottis Vaticanis, 1962) 567.

[24] See Karl Rahner, "Forgotten Truths Concerning the Sacrament of Penance," in *Theological Investigations,* vol. 2, trans. Karl-H. Kruger (Baltimore: Helicon Press, 1963) 135–74, esp. 166–74.

[25] "Interim Response to the Holy See on 'Final Report of A.R.C.I.C.,'" *Newsletter of the Australian Episcopal Conference,* no. 13, February 1984, no. 14c.

[26] For background on this matter, see, in Paul C. Empie and T. Austin Murphy, eds., *Papal Primacy and the Universal Church,* Lutherans and Catholics in Dialogue V (Minneapolis: Augsburg, 1974), the following: in the Statement itself, 30–31, 34–36; Arthur Piepkorn, "*Ius Divinum* and *Adiaphoron* in Relation to Structural Problems in the Church: The Position of the Lutheran Symbolical Books," 119–26; and George Lindbeck, "Papacy and *Ius Divinum:* A Lutheran View," 193–208. See also Carl Peter, "Dimensions of *Ius Divinum* in Roman Catholic Theology," *Theological Studies* 34 (1973) 227–50; and Karl Rahner, "Reflections on the Concept of 'Ius Divinum' in Catholic Thought," *Theological Investigations,* vol. 5, trans. Karl-H. Kruger (Baltimore: Helicon Press, 1966) 219–43.

[27] See 7b.

[28] Rahner, "Forgotten Truths," 171.

[29] An account of this process is to be had in Ludwig Bertsch and Gerhard Gäde, "'Res et sacramentum'—Zur Wiederentdeckung der kirchlichen Dimension in der Sakramentenkatechese," in *Dogmengeschichte und katholische Theologie,* ed. W. Löser, K. Lehmann, and M. Lutz-Bachmann (Würzburg: Echter Verlag, 1985) 451–78.

[30] See ST III, q. 84, a. 1 ad 3.

[31] See Aquinas's *Commentary on Book IV of the Sentences of Peter Lombard* d. 17, q. 3, art. 3, [5], ad 2, ad 3, repeated in the *Supplementum* q. 8, a. 2 ad 3.

[32] Dallen, *Reconciling Community,* 266.

[33] See RP 62. The first of these formulas is restricted by the rubrics to use in general absolutions. See also RP 46 and 55.

[34] References the same as for the preceding note.

[35] While Cyprian reconciled penitents in the full view of the congregation, today the ceremony is more likely to take place in the privacy of a confession room, in which any form of physical contact between the confessor and the penitent is prudently avoided. This is the likely reason for RP's reticence about prescribing an actual imposition of hands.

[36] See David Coffey, "Priestly Representation and Women's Ordination," in *Priesthood: The Hard Questions*, Gerald Gleeson, ed. (Sydney: E. J. Dwyer, 1993) 79–99.

[37] Edward Kilmartin, "Bishop and Presbyter as Representatives of the Church and Christ," in *Women Priests: A Catholic Commentary on the Vatican Declaration*, L. Swidler and A. Swidler, eds. (New York: Paulist Press, 1977) 296.

[38] St. Ambrose *Letter 41* 12 (*PL* 16, 1164); my trans.

[39] Tertullian *De paenitentia* 12, 9. See *La pénitence*, Sources chrétiennes 316, trans. C. Munier (Paris: Éditions du Cerf, 1984) 190.

[40] Tertullian *De paenitentia* 4, 2. See *La pénitence*, 156, where the text reads: "Eam [penitentiae vitam] . . . ita inuade, ita amplexare, ut naufragus alicuis tabulae fidem," which I translate literally as: "Seize and embrace it [the penitential life] as does a shipwrecked person the faith of some plank."

[41] See St. Jerome, *Epistola 84 ad Pammachium et Oceanum* (CSEL 55: 128, 5), and *Epistola 130 ad Demetriadem* (CSEL 56: 189, 4).

[42] See Dupuis 1943, 1642.

[43] ST III, q. 83, a. 4.

[44] *Super Iohannem* c. 6, l. 6; my trans.

[45] Ibid.; my trans.

[46] Decree on the Most Holy Eucharist, see Dupuis 1512–36.

[47] Doctrine on the Most Holy Sacrifice of the Mass, see Dupuis 1545–63.

[48] See J. F. McHugh, "The Sacrifice of the Mass at the Council of Trent," in *Sacrifice and Redemption: Durham Essays in Theology*, ed. S.W. Sykes (Cambridge: Cambridge University Press, 1991) 157–81, at 159.

[49] Ibid., 177. See also Dupuis 1548.

[50] Dupuis 1515.

[51] In the Tridentine ritual, the *Rituale Romanum* (Turin: Marietti, 1952), the formula was "Corpus Domini nostri Jesu Christi custodiat animam tuam in vitam aeternam. Amen" (May the body of our Lord Jesus Christ preserve your soul unto everlasting life. Amen).

[52] The same was true of the Tridentine formula.

[53] Dupuis 1530.

[54] See *Christian Worship: Encyclical Letter of Pope Pius XII "Mediator Dei," 1947* (London: Catholic Truth Society, 1957) nos. 75–78, 34–35.

[55] See Dupuis 1557.

[56] ST III, q. 66, a. 9 ad 5; my trans.

[57] ST III, q. 73, a. 3 ad 3; my trans.

[58] See RP 61.

[59] See Dupuis 1522 and 1536. However, Dupuis gives only the first of the two paragraphs comprising ch. 7. For the second paragraph see DS 1647.

[60] See DS 1647.

[61] DS 1647; my trans.

[62] Dupuis 1522.

[63] *The Code of Canon Law* (London: Collins, 1983) 168.

[64] Societas Goerresiana, ed., *Concilium Tridentinum, Diariorum, Actorum, Epistularum Tractatuum Nova Collectio, Actorum Pars Quarta Volumen Secundum,* Tomus VII (Freiburg: Herder, 1976) 141 (2–9); my trans.

[65] Ibid., 141 (9–18); my trans.

[66] See RP 37, and Trent's Doctrine on the Sacrament of Penance, Dupuis 1623.

[67] By Francis de Toro, theologian. See *Concilium Tridentinum* 108 (33–38).

[68] See Dallen, *The Reconciling Community,* 290.

[69] See Franco Sottocornola, "Les nouveaux rites de la pénitence: commentaire," *Questions liturgiques* 55 (1974) 89–136.

[70] See Dallen, *The Reconciling Community,* 289–90.

[71] James Corriden, Thomas Green, and Donald Heintschell, eds., *The Code of Canon Law: A Text and Commentary* (New York: Paulist Press, 1985) 653.

[72] Sottocornola, "Les nouveaux rites," 104; my trans.

[73] See ibid., "Les nouveaux rites," 102–104.

[74] See ibid., "Les nouveaux rites," 103, par. 2.

[75] *Pastoral Care of the Sick: Introduction and Pastoral Notes,* Liturgy Documentary Series 3 (Washington, D.C.: United States Catholic Conference, 1983) no. 6, 20.

[76] Here the text contains a reference to Trent's Doctrine of the Sacrament of Extreme Unction, DS 1694, from which this point is evident. For this reference, see Dupuis 1635.

[77] James Empereur states, in *Prophetic Anointing: God's Call to the Sick, the Elderly, and the Dying,* Message of the Sacraments 7, ed. Monika Hellwig (Wilmington, Del.: Michael Glazier, 1982) 94, that "if for some reason the person anointed has no access to the sacrament of penance, all his/her sins will be forgiven through anointing." While this is true, it is difficult to see why a person who had access to anointing would not thereby have access to reconciliation as well. Andrew Cuschieri, in *Anointing of the Sick: A Theological and Canonical Study* (Lanham, Md.: University Press of America, 1993), admits frankly that "a seemingly insoluble question . . . remains regarding the nature of the sins which are remitted through this Sacrament" (65).

[78] See our discussion of the ecclesial nature of the *res et sacramentum* in this chapter.

[79] The next chapter, by reference to the work of Carl Peter, explains how at the same time something can be both "instituted by Christ" *(iure divino) and* not absolutely necessary. Suffice it here to identify the principle invoked in this explanation, namely, that something instituted by Christ can present a plurality of values that, far from being equal, are given in a hierarchy in which, under certain conditions, some give way to others. We dealt with this subject in the preceding section of this chapter also.

Chapter Three

# The Parts of the Sacrament of Reconciliation

I n this chapter we shall be dealing with the acts of the penitent, contrition, confession, and satisfaction, and with the act of the priest-minister, absolution, which form the subject matter of RP 6, "The Sacrament of Penance and Its Parts." We shall treat the acts of the penitent in the order just given, inserting absolution between confession and satisfaction, because that is where it occurs in the rite. RP tells us, in no. 11, "The Penitent," that the "acts of the penitent in the celebration of the sacrament are of the greatest importance." This is because the penitent "shares by his actions in the sacrament itself," and so "celebrates with the priest the liturgy by which the Church continually renews itself." Because their acts enter into its essence, the penitent is no passive recipient of the sacrament, but is, along with the priest, a "concelebrant" of it. And because liturgy is the Church's official praise of God, penitents through their acts share with the priest in giving voice to the *exomologesis* of the Church, its confession and praise of the merciful God who forgives the sins of his people. The acts of the penitent are met by the act of the priest, namely absolution, by which, through the ministry of the priest, God welcomes, forgives, and fully reinstates the sinner in his grace and in his community, the Church, from which he or she has begun, through their sin, to fall away. Hence RP 7, which speaks of the sacrament as a whole, concludes with these words:

> The celebration of this sacrament is thus always an act in which the
> Church proclaims its faith, gives thanks to God for the freedom with

which Christ has made us free (see Gal 4:31), and offers its life as a spiritual sacrifice in praise of God's glory, as it hastens to meet the Lord Jesus.

## Contrition

We begin with contrition, the first of the penitent's acts in both time and importance. Contrition is defined in RP 6a, which asserts that it is "the most important act of the penitent." Borrowing its definition from the Council of Trent, it states that contrition is "heartfelt sorrow and aversion for the sin committed along with the intention of sinning no more."[1] Trent adds immediately that "this disposition of contrition was necessary at all times for the attainment of the remission of sins." RP avails itself of Paul VI's more scriptural way of saying this:

> We can only approach the Kingdom of Christ by *metanoia*. This is a profound change of the whole person by which one begins to consider, judge and arrange his life according to the holiness and love of God, made manifest in his Son in the last days and given to us in abundance.[2]

The pope has here invoked the Greek word *metanoia*, which is translated "penance" and denotes change of heart, or repentance. The word thus encapsulates a fundamental element of Jesus' preaching of the gospel, which was centered on the Kingdom of God. "Now after John was arrested, Jesus came into Galilee, preaching the gospel of God, and saying, 'The time is fulfilled, and the kingdom of God is at hand: repent *[metanoeite]*, and believe in the gospel'" (Mark 1:14-15). Here repentance is presented as an essential aspect of faith in Jesus, the faith that gives access to the kingdom of God that he preached.

It may strike the reader as strange that while the Gospel speaks of the kingdom of *God* (the Father), the pope (and with him RP) speaks of the kingdom of *Christ*. It is true that Jesus himself preached the kingdom, that is, the reign, of God. In so doing he revealed the true nature of God as a loving father, and called on his hearers to submit themselves anew, in mind and heart, to this God who was seeking them out through his, Jesus', ministry. This would give them a new relation not only to God, but to each other, whereby as "sons [and daughters] of the kingdom [that is, of God]" (Matt 13:38) they would become brothers and sisters of each other. We can see how this call of Jesus invited the double response of repentance and faith, but with these distinguished only as complementary aspects of a single reality, conversion. We need to recall that through his resurrection Jesus was installed as the "Christ," the anointed king who would rule on behalf of God. (This is all that the kings of Israel had ever done: far from being absolute monarchs, as sons and servants of God they only had the function of mediating his rule. He alone was absolute monarch.) For the time of the Church Christ exercises this kingship through his teaching and his sacraments. But as Paul tells us, at the end of time, Christ, having subjected all things to himself, will give back the kingdom to God his Father (see 1 Cor 15:24, 25). Paul continues, "When all things are subjected to him [the Son], then the Son himself will be subjected to him who put all things under him, that God may be everything to every one" (v. 28). The pope and RP, then, speak of the kingdom of Christ rather than the kingdom of God because penance, whether as the virtue alone or the virtue realized (made real) in the sacrament, belongs to the time of the Church.

If baptism is the fundamental way in which Christ draws us under the sway of his kingship, and if sin is *the* way in which we reject and depart from that kingship, penance is the God-given way after baptism by which we are drawn back. It is therefore one of the principal ways in which Christ exercises from heaven his kingship of and in the Church. We shall refer to this again when we consider the minister of the sacrament as Christ's representative. But this is not the only way in which the kingship of Christ is exercised in the sacrament. As Vatican II teaches, the members of the Church also exercise this kingship in overcoming in themselves the reign of sin.[3] This they do principally in approaching the sacrament of penance, in which they share Christ's royal victory over sin. Paradoxically, therefore, through penance they both submit to Christ's kingship and share in its exercise.

We have made the point that contrition is the most important act of the penitent because it alone is absolutely indispensable for the forgiveness of sins. In cases of grave sin confession and satisfaction are necessary too, but, as we shall soon see, circumstances can arise in which the penitent is excused from them, at least as long as the circumstances last. It can be asked: Is it not within God's power to forgive sin even in the absence of contrition on the part of the sinner? After all, we are urged to forgive those who sin against us, for example in the Lord's prayer (see also Matt 6:14-15), where there is no suggestion that the person who offended us must first ask our forgiveness. Can we not assume that God will be at least as generous with us as he expects us to be with our fellow human beings? In other places in the Gospel, however, for example, Luke 17:4 and Matt 18:23-35 (the parable of the unforgiving debtor), we find a different situation. In these the offender has sought forgiveness of the injured party, and the question is whether it must be given or may be withheld. The Gospel, of course, answers that it must be given, even "seven times in the day" if necessary.

Let us return, then, to our first question: What if forgiveness is not sought? In answering this question we need to realize that only when forgiveness is sought can the relationship between the two parties be restored. And while salvation is an act of God, it consists essentially in the relationship of friendship between God and us, a relationship which to be genuine friendship must be mutual. This is why we need contrition in order to have our sins forgiven. If we are not penitent, God will still "forgive" our sin in the sense that he will not harbor any antipathy toward us. But he cannot "forgive" us in the full sense of the word unless we respond positively to his offer of forgiving grace, since only then is the relationship of love and friendship between us restored (by him, who is both the offended party and the superior in the relationship). Certainly, he will continue to love us, though he will be "grieved" by our sins (Eph 4:30 tells us that by our sins we "grieve the Holy Spirit of God").

When he is said to "punish" our sins, this does not mean that he has ceased to love us. It means only that we incur the inevitable consequences of separation from him, a separation for which we have to bear complete responsibility, as we shall have brought it about entirely by ourselves. If not remedied in time, this separation will be felt in eternity as profoundly painful to us, because God made us for himself alone, and at its deepest level our being will yearn for him unceasingly though our hearts be hardened in their rejection of him.

Penance, then, in the sense of repentance, is the most important of the acts of the penitent. It alone of these acts is absolutely indispensable as the condition, God-given as well as supplied by us, for the forgiveness of sins. But there is a further ground for our assertion of its primary importance. This is that it underlies the other acts, confession and satisfaction. Without repentance these acts would be rendered meaningless. If true repentance is present, it will come to expression and completion in the other acts because of the social nature of sin and the consequent social and sacramental nature of its forgiveness. The fact of this connection, though not the reason for it, is stated by RP in no. 6: "It ['inner conversion of heart'] *is expressed* [emphasis mine] through confession made to the Church, due satisfaction, and amendment of life." Speaking of confession in no. 6b, it says that "the confession of sins . . . comes from true knowledge of self before God and *from contrition for those sins* [emphasis mine]." And on satisfaction, in no. 6c, it says that "true conversion *is completed* [emphasis mine] by acts of penance or satisfaction for the sins committed, by amendment of conduct, and also by reparation of injury."

St. Thomas Aquinas supports this line of thought.[4] He teaches that the acts of the penitent, contrition, confession, and satisfaction, are "integral" parts of penance. Here "integral" means, as St. Thomas says, that "the whole is not found, either in its full power or its essence, in the parts taken singly, but is found rather in their ensemble." Thus, for example, a building consists not in its foundation or any of its particular floors but in the totality of foundation and floors. But this does not mean that contrition is completely separated off from the other two parts. In the sense that the foundation implies, and so includes, the whole building, contrition implies and includes confession and satisfaction. Thus we have the second ground for our assertion that contrition is the most important of the acts of the penitent.

A little earlier in no. 6, RP had said that "inner conversion of heart embraces sorrow for sin and the intent to lead a new life." It requires only a little reflection to see that the *intention* to amend one's life is implied by genuine repentance. For how could a person's repentance be sincere if they intended to repeat the very sin for which they were supposed to be repenting? The only kind of repentance that would be compatible with such an intention would be one that amounted to a regret arising from some utterly selfish motive unable to connect us to God, for example that my sins might land me in inconvenience of one kind or another. With this statement I have introduced the question of the motivation of contrition, which must direct us to God in some way, whether by love or some other virtue. We shall speak of this in more detail soon. But we need to anticipate it now, for it supplies the ground for RP's assertion that true repentance must include the intention to amend one's life. Since all sin harms our relationship with God, true repentance must in principle exclude all sin in the future, and so must be motivated by some virtue linking us directly to God.

This matter of amendment of life constitutes a sticking point for some people, keeping them away from the sacrament. Reflecting realistically

on their lives, they have to admit that it is unlikely that they will succeed in avoiding all sin in the future. Indeed what seems to them most
likely is that they will relapse quite frequently into the very sins that
trouble their conscience now. They therefore reason that any promise of
amendment on their part would only be insincere, and that therefore
they would be better off not approaching the sacrament at all. Such
people need to be reassured that the commitment to amendment required by the sacrament centers only on intention and not on actual
performance. It has to do only with the present dispositions of the person. What is important is that in their self-commitment to God they
exclude all intention of sinning in the future; and though they admit in
all honesty that they probably will in fact sin again, nevertheless their
present intention is not to do so. Most importantly, in this they rely not
on their own weakness, which they know only too well, but on the
strength that comes from God. Realistically, they have to be ready for
the likelihood that this strength will come only with time and perseverance. In the meantime they have the help of the sacrament to inspire and
empower them in their endeavors to serve God. They need to keep pa-
tience, hope, and humility alive in their hearts, and they should resolve
that no matter what happens, they will never give up the sacrament. They
would do well to remember the words of the risen Christ to St. Paul when
the latter prayed to be delivered from the "thorn in the flesh" that so
troubled him: "My power is made perfect in weakness" (2 Cor 12:9).

It is significant that a distinction between two kinds of contrition
made much of in the Council of Trent is not mentioned in RP, though
it is alluded to. I refer to the distinction of "perfect" and "imperfect"
contrition, also called, in Trent itself, the distinction of "contrition" and
"attrition," respectively.[5] It will be clear from this that the term "contrition" can be used in either of two senses: the first a general sense of sorrow for sin, and the second a particular sense in contradistinction to
"attrition." When it is used in the first sense, the user can make it specific, if they so desire, by calling it either perfect or imperfect. For the
reader, the sense in each case is to be gleaned from the context. I shall
now briefly summarize the history of this distinction within sorrow for
sin and discuss its relevance to penance in the post-Vatican II period,
especially in view of the fact that it finds no place in the council documents.[6] Finally, we should note that the distinction was recently revived in the *Catechism of the Catholic Church*.[7]

The early scholastics (roughly the twelfth century) distinguished between two kinds of sorrow for sin, one based on the fact that sin drew

God's punishment upon the sinner, the other on the consideration of sin as such, that is, as an offense against God.[8] While the first kind was regarded as useful, only the second was recognized, at this stage, as prompted by grace and effective in obtaining forgiveness. At the end of the twelfth century, a distinction was made between contrition and a lesser form of sorrow called "attrition," perhaps first by Alan of Lille and Simon of Tournai. Soon the distinction was made on the basis of whether the sorrow was "informed" (characterized) by the grace of justification or not. This led to the insight that the grace in question was sanctifying grace (as it is called today) and the love that accompanied it the virtue of charity. William of Auvergne (d. 1249) concluded that contrition corresponded to charity while attrition preceded sanctifying grace and charity and strove toward their acquisition. This teaching was taken over by the theologians of high scholasticism (thirteenth century), including Aquinas, Bonaventure, and Scotus.

At this stage the thinking remained metaphysical; there was as yet no "psychologizing" of contrition and attrition, no tendency to distinguish them, respectively, as "perfect" and "imperfect," or as inspired by nobler and less noble motives. This development came around the end of the century with Richard of Middleton and was taken up by Scotus and his school. We have already met St. Thomas's teaching that in the sacrament itself attrition turns into contrition, that is, that the "attrite" person becomes "contrite," though he was here referring only to a higher kind of attrition. He also believed that there was a lower kind not susceptible to this conversion. According to him, the normal requirement for the fruitful reception of the sacrament was contrition, and attrition was acceptable only when the penitent sincerely believed themselves to be contrite (though really, in the sight of God, they were only attrite). Scotus softened this requirement by teaching that conscious and actual attrition was always acceptable provided the penitent desired a fruitful reception of the sacrament and placed no obstacle in the way of grace. This milder doctrine was widely accepted. But with this emphasis on motivation the distinction of contrition and attrition came to be grasped in purely psychological terms, that is, as arising, respectively, from love and fear, and their relationship to habitual grace was forgotten.

A final development from early in the fourteenth century deserves to be mentioned. This was the contribution of the Dominican nominalist, Durandus of Saint-Pourçain. He agreed with St. Thomas that the norm was that only the already justified contrite person should approach the sacrament, but unlike St. Thomas he did not accept that it was only in some circumstances that the attrite person was rendered contrite in the sacrament. His view was that for any attrite person approaching the sacrament their simple attrition sufficed. In practical terms this teaching had the effect of placing the Thomist school on the same footing as the Scotist on the issue of the penitent's sorrow for sin: each had now established attrition as the minimum requirement for the sacrament.

The Council of Trent treated contrition (in the general sense) in its fourteenth session, in 1551, in chapter 4 of its Doctrine of the Sacrament of Penance. It defined contrition as "the soul's sorrow and detestation of the sin committed, with the resolve to sin no more."[9] The council continued:

> Although it sometimes happens that this contrition is perfect through charity and reconciles the person to God before this sacrament is actually received, this reconciliation, nevertheless, is not to be ascribed to contrition itself without the desire of the sacrament, a desire which is included in it.[10]

We have already covered this point in chapter 1, but a repetition will not go amiss here. Sin is primarily an offense against God, but it is also an offense against the Church. Hence for forgiveness to be complete grave sin needs to be forgiven in the Church, though God will accept simple (perfect) contrition if approach to the sacrament is impossible. He also forgives us if we turn to him again in love before approaching the sacrament, though, as the council says, we are still obliged to receive the sacrament. A further reason for this requirement is that God has revealed that our sins are forgiven through his Son, Jesus Christ, who not only died for them but established the Church as, among other things, his way of bringing forgiveness to us through its sacraments of baptism and penance. If we refuse to avail ourselves of the means that God has revealed as *his* way of forgiving sins (sin being against *him*, be it remembered), such a refusal is an indication that our contrition is not sincere. In this hypothesis we would be laying down to God the conditions under which we would accept forgiveness from him, or at best we would be presuming that he will forgive our sins *our* way rather than the way he has actually revealed as *his* way. Unless excused through ignorance, we would thus be placing ourselves outside the scope of his forgiveness, whether through the sacrament or any other means, as there is no forgiveness of sin without true repentance.

The council then goes on to speak of imperfect contrition or attrition, listing its characteristic motives as the heinousness of sin and the fear of hell and of punishment.[11] The council declares that "if it [attrition] excludes the will to sin and implies the hope for pardon," it is "a gift of God and an impulse of the Holy Spirit, not indeed as already dwelling in the penitent but only as moving them, an impulse by which the penitent is helped to prepare for themselves a way to justice."[12] Thus the penitent who is not already justified at the beginning of the sacramental celebration receives justice through the sacrament. The council further states that while attrition cannot justify a person without the sacrament, it "disposes them to obtain the grace of God in the sacrament." Thus the council, without distinguishing between higher and lower forms of attrition, teaches that simple attrition suffices for forgiveness in the sacrament, though clearly it recommends (perfect) contrition if that is possible. The current teaching of the *Catechism of the Catholic Church* on this topic is nothing more than a re-presentation of the essential elements of the Tridentine doctrine.

Bearing in mind that RP is silent on the distinction of contrition and attrition, it is helpful to note Karl Rahner's comment on the subject. First, he bluntly states that "traditional theology has expended a great deal of needless energy" on this distinction.[13] He concedes that the distinction is "theoretically correct," but adds immediately that "it does not have much importance in actual practice." Then comes his reason:

> For whoever is really capable of turning away from guilt, whoever no longer absolutizes a finite good, for such a person the real difficulty of loving God no longer exists; for, just as the heart of man cannot contain the fullness of its own love but must be ever-giving; so, too, the love of God which man is constantly receiving and by which man lives, is constantly giving itself to man.[14]

Unfortunately, this statement is not as clear as it might be. Let us try to fill it out and interpret it. First, it seems correct to say that if by the help of grace a person becomes truly detached from the object of their sin, there is then nothing to stop them from once again loving God (above all else), especially as grace will be moving them in that direction. But why in this circumstance would it have to be precisely *love* for God that they achieve? Might it not be something positive and good relating them to God but falling short of love? Yes, theoretically that is possible, says Rahner, but it is not very likely. For God is constantly offering himself to us precisely in love, and love offered calls for love in return. Hence in practice there is nothing to stop the response of the penitent from being the love of God above all else. This would mean that the person would have contrition, not just attrition. Indeed, Rahner observes by way of conclusion that the two kinds of contrition can coexist simultaneously in the same person, "though one or the other may emerge more strongly in our consciousness at a particular time."

Here Rahner skillfully marries the metaphysical and the psychological aspects of repentance. Metaphysically a person may have (or, more likely, does have) true charity and grace, and thus contrition, but psychologically they may be moved to focus on a motive less than love, thus indicating that they also have attrition. We need to bear in mind that the presence of charity is not known through the intensity of emotion felt or avowals uttered (though these are admirable and not to be despised), but through the calm and lived decision to place God and his service at the center of our lives, and even then it can only be prayerfully discerned (as distinct from known directly).

We conclude our reflection on contrition with the observation that as far as the sacrament of penance is concerned there was no need for RP to mention the distinction between perfect and imperfect contrition, as Trent had already established that the lesser of these, attrition, was sufficient. Outside the sacrament and in the matter of grave sin, it could be a different matter. There contrition needs to be perfect, though, even so, it must include the intention of approaching the sacrament, as RP 37 states. But if Rahner is right, even there the distinction lacks practical importance, as most likely the person will actually be contrite in any case. A final comment is that if Rahner is wrong on this, St. Thomas is probably right in saying *"ex attrito fit contritus"* ("the attrite person is rendered contrite [in the sacrament]"). For grace and, with it, charity are definitely given in the sacrament. In St. Thomas's theology the first gift of grace, charity, is at the same time the last disposition of the penitent for forgiveness. Here, of course, charity is considered not psychologically, but metaphysically. Psychologically, the motivation would remain something less than love. But if this seems too artificial to be believed, the alternative, so it seems to me, is to accept without further ado the position of Rahner.

## Confession

We come now to the subject of confession, the recounting of one's personal sins in the sacrament of penance for the purpose of gaining absolution and reconciliation with the Church and with God. From a pastoral point of view this is the most contentious of the four parts of the sacrament and the most challenging for both penitents and Church authorities. It is also the part least understood in the contemporary Church. For these reasons this section of the chapter will be longer than its fellows, and though I shall be careful to present all that RP has to say on the subject, I shall depart from the expository style I have employed hitherto, and invoke RP in the context of facing up to this difficult issue in my own way. Confession is challenging for the authorities because since the council, in the developed, Western world, great numbers of people have turned away from the sacrament. It is probably no exaggeration to say that at the present time the sacrament is facing a crisis comparable to that which confronted canonical penance in the early Middle Ages, when for the sake of preserving the place of the sacrament in the Church the authorities found it necessary to introduce fundamental changes to its structure. And the problem is only partly the idea of the sacrament itself: witness the packed congregations that invariably assemble for celebrations of the third rite (general absolution), probably in the mistaken belief that confession is simply dispensed with under these circumstances.[15] For many of these people the problem is not so much the sacrament itself as the need for confession as one of its parts. (Some among them would hold also that the sacrament is only one among several ways of obtaining forgiveness, even of grave sins.) If this diagnosis is correct, we have switched our perspective on confession from the challenge to the authorities to the challenge to penitents.

## Confession: A Contemporary Problem

Why, then, is confession now so widely viewed as too great a burden to be borne? In a study document issued by the United States bishops in 1990 the difficulty most commonly listed by lay respondents (to the survey conducted in the preparation of the document) centered on the availability of suitable confessors.[16] Most complained that they were too well known to their pastors to feel comfortable about confessing to them. Others said that conflicts or differences they had had with their pastors kept them away. Others felt that their confessors did not take their search for spiritual growth seriously enough. High percentages mentioned ways other than the sacrament, such as receiving the Eucharist or personal prayer, in which they experienced reconciliation. In itself this latter finding is not significant, given that to list such ways was precisely what they were invited to do by the survey.

Unfortunately, the respondents were not asked whether the reason for the infrequency of their reception of the sacrament was that they believed that it was not necessary (since reconciliation could be had by other means). I have already stated my personal conviction that this latter belief is widespread. For these people, the sacrament is only one among several ways in which sinners can be reconciled. It must be granted that in some circumstances this view is justified. In the many cases in which sins are not grave, the sacrament is not necessary, and the alternative means listed in the survey suffice. But to claim that even when access to the sacrament is possible, these means suffice in the case of grave sin is, as I have already suggested, sheer wishful thinking, unless the person happens to be excused through ignorance. Recall also that I have argued that a theology of fundamental option commends the view that grave sin, though far from impossible, is not as common as has been thought in the past.

The conclusion must be that there are doubtless many cases in which the sins committed do not require the sacrament for forgiveness, and can be forgiven through other means. But this conclusion does not cover all cases, and it is precisely these other cases that cause such grave concern to Church authorities at the present time.

It must be admitted that addressing the problems identified in the survey would not, and does not, of itself solve the predicament in which the Church now finds itself. That people experience a difficulty in confessing to a priest with whom they have a personal relationship, whether positive or negative, is understandable. In general, it is advisable to keep personal relationships separate from professional ones, and the relationship of penitent and confessor is just as professional as that of client and lawyer or patient and doctor. But if this were the main problem, the situation could be easily remedied: the pastor need only invite a visiting confessor to the parish, or people could go to neighboring parishes to receive the sacrament. These things are done already, but they have had little impact on the problem.

The difficulty about confessors not taking penitents seriously has to do with the level of maturity, spirituality, and education of the confessor. These are important qualities, and cannot be presumed to be equally present in all confessors. Penitents, therefore, need to be just as careful in selecting their regular confessor as they are in choosing their doctor or lawyer. And church authorities need to do more to prepare clergy for the demanding role of confessor. But as a general statement we can assert that even at present there are enough sufficiently qualified priests available to enable discerning penitents to choose their confessors wisely and well. This opportunity is already factored in to the serious situation that we currently have. While recognizing that improvements in the two areas mentioned are highly desirable, even necessary, we need to probe deeper if we are to discover the truly influential reasons for the present malaise of the sacrament.

I would like to suggest the two following reasons. First, there exists a resistance on the part of many of the faithful to being instructed by the Church on moral matters. And secondly, the demands made by RP on the maturity and spirituality of the penitent are considerably greater than under the former rite.

### First Reason: Resistance to Authority

We begin with the first reason. People now tend to form their own ideas about right and wrong, or simply to imbibe them uncritically from the society in which they live, and these ideas are often at variance with Church teaching. Rather than risk getting into a confrontation with their confessor, they prefer to turn to other means of seeking peace with God. Several factors have given rise to this situation. The spirit of independence here evident is encouraged by the pluralism and individualism of the secular culture. Further, in post-modern society there exists a general disillusionment with major institutions of whatever stamp, whether secular or religious. Largely responsible for this is the regular occurrence of scandals and corruption among officials in these institutions, and the detailed revelation of these events in the media. Where at one time these institutions were trusted and believed, now the opposite is largely the case. The Church is by no means exempt from this mistrust.

In the Church the decline began with the publication of the papal encyclical on planned parenthood, *Humanae vitae*, in 1968. Prior to this, official teaching on moral matters was generally accepted without question throughout the Church; after it, and as a result of it, such teaching has often been met with hostility, disagreement, skepticism, or indifference. The situation has not been helped by scandals involving clergy and religious, incidents in some cases of the misuse of power and money, but more often of pedophilia and child abuse, not to mention other sexual activity incompatible with Church teaching and with commitment to celibacy or the vow of chastity.

This grim situation is not going to be overcome easily or quickly. The Church can respond by being more careful in its screening and training of prospective clergy and religious, but the sharp decline in vocations, which shows no sign of abating, will continue to augur badly for the existence of a truly effective clerical and religious workforce in the foreseeable future. The presentation of Church teaching in official documents, instructions, and homilies needs to be made more persuasive and to be more clearly shown to be based on the Bible, on reason, and on the experience of the faithful. In the face of the individualism and general disillusionment of secular society the Church should show itself as openly countercultural, but at the same time careful not to condemn itself thereby to irrelevance. In large part this danger can be avoided through a "preferential option for the poor," which needs to be unmistakably evident in the Church's social action. In the face of such challenges, dramatic successes with such barometers as the quality of the celebration of the sacrament of penance are hardly to be expected, and the Church must learn to be satisfied with small gains merely suggestive of a brighter future.

Illustrative of the spirit of independence and resistance of which I have been speaking is a letter that appeared recently in the London Catholic weekly, *The Tablet,* from Dr. Jack Dominian, Catholic psychiatrist and writer on marriage and sexuality.[17] I wish now to comment briefly on two points made in this letter. Speaking of "sexual matters" and "infringements of rules and regulations of the Church," Dominian writes: "These no longer impinge. As the people of God have matured, the paternalistic stance of parent to child in the confessional has come to seem unacceptable." It would be deplorable if church regulations, grounded as they always are in divine law, and sexual conduct, which bears strongly on right relations to ourselves and others, were no longer regarded as matters of conscience by Christian people. This part of Dominian's assertion can simply be disregarded as overstatement.

That people are more mature now than in previous generations is a highly questionable assertion. It can be granted, however, that prior to the council confessors often adopted toward their penitents a paternalistic attitude that was evident in their general style. (For example, they often addressed penitents as "my child," "my son" or "my daughter," and, even if kindly, behaved in an authoritarian way.) It should be added that this attitude was taken for granted by everyone and, except in a very few cases, not resented. But today the social climate is very different, and I greatly doubt whether this situation now occurs with any frequency. Nowadays the conscientious confessor strives to present himself to his penitents as a compassionate brother in Christ. However, RP, in no. 10 ("The Pastoral Exercise of This Ministry"), as well as describing the confessor as brother, has him as healer, teacher, judge, father, and pastor, and we should now devote a little space to examining exactly what this means.[18]

In this list the two analogies that confront the eye of the modern reader are those of father and judge. The idea of the confessor as father is presented in RP 10c and is derived from the motif of the fatherhood of God. It is there combined with that of Christ as the Good Shepherd, that is, pastor. In combination these motifs convey a sense of authority, that is, of divine authority mediated by a human being. This, far from being arbitrary, should be wise, compassionate, and provident. The respect that a penitent has for their confessor is in one way like that of a client for their lawyer or doctor, that is, beyond regard for their personal qualities, it is respect for, and deference to, their professional competence and prudence. But it goes beyond this also. It is first and foremost a recognition that the confessor has been entrusted with a divine ministry. It is not as though he is confused with God, but rather that he is respected as the representative of Christ and the Church. This is a respect stemming from faith and transcending all purely human honor.

As for the second role, that of judge, for believers this accrues only to those invested with authority from above, those called to exercise judgment with Christ and God (see 1 Cor 6:2); the normal rule within the community is that the Christian is to refrain from judgment (see Matt 7:1-2).[19] A tremendous responsibility is thus placed on the bearer of judgment to exercise it wisely and well in the name of God. In the context of the sacrament it is explained by RP, in 10a, as discretion, that is, the discretion to guide and advise appropriately, a discretion that is not innate but acquired from God through study, the guidance of the magisterium, and prayer. It is, as RP says, the "discernment of spirits." Implied here, though not stated, is a more fundamental exercise of judgment, namely the decision either to grant or to withhold absolution according to the gospel injunction (John 20:23). This is no arbitrary decision, but is based on the confessor's "discernment" of the dispositions, that is, the genuine repentance, of the penitent. This is necessary both out of respect for the sacrament, whose principal guardian the confessor is, and out of pastoral concern for the penitent. For if the latter is not properly disposed, no benefit is gained from granting absolution.

When it appears that the confessor may be obliged to withhold absolution, he has the opportunity to do what he can to bring the penitent to the right dispositions. If this fails, it is not so much a matter of refusing absolution as of deferring it until such time as the penitent attains repentance. Perhaps they need more time, more prayer and reflection, to be able, under God's grace, to accomplish this. There is no need for this situation to become confrontational; the penitent, even if disappointed, will usually see that this is the best, indeed the only way to proceed, and will agree happily enough to seek further guidance in prayer and perhaps consultation. It would be good for the confessor, pastor and brother as well as judge, to promise to keep the penitent in his own prayers. Finally, judgment is also, as Trent says, the actual imparting of divine forgiveness and not just a declaration that sins are forgiven.[20] This places the issue of judgment in its proper perspective: it is always a decision of charity, one either of merciful forgiveness from God, or of its deferral until such time as God's grace has brought the penitent to the repentance without which there is no forgiveness of sins. In addition to the four qualities required of the confessor by RP 10 and already considered, namely brother, father, pastor, and judge, there remain two still not dealt with, namely healer and teacher. About these we need say no more here than that each, like pastor and judge, is a role calling for due professional competence and prudence, to which appropriate deference is due on the part of the penitent.

Our reflections have brought us to the point of seeing that when Dominian objects to "the paternalistic stance of parent to child in the confessional," what he is objecting to must be either the concept of the confessor as a professional person, or the idea of the mediation of divine authority (or both). Whichever of these be his object, he errs by excess. That the role of confessor is by nature professional is obvious, and I shall not attempt to argue it here. Now any professional person faces the danger of lapsing into an arrogance amounting to paternalism (or worse). The confessor, therefore, *can* be like this, but he does not have to be. Similarly, the mediation of divine authority in the sacrament can be exercised either in a way that adequately takes account of the gap between divine authority as such and its mediation, conditioned and subject to limitations, in a human institution, or in a way that does not, and so results in an arrogant attempt on the part of the confessor to arrogate divine authority without remainder to himself.[21] Again, it is possible for the confessor to follow the latter alternative, but he does not have to, and of course should not.

The corrective for each of these dangers is for the confessor to realize his commonality with the penitent, the fact that he is the penitent's brother, standing under the same law of God and the Church and subject to the same weaknesses. His is a humble role, a service, a *diakonia*. He would do well to remember the sentence from St. Augustine, "I am a bishop for you, and a Christian with you,"[22] or better still the verse from the letter to the Hebrews (4:15), speaking of his master, Christ, "We have not a high priest who is unable to sympathize with our weaknesses, but one who in every respect has been tempted as we are." The flaw in Dominian's assertion is that with each set of possibilities he overlooks one alternative and asserts the other as solely operative, even though it is extreme and occurs in practice only rarely if at all.

There is therefore no need for the experience of confession to be for the penitent a regression to a childish state. It can be, and ideally is, a structured meeting of two adults, brothers, or brother and sister, from the one Christian community, with one by virtue of his office and competence ministering to the other, to help them discern their fidelity or lack thereof to the law, of God and the Church, under which they both stand; to help this person attain and express a true repentance for their sins thus confessed; to mediate God's pardon to them in the Church, the divinely appointed place of reconciliation; and with them to give praise to God for his mercy. There is no reason why the relationship thus characterized should be paternalistic.

The second point from Dominian on which I wish to comment is his assertion that certain of the human sciences have rendered confession obsolete:

> Whilst the sense of right and wrong remains, a deeper understanding of responsibility has been attained through 100 years of psychological insights. Psychoanalysis, psychotherapy and counselling offer a rich way of healing and are widely used.

This assertion exemplifies a reductionism typical of many educated Catholics, and for this reason merits our consideration. What Dominian is doing here is reducing the spiritual life to the psychic life, with which, admittedly, it is closely related, but from which it needs to be distinguished. Their distinction becomes clear when it is realized that the psychic life has to do with our mental health, while the spiritual life has to do, ultimately, with our relationship with God. The "healing" to which Dominian here refers is presumably deliverance from neurosis. But when this is done, there still remains the need for forgiveness, the acquisition of virtue, and help toward the deepening of prayer.

These constitute the task of the confessor and the spiritual director, not of the therapist. The confessor should know just enough of the behavioral sciences to be able to recognize a problem in this area when it exists, and encourage the penitent to seek appropriate help. Even if qualified (and, obviously, all the more if unqualified), he should not attempt it himself, for to do so would be to mislead the penitent as to the nature and purpose of the sacrament. Many Catholics, who otherwise would not consult a therapist, do so because their confessor has urged them thereto. However unwittingly (as in the case of Dominian), disseminating the belief that the clinical practitioners of the behavioral sciences can replace the confessor strikes a blow at the heart of religion, because in reducing sin to the psychic order it embodies a form of naturalism that effectively denies the "supernatural" dimension of human being and activity, seeing it purely in terms of containment within this world. Authentic Christianity, on the other hand, has to do with the fact that by his grace God has raised human beings above their natural station to a life shared with him, both here below and in heaven.

### Second Reason: The Greater Demands of RP

There is a second reason for the present malaise of the sacrament of reconciliation, namely, the fact that in regard to confession RP makes far greater demands on the maturity and spirituality of the penitent than did the previous discipline, demands that many present-day Catholics feel unable to meet. This is evident in the admission they so often make, "I don't go to confession any more, because I don't know what to say." The reason for this is that Catholics, being instructed and prepared for this sacrament at age six or seven, generally receive no further education in this regard. They feel foolish making the kind of confession they made as children; they know in a vague kind of way that the new rites expect them to confess as adults; but they do not know how to do this.

Earlier I criticized Jack Dominian's rather rosy estimate of the maturity of adult lay Catholics. By this I did not mean the general maturity of their everyday lives, a maturity which to me seems to be pretty much on a par with that of previous generations, but only the maturity they manifest in their spiritual lives. In the sacrament of reconciliation this want of maturity and spirituality comes to the fore in their approach to confession. With the problem stated like this, it is clear that the remedy is education, ongoing adult education. A certain amount of this can be done in the homily at Sunday mass, but not a great deal without subverting the nature and purpose of the homily. The greater part of the remedy lies in retreats, adult education groups and courses, parish libraries, diocesan newspapers, and periodicals, with the last two recommended from time to time from the pulpit (not every Sunday, as people quickly become immune to this level of bombardment).

## 1. Comparison of Trent and RP: Integral confession

That the demands of RP are greater than those of Trent can be seen from a simple comparison on the matter of "integral confession." The teaching of Trent is to be found in chapter 5, "Confession," of its Doctrine on the Sacrament of Penance, 1551. In the Dupuis translation, the first paragraph speaks of the "complete confession of sins,"[23] thus rendering the council's expression *integra peccatorum confessio*. The technical term for the word Dupuis has translated as "complete" is "integral," and it is this term that we shall use from now on. It is clear from the next paragraph that only "mortal" sins are intended by this term, though the confession of venial sins as well, or of venial sins only (if there are no mortal sins), is neither excluded nor imposed. In fact this last type of confession, later called "the confession of devotion" or "devotional confession," is encouraged. The main point of the first paragraph is that integral confession was "instituted by the Lord," which Trent understands in a simplistic historical way. The reason Trent gives for integral confession is that without it the priest would be unable to exercise properly the discretion to grant or withhold absolution or to "observe equity" in the imposition of penances.

The second paragraph contains Trent's requirements for confession: "All mortal sins of which penitents after a diligent self-examination are conscious must be recounted by them in confession, though they may be most secret and may have been committed only against the last two precepts of the decalogue (see Exod 20:17; Matt 5:28)."[24] The point of the last stipulation is that sins against these particular precepts are sins of thought only, and hence are even more secret than the most secret of acts. Thus it is not only public sins that have to be confessed but secret ones as well. The fourth paragraph makes it plain that the integrity demanded for the sacrament encompasses only those mortal sins brought to memory by careful reflection.[25] In scholastic language, this is called "formal" integrity. ("Material" integrity would encompass *all* actual mortal sins, whether remembered or not.)

The council goes on to say that in confessing remembered sins the penitent actually submits for forgiveness all their mortal sins, including forgotten ones, since nothing has been deliberately withheld. In the second paragraph, it describes this formally integral confession, as "open and humble." It follows that if forgotten sins are later remembered, they must be confessed at the next confession, since, as the first paragraph says, all mortal sins must be submitted to "the power of the keys" (see Matt 16:19), that is, to the Church's jurisdiction over sin. But, says the second paragraph, if a person knowingly withholds a mortal sin in confession, nothing is forgiven. Though the council does not say so, their guilt in this case is compounded by a new sin, of sacrilege. The third paragraph adds that circumstances changing the kind of sin must also be confessed, as these will affect the sacramental judgment that the confessor must make.[26]

A reader learning of these requirements for the first time might wonder how RP could possibly be more demanding. It must be conceded that in an intellectual sense the Tridentine discipline was quite demanding. But it was not particularly so in a personal sense. It presupposed that mortal sins could be clearly known and distinguished from venial sins, and that they were quite common, as on any given occasion a penitent might have several to confess. Hence it was generally not necessary for the penitent to enter into a discernment process with the confessor. While the penitent might have been concerned about venial sins in their life, they did not need to complicate their confession with this concern, as these sins did not have to be confessed in any case. The main task was to compile and recount a complete and accurate list of mortal sins committed since the last confession.

This is what Trent meant by an "open and humble confession." For this task a certain amount of technical knowledge was necessary, and if the penitent lacked it, the confessor was supposed to help them in order to ensure an integral confession, but this usually required only one or two quick questions. Granted that the confession of one's sins to another under any circumstances demands the virtue of humility, it was likely that for a person who possessed the requisite knowledge and had made an adequate examination of conscience, the self-accusation and contrition preceding the confession were considerably more demanding in a personal sense than the confession itself. In making this judgment, we need to bear in mind that the sins confessed were objectivized in an almost scientifically concise and precise way, and that the confession was protected by the anonymity of the confessional.[27] It was possible, therefore, for it to be a relatively impersonal exercise, though of course it did not have to be. Eventually these factors combined to form the mentality of the "shopping list" of sins brought to confession. Though the expression is a parody, it contains more than a grain of truth, and it emphasizes the point that the Tridentine discipline lent itself to the reduction of confession to the level of a relatively impersonal and noninvolved exercise.

Reflecting on Trent in the light of contemporary concerns, we need to realize that nothing that it required as truly *iure divino* can later be overturned by Church authority.[28] As the Church exists only to serve God, it cannot abolish or disregard anything that it has accepted as revealed as God's gift to itself. Admittedly, there has been some discussion as to exactly what *iure divino* meant at Trent. It could cover several meanings ranging from "instituted by Christ" to "prescribed by the Church," and the meaning in any given case would have to be determined by the context.[29] On the matter of integral confession, Carl Peter argues persuasively for "instituted by Christ," which, in an updated form, is the meaning the expression has today:

> As to the basic, hard fact of integral confession, that comes from God. At least for the Fathers of Trent, integrity was not one of those elements arising solely from the Church's determination of the sacrament; it was contained in or followed from Christ's institution. Concretely they differentiated between it and other prescriptions. It alone was necessary because of divine law.[30]

The council based this position on Scripture, the texts most commonly invoked in the discussion being John 20:21-23; Matt 18:17-18; 16:17-19; and Jas 5:16. As suggested above, the institution of confession by Christ was understood either in the straightforward, obvious sense, or in the sense of being insinuated by him as necessary. Integrity was understood either as contained in this or as presupposed for it.[31] Today the *iure divino* character of integrity would not be based so directly on Scripture, but rather on the essence of the sacrament: if reconciliation is a sacrament and hence *iure divino*, then so is integrity, because it is inseparable from its sacramental nature. I know of no one who has in fact explained this point more clearly than Clement Tierney, though, as we shall soon see, this was not what he had in mind in penning these lines:

> In his integral confession the penitent is giving a sacramental shape to that inner confession of sins which he makes to God in his heart. He must confess to God in his heart because he has sinned against God and is seeking forgiveness from God and reconciliation with

God. But this personal and intimate dialogue between the sinner and God must also be drawn into God's historical plan of salvation which takes visible and sacramental shape in the Church. In other words, the personal dialogue with God must become a sacramental dialogue with God.[32]

This argument of Tierney establishes the *iure divino* character both of confession as a necessary element of the sacrament and of integrity as a necessary quality of confession. It also places integral confession in its correct perspective, so that its importance will be neither undervalued nor exaggerated. It will not be undervalued, because the sincerity of the penitent must be truly signified, and under normal circumstances this will require an honest, and therefore complete, confession of whatever has separated them from God. But it will not be exaggerated either. As Louis Monden has pointed out, the confession is the bringing of sins to verbal expression; it is not the sins themselves, nor is it identical with the sinful person who is responsible for them. It is merely a *sign* of the sins that are the true object of pardon, and of the person who is ultimately forgiven, in this sacrament.[33]

There should therefore be no excessive concentration on the actual confession by either the penitent or the confessor. Monden thinks that this defect, particularly on the part of penitents (and because of the unbalanced catechesis they have received), has contributed significantly to the present-day decline of the sacrament.[34] Trent recognized this point by requiring only formal, rather than material, integrity. However, by its detailed attention to the precise matter to be confessed it must bear its share of the blame for the misplaced emphasis on objective precision that still obtains today.

This reflection enables us to answer a question that has puzzled theologians. We know that when integral confession is impossible, a penitent can be absolved without it (though when the impossibility is overcome the obligation returns). Canon 960 of the 1983 Code of Canon Law recognizes that this impossibility can be either "physical" or "moral" in nature.[35] As the commentary commissioned by the Canon Law Society of America states, "these kinds of impossibility may embrace a variety of physical and moral (even psychological) incapacities on the part of the penitent, the latter's relationship to the only available minister, circumstances of time or place, etc."[36] The question is: How can an obligation be at the same time *iure divino and* not binding under all circumstances? Tierney assumes that it cannot, which must mean that, unlike Carl Peter, he does not understand Trent's use of *iure di-*

*vino* in this instance as being in the strict sense. All he requires as of "the very nature of the sacrament" (the equivalent of *iure divino*) is "some confession of sin, some external manifestation of sinfulness." For him integral confession is a requirement of *the Church,* and this explains why it can be dispensed with under certain conditions.[37] As we saw from Peter, he is on weak ground here. Peter, in seeing integrity as one value among several, has given what is to me a more convincing answer. Referring to Trent, he says:

> It asserted integrity as a value, recognized that the latter exists concretely in the midst of other values that taken together form a hierarchy. Sometimes those other values take precedence; sometimes they do not. Which ones do and which ones do not? To make Trent decide that is to do violence to its teaching. To assert that integral confession is required by a purely disciplinary law is the other extreme and no less prejudicial. If divine revelation points out a religious value as obligatory, let us not pretend the case is otherwise. If it recognizes that value as coexistent with others, let us not make that value obligatory in all circumstances or without any further consideration.[38]

Integral confession would not be able to be thus relativized if it were not already secondary to the one truly indispensable act of the penitent, repentance/conversion, to which it stands in the relation of a sign. Peter's account, giving, as it does, appropriate recognition to each horn of the dilemma posed by our question, alone appears to be a fully satisfactory solution.

Turning to RP, we note that it deals with confession in two places, nos. 6b (no. 6: "The Sacrament of Penance and Its Parts," and b: "Confession") and 7a and b ("The Necessity and Benefit of the Sacrament," no subheading). No. 7a resumes the doctrine of Trent, though it expresses it in updated language: "To obtain the saving remedy of the sacrament of penance, according to the plan of our merciful God, the faithful must confess to a priest each and every grave sin which they remember upon examination of their conscience." This clearly conveys the requirement of integrity, and the phrase "according to the plan of our merciful God" covers the doctrine that this is *iure divino,* though it transcends its juridical character by using personal and biblical language. No. 6b gives RP's own treatment of confession, and hence we shall quote it in full:

> The sacrament of penance includes the confession of sins, which comes from true knowledge of self before God and from contrition for those sins. However, this inner examination of heart and the exterior

accusation should be made in the light of God's mercy. Confession requires in the penitent the will to open his heart to the minister of God, and in the minister a spiritual judgement by which, acting in the person of Christ, he pronounces his decision of forgiveness or retention of sins in accord with the power of the keys.

Note the personal emphasis of this entire paragraph. Sins are no longer items to be put on a list, but manifestations of the discerned relationship of this person to God, a spoiled or damaged relationship about which the penitent is truly repentant. If the emphasis were to remain on the human person, there would be a temptation to despair, but this is not where it finally settles. It is firmly directed to our merciful God, who inspires in our hearts hope and gratitude. What the penitent now does is "open his heart" to the minister. This beautiful expression sweeps up Trent's requirement of integral confession into the personal perspective of the paragraph as a whole. It reproduces exactly the right balance between what is known and repented in the heart and what is expressed in faltering human words. At this point we can fruitfully quote the words of Rahner:

> All scrupulousness in the examination of individual sins, their precise listing, etc., would be a sign that one has not understood the true significance of this sacrament which, in its last analysis, is not a question of sins but rather of a sinful man who is encompassed by God's mercy and who can grasp, who can accept, historically and socially, this situation in the word of forgiveness of the Church, coming from God, and superabundantly overcoming all his guilt.[39]

What matters, as far as confession is concerned, is that the person be truly repentant, that they be sincere of heart, and that in their confession they do their human best (which is not necessarily an absolute best) to express whatever they find in their heart needing to be said on this occasion of grace. If the confessor suspects they need help in doing this, he can and should provide it.

This opening of the heart of which RP speaks takes into account the fact that grave sin is not as easily identified as was previously thought. The penitent simply does their best in confessing their guilt as they see it. But this does not mean that the requirement of integrity is not respected and observed. If anything, more rather than less is confessed than the Tridentine injunction requires. For the penitents do not say to themselves, "This I shall confess because it is a grave sin, but this I shall not, because it is only a venial sin." Rather, they say, "I want to confess whatever my heart tells me is an obstacle that I have erected between myself and God." I am not suggesting that RP *obliges* the penitents to confess all that is in their hearts: they remain obliged to confess only their certainly grave sins. But in deliberately not distinguishing here between grave and non-grave sin and choosing the expression "open his heart," RP is urging the penitent to confess in the way I have suggested. The penitent is exhorted to lay aside any calculating, minimizing spirit, and to be completely open with their confessor. Perhaps the reader will now understand why I said earlier that RP is more personally demanding on the penitent than was Trent.

### 2. Comparison of Tridentine discipline and RP: The anonymity of the penitent

Further, recall that the Tridentine discipline protected the penitent through the anonymity of the confessional. All that RP has to say on this matter is that the sacrament is celebrated in the place prescribed by canon law.[40] It presumes, however, that confessor and penitent are present to each other in a way that is normal for a human encounter. Thus the rubric accompanying the giving of absolution, in RP 46, prescribes that the priest extend his hands, or at least his right hand, "over" (Latin: *super*) the head of the penitent (thus approximating to the ancient imposition of hands without making actual physical contact). This would make no sense if penitent and confessor were separated by a grill.[41] The 1983 Code of Canon Law, in canon 964, after stating that the proper place for confessions is a church or oratory, goes on to say that confessionals should be located in an open space and provided, "for those who desire it," with a fixed grill between the penitent and the confessor, and that without a just reason confessions should not be heard outside the confessional.[42]

This provision is now incorporated into RP by the "particular decree" of the Congregation for Divine Worship mentioned in the Preface. In the United States, as in other countries, the law is interpreted as the requirement to provide in churches small chapels or rooms in which penitents are given the choice of either a face-to-face exchange with the confessor or an anonymous encounter through the use of kneeler and grill, thus making possible the exact observance of the RP rubric (hand or hands extended *over* the head of the penitent) for at least the first of these alternatives.[43] The "just reason" for hearing confessions elsewhere does not have to be a strong one, though the normal place will remain that provided in the church. Sottocornola expressed a truth when he wrote that most confessionals, "old, dusty, and dark, which oblige us to whisper, and which convey no sense of the presence of an interlocutor, lead to a very negative experience of the sacrament, which is, by contrast, a meeting with a brother in whom Christ makes himself visible and humanly present for us."[44]

This criticism, while not directed at kneelers with grills, applies in some degree to them also, for they provide a means of avoiding a truly personal fraternal encounter. The penitent and the confessor should have a normal "heart to heart" conversation. This means that the confessor should be related to in a human way, and not used as a microphone through which the penitent addresses God or Christ directly. (Again, some penitents have been given misleading instruction on this point, for example, being told that in the sacrament they are speaking *not* to the priest, but to Christ or God.) While we are still in a period when the grill must be provided for those who want it, most people, so far as I can see, realize instinctively that taking refuge behind a grill is not a particularly human way of conducting a conversation. But as we move toward a more open and personally involved form of confession, we need to recognize that in urging this RP asks considerably more of the penitent than did Trent. As I remarked at the introduction of this subject, this could constitute an additional factor for the present-day decline of confession: many people simply feel unable to cope with this more demanding situation, and therefore avoid it as far as possible. The answer is to provide the grill for as long as necessary and at the same time through public education and reeducation to encourage people to adopt the more open form presumed by RP. In this connection it is interesting to review from the vantage point of a quarter century later the following words of Sottocornola:

> Today it has become more and more disagreeable, particularly for young people, to go to confession in a confessional. Perhaps it should even be recognized that the decrease in confessions is due in part to the fact that in this area innovations were not made in due time.[45]

In fact, experience has shown that very few people, even of the relatively small number still receiving the sacrament, choose the option of open confession, and of these almost none are young people. The challenge to the tact, prudence, and perseverance of Church educators is obvious.

Going to confession was never easy. It always called for a high level of self-transcendence. We saw in our brief history of the sacrament that in the twelfth century expiation was transferred from the work of penance to the confession itself, in as much as the latter involved difficulty and humiliation. Under any circumstances to confess one's sins to another requires the virtue of humility. And there have always been, as there always will be, some people too proud to go to confession. But at the present time two new factors have combined to make this humility even more difficult. These are, first, the more exacting demands of RP, which we have just presented, and second, in Western culture, the fact that a fiercely competitive society pushes people always to project the most positive possible image of themselves, an image which allows no room for the admission of weakness, let alone failure. This means that humbly confessing one's sins to another, seen as madness by our society, is rendered all the more difficult. Part of adult catechesis, therefore, should be a frank recognition that confession is a counter-cultural exercise embarked on in faith, in which we put ourselves on the line. But its reward is the experience not of the contempt, rejection, or derision that our worldly involvement might lead us to expect, but the acceptance, understanding, compassion, and love of a brother in Christ, and the merciful forgiveness of God.

## Devotional Confession

We come, finally, to the question of frequent devotional confession, or "devotional confession," as we shall call it. This is recourse to the sacrament when there are no grave sins to confess. In order to have the sacrament at all, it is necessary that *some* sin or sins be submitted to the power of the keys. In devotional confession, therefore, what is confessed is non-grave sins, or grave sins already absolved on a previous occasion (indicated by some such formula as "sins of my past life"), or a combination of both. As it is for the penitent to decide what they want to confess, the issue of integral confession does not arise under these circumstances. The title of this type of confession flows from its nature: as it is not *necessary* to receive the sacrament for non-grave sins, to do so is to perform a "devotion," a pious exercise oriented to growth in the spiritual life.

RP has the following to say on devotional confession, in no. 7b:

> Frequent and careful celebration of this sacrament is also very useful as a remedy for venial sins. This is not a mere ritual repetition or psychological exercise, but a serious striving to perfect the grace of baptism so that as we bear in our body the death of Jesus Christ, his life may be seen in us ever more clearly. In confession of this kind, penitents

who accuse themselves of venial faults should try to conform more closely to Christ and to follow the voice of the Spirit more attentively.

In order that this sacrament of healing may truly achieve its purpose among Christ's faithful, it must take root in their whole lives and move them to more fervent service of God and neighbor.

The main idea running through this entire provision is process. Sin is forgiven in an instant, but pulling up the roots of sin, as an essential component of becoming conformed to Christ, is a process, the work of a lifetime. While baptism stands for the instantaneous and total victory of Christ over sin *for* each of us individually, penance, repeated as it is from time to time, stands for the process of the gradual appropriation of this victory *in* each of us, and not just penance as brought to bear on our grave lapses, but penance as burrowing ever deeper into our lives and gradually removing from them even the roots of sin, that is, penance as the practice of devotional confession. Hence the emphasis on perfecting the grace of baptism, conformity to Christ, heeding the Spirit, penance as sacrament and virtue taking root in life, and fervent, persevering service of God and neighbor. To place this positive teaching in clearer relief, RP rules out two things that devotional confession is not. It is not a mere ritual repetition, a fruitless and obsessive raking over of fields already plowed. Nor is it an opportunity for psychological counseling. Even spiritual direction, which in a limited form can be given on this occasion, is not its justifying principle.

As Rahner has pointed out in his important article on the subject, what justifies and provides the *raison d'être* of devotional confession is that in it God's pardon comes to us visibly and historically through the ministry of Christ and the Church.[46] It matters not that the sins submitted are either certainly (in the case of sins already absolved) or probably (in the case of non-grave sins, through the repentance that moved us to seek out the sacrament in the first place) already forgiven. That the sentence of pardon is pronounced or repronounced in precisely this forum adds greatly to the power of the process of eradicating sin from our lives and thus becoming more perfectly conformed to Christ. It is no wonder that the practice is recommended to all who seek to follow Christ more closely, and especially to clergy and seminarians.[47]

Other reasons advanced for devotional confession, for example, obtaining spiritual direction and growing in God's grace, are valid and important, but do not in themselves constitute justifying reasons, as these benefits can also be had in other ways. A very practical subsidiary reason for retaining the practice is that if it were not permitted, to be known to have gone to confession would be tantamount to a public admission of grave fault, in which case people would either shun the sacrament altogether, or approach it only under conditions of utmost secrecy. Clearly, it is to the advantage of the sacrament itself that it be available not only to those with grave sin but to all.

## Absolution

The remaining parts of the sacrament, absolution and satisfaction, can be dealt with much more briefly. RP treats absolution in no. 7d, calling it the sign of God's pardon. Note that in this place where we might expect it, there is no mention of reconciliation with the Church. The paragraph states also that absolution completes the sacrament. To this we might want to raise the perfectly valid objection that the sacrament is really only completed through satisfaction. RP's assertion, however, can be defended by pointing out that in commenting on the four parts of the sacrament it treats absolution in last place. Also, in considering satisfaction, in RP 7c, it calls it the completion of conversion rather than of the sacrament. And it is true that satisfaction is the completion of conversion. The full truth is that both positions are correct: absolution completes the sacrament logically, and satisfaction completes it chronologically.

Let me mention two further stipulations of RP concerning the confessor. In no. 9 b, on the minister, it says that the competent minister is a priest "with the faculty to absolve in accordance with canon law." Normally this faculty, or permission, is given either by the bishop or by the law itself. The law deals with this subject in canons 966 to 976.[48] It should be remarked that the faculty is a requirement not just for legality but for validity, that is, for a true celebration of the sacrament, though if the confessor is in error or doubt as to whether he has it, this is one of the cases in which the law provides it.[49] Such a case, however, would be rare. The wisdom of the provision is obvious. The Church universal and the local bishop in particular have a serious responsibility to see to it that confessors are competent and trustworthy ministers, a quality that does not come automatically with priestly ordination. This responsibility arises from the respect due both to the sacrament itself and to penitents, who have a right to expect suitable confessors. The suitability of confessors, therefore, needs to be established and supervised over time, and this is done through the mechanism of granting or withdrawing the faculty to hear confessions.

The second stipulation, in RP 10d, concerns the so-called "seal of confession," the solemn obligation on the confessor not to reveal to any third party what has been confessed in the sacrament. RP simply says that the confessor must keep the seal "absolutely inviolate." Canon 983 adds that there is never any justification for breaking the seal either by word or in any other way, and extends the obligation to any interpreter (if one is used, which would be very unlikely) or anyone who may have come to know what was confessed (for example, someone who has overheard the confession).[50] From time to time civil governments legislate that professional people, for example doctors, must under certain conditions reveal to the appropriate authority what they have heard in professional consultations, a general provision that in principle would include confessors. When this looks like happening, the Church can normally gain an exemption for the case of sacramental confession. However, if such application should fail, the confessor remains bound by the higher law of God never to break the seal under any circumstances, even if this should mean his punishment by imprisonment or death at the hands of civil authorities. This would be civil disobedience not only sanctioned, but demanded, by the Church.

RP first gives the formula of absolution in no. 46. I have already referred to the confessor's accompanying gesture approximating to an imposition of hands. In the last chapter we briefly discussed this gesture and the meaning of its full antecedent in antiquity as reconciliation with the Church and, indirectly, the giving of the Holy Spirit, that is, in as much as the Spirit is the life of the Church.[51] We also suggested, in a footnote, that the weakening and reduction of the imposition of hands in RP is probably explained by a pastoral prudence that would counsel against any actual physical contact between confessor and penitent under present-day conditions.[52] However, the meaning of the gesture is basically the same as that of its antecedent, though probably enriched by the addition of the idea of a direct giving of the Holy Spirit in accordance with the New Testament usage (see Acts 8:17; 19:6). In the sacrament the Spirit in effecting communion with God overcomes sin, which alone disrupts this communion. This idea is forcefully presented in Titus 3:6 in connection with baptism.

If reconciliation with God is conceived no longer as indirectly but as directly bestowed by the minister (though, of course, still and always sacramentally), the same extension of meaning should be allowed for this imposition of hands, that is, as indicating no longer only an indirect giving of the Spirit but a direct (though sacramental) one. This, then, so I argue, is the present meaning of the quasi-imposition of hands that we have in the sacrament: it is the visible sign of the reconciliation with the Church and with God that takes place in the sacrament through the giving of the Holy Spirit. Its importance is increased by the fact that reconciliation with the Church is not verbalized in the formula in either of the formulations presented in RP (recall that we mentioned that RP 62 allows an alternative formulation to that in no. 46, in the case of the third rite).[53] All the more reason, then, why it should never be omitted. Further, it should be seen by the penitent, and its meaning should be carefully explained to the faithful in homilies and instructions.

Of the two forms of absolution, that in RP 46 is the regular one. To it the penitent answers, "Amen." The text contains an indication that the minister should make the sign of the cross while invoking the Trinity. Here, then, is the form laid down in RP 46:

> God, the Father of mercies, through the death and resurrection of his Son, has reconciled the world to himself and sent the Holy Spirit among us for the forgiveness of sins; through the ministry of the Church may God give you pardon and peace, and I absolve you from your sins in the name of the Father, and of the Son, and of the Holy Spirit.

This is an imperfect translation of the Latin original, which is given in a note.[54] My own literal translation of the original is as follows:

> May God, the Father of mercies, who through the death and resurrection of his Son has reconciled the world to himself and poured out the Holy Spirit for the remission of sins, grant you pardon and peace through the ministry of the Church. And I absolve you from your sins in the name of the Father, and of the Son, and of the Holy Spirit.

The first sentence (of the Latin original and also of my translation given above), a prayer, contains at least three scriptural allusions, the last and arguably the most important of which has been lost in the official translation. God is called the Father of mercies in 2 Cor 1:3; the long adjectival clause introduced by "who" has two parts, the first echoing 2 Cor 5:18, and the second Titus 3:6 and Acts 2:33 and 10:45, all three of which allude to Joel 2:28's use of the expression "pour out" in regard to God's Spirit. The official translation has lost the last mentioned allusion by replacing "poured out" with the relatively weak word "sent," and has added the ambiguous phrase "among us." The phrase "through the ministry of the Church" expresses the Church's total ministry of reconciliation, which combines the work of the common priesthood of the baptized with the special priesthood of the ordained.[55] The whole Church "by charity, by example and by prayer labors for their [that is, sinners'] conversion,"[56] while the special priesthood is exercised principally in absolution. The Latin original (see also my translation) manifests a structural defect that translations cannot overcome: the lack of a logical connection between the first and the second sentence. The transition from a prayer about the ministry of the Church as a whole to a performative statement of a particular priest is too abrupt, and not at all explained by the conjunction "and" (Latin: *et*). Had the Latin had the *deinde* ("in fine," "accordingly," "wherefore," "and so") of the previous rite,[57] matters would not have been so bad, though the transition just mentioned would still have been too abrupt. It is clear why the second sentence has been included: being the Tridentine formula, it marks, as just intimated, a direct connection with the Council of Trent. But it can be asked: Was this really necessary?

The same difficulty is also to be seen in the official translation, which consists of one long sentence, divided, however, into three main parts: a declarative statement, a prayer, and finally the performative statement of the priest as mentioned above. It is to be hoped that a future revision will address this problem, which, relating as it does to the form of the sacrament, cannot be dismissed as minor. The biblical richness (provided it be allowed to come through in translation) and the Trinitarian form of the first sentence (of the Latin and my translation) are praiseworthy. The only material lack is the absence of the theme of reconciliation with the Church, again a fault that cannot be described as minor, particularly as the accompanying gesture, being a weak form of the imposition of hands, only hesitantly suggests it.

The alternative form, in RP 62, is longer and better, but is restricted to celebrations of the third rite. In RP 62 it is offered as the first alternative, which is probably to be interpreted as an indication that it is considered the more suitable of the two for these occasions. If it is so considered, I would agree. It begins with three prayers, one to each of the persons of the Trinity in turn, and concludes with the same Tridentine formula as the first form. The answer to each of the four parts is "Amen." The minister is instructed to extend his hands over the penitents while reciting it, and in the last part to make the sign of the cross at the invocation of the Trinity at the end. Each of the prayers focuses on the work of a particular divine person in the work of reconciliation (with God), and is rich in biblical allusions, which are faithfully transmitted in the official translation.

In one instance the translation actually improves on the original. The second prayer, to Christ, recalls his death, resurrection, and giving of the Holy Spirit to the apostles, but once again, in relation to the Holy Spirit, "poured out" (Latin: *effudit*) is replaced by "sent." However, in John 20:22, the text referred to here, Jesus only says to the apostles, "*Receive* the Holy Spirit." It can be reasonably argued, therefore, that "he sent the Holy Spirit" is more faithful to the spirit of the text than "he poured [the Spirit] out." Structurally, the Tridentine performative formula, following, as it does, three prayers (rather than just one), does not jar as badly as in the first form, but it is still incongruous, and again it can be asked: Was it really necessary? As already mentioned, reconciliation with the Church is not verbalized in this form either.

Finally, I wish to address the question as to why the priest says "I absolve" rather than "I forgive" in the absolution formula. There are two reasons. The first is that it is an element of a sentence from the Tridentine ritual, and hence is traditional, providing a link with the previous sacramental practice of the Church. The sentence of RP, "I absolve you from your sins in the name of the Father, and of the Son, and of the Holy Spirit," is identical to that of the ritual published in 1614 at the command of Pope Paul V to incorporate the reforms of Trent, the *Rituale Romanum*, except that while the former is introduced by "and," the latter is introduced by *deinde* ("in fine," "accordingly," etc.), as was just mentioned in another context. The Tridentine formula has three additional occurrences of the word, the first being in a prayer that God will grant "pardon, absolution, and remission" of the penitent's sins, where, obviously for the sake of solemnity, the same idea, forgiveness, is stated three times by use of synonyms or near synonyms. The second and third occurrences, which have to do with any ecclesiastical censures (excommunication, suspension, or interdict) by which the penitent might be bound, are, respectively, in a prayer that "Jesus Christ may absolve you," and in the statement "and I, by his authority, absolve you"; and in these the term clearly carries a technical, legal connotation alien to the meaning of "forgive."

We saw in the last chapter that the term "absolution" was originally used for the blessing terminating the reconciliation ceremony. In this context it was a ministerial act only indirectly indicating divine forgiveness (that is, in as much as it concluded the process). In the thirteenth century the term came to acquire a deeper meaning as it was understood to be the sacramental act in which divine forgiveness was actually imparted. It is clear from this that "to absolve" from sin was never anything more than a priestly act; it was not something that God did himself, despite the fact that the Roman Ritual could use the noun form ("absolution") along with other synonyms to indicate divine forgiveness.

This leads us to the second reason. To forgive is a personal, or better, interpersonal, term, properly used only of the person offended in regard to the person offending. In other words, it is for God, and no one else, to forgive the sinner. It would be inappropriate and presumptuous of the minister to use this term for what he himself does. The Church respects this fact by having him say "I absolve."

There is, of course, a sense in which the minister does forgive sin, that is, in as much as he acts on God's behalf. This is exactly what he does in the sacrament, and it is the sense intended by John 20:23 ("If you forgive the sins of any, they are forgiven"). But this is so only because the minister's action is the sacrament of God's action. For the sake of clarity on this matter, the Church has wisely reserved the word "forgive" for God and assigned "absolve" (as the specifically sacramental action) to the priest. It is likewise inappropriate to say that as the representative of the Church the priest "forgives" in as much as sins against God are also sins against the Church. For we do not have a case of interpersonal relations here either. The sinner is a person, but the Church is a society or community. When the state pardons an offender, it does just that, it pardons; no one says that it "forgives." Likewise, the Church can grant pardon and absolution, but for forgiveness we look to God.

Finally, early in this chapter I mentioned the two ways in which the kingship of Christ is exercised in this sacrament. The first is by the penitent, in as much as through their repentance and confession the sacrament is a celebration of Christ's royal victory over sin, *their* sin; and the second is by the minister, representing Christ the King, in as much as he (the priest), through absolution, actualizes this victory once more in this historical instance. Each celebration of the sacrament, therefore, is a celebration, a partial actualization, an anticipation, of the perfect kingship of Christ, contributing to the eschatological subjection of all things to him, so that at the end he in turn can give back the kingdom to the Father, "that God may be everything to every one" (1 Cor 15:28).

## Satisfaction

Finally, we come to the chronologically last part of the sacrament, satisfaction. Here is what RP, in no. 6c, has to say on the subject:

> True conversion is completed by acts of penance or satisfaction for the sins committed, by amendment of conduct, and also by the reparation of injury. The kind and extent of the satisfaction should be suited to the personal condition of each penitent so that each one may restore the order which he disturbed and through the corresponding remedy be cured of the sickness from which he suffered. Therefore, it is necessary that the act of penance really be a remedy for sin and a help to renewal of life.

RP 18, as part of an instruction on the right conduct of the first rite, that is, the reconciliation of individual penitents, adds that "as far as possible, the penance should correspond to the seriousness and nature of the sins." It further recommends that the prescribed act or acts fit into one or more of the three traditional forms of penance, that is to say, prayer, self-denial, and (and here it adds the word "especially") service of the neighbor and works of mercy, as these emphasize "that sin and its forgiveness have a social aspect."

What comes through in these statements is that the penance is truly the completion of conversion, that is, the establishment of inner conversion of heart in the whole being of the penitent, body as well as soul, and, through the body, the extension of this conversion into the community of which the penitent forms a part, and which has been harmed by their sin. It *presupposes* a willingness to make restitution for any injustice done, this point being underscored in RP by the fact that it deals with restitution when treating, not the penance, but the minister's dialogue with the penitent *prior* to giving the penance.[58] This in no way opposes RP's general stipulation, already cited, that one of the aims of the penance is to restore the order disturbed by the sins committed and confessed.

To give an appropriate penance remains an ongoing challenge for confessors. It should not be a formality. Nor need it be something that can be done immediately, for its purpose is to help the penitent establish the *virtue* of penance in their everyday life. On the other hand it should be something specific, not something so nebulous as to be a source of anxiety for the penitent, as when, for example, they find it impossible to decide when they have finished performing it. (An example of the latter would be, "Be more kind to your next-door neighbor in future.") Most confessors settle for prayer, which can be said immediately on leaving the confession room, but the problem with this is that it is not necessarily the best form of penance in every instance.

It is clear that the penance is an important part of the sacrament little understood by penitents and, sadly, by some confessors as well. It calls for ongoing education of both priests and people. To give no penance at all or to give the same for all comers, are equally abuses crying out for remedy. Occasionally confessors will ask penitents to suggest their own penance. This practice is not against the requirement that the confessor himself prescribe the penance, since it can still be said to be prescribed when the confessor agrees to the penitent's suggestion. I therefore do not wish to criticize this practice, beyond saying that some penitents are embarrassed by such a request and would be much happier for the confessor to take the initiative. However, it would be wise of the confessor, if inclining to prescribe an unusual penance, first to check that the penitent understands what is being asked, knows how to do it (confessors have been known to prescribe prayers that penitents do not know), and is comfortable with the prospect of carrying it out. Unsuitable penances, which penitents are unwilling or unable to perform, can be changed by the same or another confessor on the occasion of a subsequent confession.

A common misunderstanding, reinforced by the catechesis that has come down to us from the Council of Trent (that is, in both the conciliar documents and the *Rituale Romanum* of 1614),[59] is that the penance is a punishment for the sins confessed. The length of Trent's treatment of satisfaction[60] is explained by the fact that the doctrine that ordinary Christians (in contradistinction to Christ) can make satisfaction for their sins and the linked doctrine and practice of indulgences as well as the doctrine of purgatory were primary targets for the attacks of the Reformers. In dealing with all this, Trent made no concessions. It taught that when the guilt of sin is forgiven, the debt of "punishment" due to sin is not necessarily fully remitted (purgatory being where this debt is paid off if this has not already been done through works of penance in this life). The satisfaction imposed in the sacrament of penance is a salutary means of paying at least part of this debt.

It was the Church's power to dispense graces from its own "treasury" (which was nothing more than its participation in the grace of Christ) that allowed it under certain conditions to apply the merits of others (also based on the merits of Christ) to penitents, and so either lessen or abolish altogether the punishment they still had to undergo. This was the doctrine of "indulgences."

The Church maintains these doctrinal positions to the present day, but since the sixteenth century theology has been able to add significant clarifications. First, hear what Rahner has to say on the treasury of the Church:

> If the concept of "the treasury of the Church" was developed in regard to justifying the practice of indulgences since the fourteenth century, the reality denoted by the expression, independently of its historical occasion, and indeed the very expression itself, only says in a different form what already and always had been expressed just as clearly without it, namely, that God wills the salvation of every person in *every* aspect that salvation possesses, in reference to Jesus Christ, his infinite satisfaction and "merits" on the cross, and in reference to the whole body of Christ, which possesses whatever operative power it has from him and in him, and God allows this to come to the aid of every person (see 1 Cor 12:25f). In so far as the totality of the saving reality of Christ and his body works for the remission of the temporal punishment due to sin, and particularly by means of indulgences, it is called "the treasury of the Church."[61]

Add to this the observations of Gerhard Ludwig Müller on indulgences, for whose necessary length I apologize in advance:

> Rahner has offered a necessary theological depthing of such concepts as guilt, punishment, suffering and divine justice and mercy, which in any case were only to be understood analogically: God does not vindictively impose punishment to exact satisfaction for an insult he has suffered. Rather, it is a matter of an immanent consequence of guilt, which brings one into a painful negative relation to oneself and one's environment of persons and things. Just as after baptism the Christian continues to live under the conditions of the old world, which he or she steadfastly bears in active love, consolation and trust, so it is with the healing and sanctifying influence of the Church—intended through indulgences—on bearing and working off the evil consequences set in train by subjective sin. The object is to bring into effect, in the plurality and complexity of the finite, existential, social and natural dimensions of human existence, the mercy of God already definitively extended to the sinner, and reconciliation with the Church. The objective participation of the Church in subjective penance is based on the present saving power of Christ (the "treasury

of the Church"), which comes to light in the life of the Church as the holy community. Invoking this "treasure" bestows on the official ecclesiastical intercession a greater and different assurance of being heard than private prayer has. It shows that the Church's sanctifying ministry operates out of the grace of Jesus Christ, and does not just have to appeal to God's will to reconcile. Indulgences are neither able nor intended to replace subjective penance, but rather to facilitate it. But they make clear that reconciliation is more than just a passive acceptance of a declaration of forgiveness of sin by God. They have to do with the acceptance and historical realization of the self-communication of God and his reconciling action in the historically extended course of the Church's life.[62]

Helped by these quotations from modern theologians, we can draw the following conclusions. That God and even the Church "punish" us for our sins was not the direct object of what Trent wanted to teach or actually taught. What did constitute this direct object were the doctrines of the remnants of sin (consisting principally in continuing attachment to past sins, and manifest in the strength of our evil inclinations), purgatory (the condition supervening on death whereby we are "purged" of these remnants so as to be able to pass into the eternal presence of the all-holy God), and the treasury of the Church (as the foundation for the doctrine and practice of indulgences). In resorting to the terminology of punishment, Trent was uncritically (but without fault) employing the anthropomorphic language of Scripture to speak of the difficult and often painful efforts we must make, under God's grace, to root out the remnants of sin from our lives even after we have been forgiven, and gradually but constantly to grow in Christian discipleship. And it adapted this language to our present life, having borrowed it from Scripture's use of it for the afterlife, specifically for hell. But as Müller has pointed out, ours is not a punishing God.

What we have called divine punishment is nothing other than the inevitable working out of the consequences of our own evil decisions. If we have deliberately and definitively separated ourselves from God despite the fact that he has made us for himself, then he respects and accepts our decision, for the afterlife as well as for this. The pain inseparable from this decision in the afterlife, Scripture, along with the consequent tradition until quite recent times, has anthropomorphically called divine punishment. Admittedly, the concept of a punishing Church stands at some remove from that of a punishing God, but the two are connected. What is at stake here is our very concept of God, which exercises an enormous influence over our religious attitudes and on how we live our spiritual lives. A God who "vindictively imposes punishment" (to quote Müller) is not the Christian God. The penance given in the sacrament, therefore, is not a punishment for sins, and to its credit RP nowhere gives the impression that it is.

I conclude with the observation that it was a wise and providential decision on the part of the Church to transfer satisfaction from before to after absolution. Thus any false impression that we win forgiveness from God through our own efforts is effectively countered. This impression suffers from the further defect that satisfaction before absolution would rightly be seen as an exercise of purely human effort. Since in any case it would be supported by God's grace, this impression is shown up as doubly false. By placing satisfaction after absolution the Church has allowed the lesson to shine through with crystal clarity: divine grace precedes and empowers whatever satisfaction we might make. This allows it, now seen as inadequately named satisfaction (better: the work of penance), to emerge in full clarity as what RP says it is: the completion of conversion, the removal of the traces of sin, and the renewal of our (baptismal) dedication to the Christian life.

## Conclusion

In this chapter we have reflected on the four essential parts of the sacrament of reconciliation: contrition, confession, absolution, and satisfaction. The two most important are contrition and absolution: without them there can be no sacrament. But confession and satisfaction remain essential also, in the sense that they constitute the normal working-out of contrition once it is drawn from the privacy of the heart into the sacramental and social arena. The confession of grave sin, therefore, can never be made optional by the Church, no matter how great a pastoral problem this may present. Even in the third rite, which, as we shall see in the next chapter, must always include a general confession of some kind, the need for individual confession is not dispensed with in the case of grave sin. Here the requirement is that such sin be confessed at some later time. Of course, if sins are not grave they do not need to be confessed, but there never was an obligation to confess non-grave sins anyway. However, devotional confession is still a practice strongly recommended by the Church, and is certain always to remain so.

Where culture begins to conflict with divine revelation, the Church may be able, indeed should, adapt its practices up to a certain point, but it cannot cross the line where revelation is threatened, let alone compromised. In these circumstances it has no option but to encourage people to be consciously counter-cultural, to strive to appreciate the intrinsic value of what it must insist on, and to learn to be comfortable with this. After all, such things, as coming from God, must be deeply consonant with human well-being at every level, if only we could see it. The practice of the sacrament of reconciliation as inclusive of confession is a prime instance of this.

## Notes, Chapter 3

[1] The Council of Trent, 14th session, Doctrine on the Sacrament of Penance, Dupuis 1622.

[2] Paul VI, Apostolic Constitution *Paenitemini,* February 17, 1966, *AAS* 58 (1966) 179. See *Penitence* (London: Catholic Truth Society, Do 450, 1973) 6–7 (different trans.).

[3] See Vatican II, Dogmatic Constitution on the Church *(Lumen gentium)* no. 36, Flannery, 54.

[4] See ST III, q. 90, a. in corp. and ad 2.

[5] RP's allusion to this distinction occurs in no. 37, which encourages penitential services in places where no priest is available. It states that such services help people attain the "perfect" contrition that enables them to find forgiveness and grace through a desire for the sacrament. Imperfect contrition is not mentioned.

[6] Vatican II's sole reference to the virtue of penance occurs in its Constitution on the Sacred Liturgy *(Sacrosanctum concilium),* no. 109, where it is defined as "a detestation of sin because it is an offense against God." See Flannery, 151.

[7] Nos. 1452, 1453.

[8] This historical survey up to the Council of Trent is based on Herbert Vorgrimler, *Busse und Krankensalbung,* vol. 4 pt. 3 of Handbuch der Dogmengeschichte (Freiburg [Germany]: Herder, 1978) 138–45.

[9] My translation. See Dupuis 1622 (DS 1676).

[10] Dupuis 1623. I have changed the word "humanity" to "person."

[11] See Dupuis 1624.

[12] My trans.

[13] See Karl Rahner, *Allow Yourself to Be Forgiven: Penance Today,* trans. Salvator Attanasio (Denville, N.J.: Dimension Books, 1975) 37–38.

[14] Ibid., 38.

[15] We have already seen that confession is indeed not necessary when the sins are non-grave, but that it *is* necessary, at some later time, when they *are* grave. Many people do not know this requirement.

[16] Committee for Pastoral Research and Practices, *Reflections on the Sacrament of Penance in Catholic Life Today: A Study Document* (Washington, D.C.: United States Catholic Conference, 1990) 8–9.

[17] *The Tablet* 253:8308 (November 13, 1999) 1542.

[18] It has been necessary here to have recourse to the original Latin text, as the English is defective at certain points. Thus, in 10a, the English says that the confessor should "understand" the disorders of souls, but the Latin has "discern" or "diagnose" *(dignoscat)*, which brings out much more clearly the role of healer. And 10d, in speaking of the matter confessed as "the secrets of *another's* conscience [my emphasis]," where the Latin has "the secret conscience of his *brother* [my emphasis]" *(secretam fratris sui conscientiam)*, suppresses the role of the confessor as brother altogether.

[19] In fact there are two different *kinds* of judgment here, which can be characterized as professional and personal, respectively. The first, calling for competence and prudence, is made by virtue of one's office. In the context of the sacrament, far from being cold and detached, it stems from pastoral charity and has the best interests of the penitent in view, but also the good of the community and the respect due to the sacrament. The second is purely personal, in that it consists simply in either the affirmation or the rejection (or condemnation) of another person for whatever reason. Of these, it is the last, personal condemnatory judgment, that is forbidden to Christians, including people making professional judgments. Hence the confessor's role of judge by no means implies that he is required, or even permitted, to reject or condemn a penitent.

[20] See the Council of Trent, Decree on the Sacrament of Penance, Dupuis 1628.

[21] See Peter Meinhold, I. Self-Understanding, in "Protestantism," SM 5, 113b–130b, at 113b–120a.

[22] St. Augustine, *Serm.* 340, 1; PL 38, 1483 (my trans.).

[23] Dupuis 1625.

[24] Dupuis 1626.

[25] DS 1682.

[26] DS 1681.

[27] The introduction of the confessional was part of the Tridentine reform. See Franco Sottocornola, "Les nouveaux rites de la pénitence: commentaire," *Questions liturgiques* 55 (1974) 89–136, at 133.

[28] The reader is reminded that the expression *iure divino* was explained in chap. 2.

[29] See Carl Peter, "Auricular Confession and the Council of Trent," *CTSA Proceedings, 22nd Annual Convention, 1967* (Yonkers, N.Y: St. Joseph's Seminary, 1967) 185–200, at 196, 198.

[30] Ibid., 194.

[31] Ibid., 194, n. 31.

[32] Clement Tierney, *The Sacrament of Repentance and Reconciliation* (New York: Costello, 1983) 72.

[33] See Louis Monden, *Sin, Liberty, and Law,* trans. Joseph Donceel (New York: Sheed and Ward, 1965) 46–47.

[34] Ibid., 46.

[35] See The Canon Law Society of Great Britain and Ireland, *The Code of Canon Law* (London: Collins, 1983) 174.

[36] James Coriden, Thomas Green, and Donald Heintschel, eds., *The Code of Canon Law: A Text and Commentary* (New York: Paulist Press, 1985) 677b.

[37] See Tierney, *The Sacrament of Penance and Reconciliation,* 72–73.

[38] Peter, *Auricular Confession and the Council of Trent,* 199–200.

[39] Rahner, *Allow Yourself to Be Forgiven,* 37.

[40] RP 12.

[41] Admittedly, the Tridentine ritual had a similar requirement: the priest was to "raise his right hand toward the penitent" (*Rituale Romanum* [for publishing details of which see n. 52] 70), even though this gesture would not be seen by the latter. I concede that on this point I am attributing a greater rationality to RP than to the *Rituale.*

[42] See *The Code of Canon Law,* 175.

[43] See *Bishops' Committee on the Liturgy Newsletter 1965–1975* (December 1974) 450.

[44] Sottocornola, "Les nouveaux rites de la pénitence," 133.

[45] Ibid.

[46] See Karl Rahner, "The Meaning of Frequent Confession of Devotion," *Theological Investigations,* vol. 3, trans. Karl-H. and Boniface Kruger (Baltimore: Helicon Press, 1967) 177–89, at 183–87.

[47] See Vatican II, Decree on the Pastoral Office of Bishops in the Church *(Christus dominus),* no. 30 (2), Flannery, 304, and Decree on the Ministry and Life of Priests *(Presbyterorum ordinis)* no. 18, Flannery, 355. See also Pope John Paul II's Post-Synodal Exhortation "I Will Give You Shepherds" *(Pastores dabo vobis)* (Boston: St. Paul Books & Media, 1992) no. 48, 95–96. See also Pope Pius XII's encyclical letters, *Mystici corporis* (Washington, D.C.: National Catholic Welfare Conference, 1943) no. 88, 33–34, and *Mediator Dei* (Washington, D.C.: National Catholic Welfare Conference, 1947) no. 177, 63.

[48] See *The Code of Canon Law,* 175–77.

[49] Ibid., can. 144, 23, with cross-reference to can. 966.

[50] Ibid., 177.

[51] See also Cyrille Vogel, "Handauflegung I (liturgisch)" RAC 13, 482–93, at 487.

[52] It is of interest, and not a little ironic, to note that the frontispiece of the Latin original of RP, the *Ordo Paenitentiae,* is an engraving showing a confessor, seated, resting his right hand affectionately on the shoulder of the kneeling young man going to confession. This sort of contact would be strongly discouraged in the United States. Needless to say, there is no confessional grill to be seen in the picture.

[53] Note further that "in imminent danger of death" the formula may be shortened to simply, "I absolve you from your sins in the name of the Father, and of the Son, and of the Holy Spirit" (RP 65).

⁵⁴ "Deus, Pater misericordiarum, qui per mortem et resurrectionem Filii sui mundum sibi reconciliavit et Spiritum Sanctum effudit in remissionem peccatorum, per ministerium Ecclesiae indulgentiam tibi tribuat et pacem. Et ego te absolovo a peccatis tuis in nomine Patris, et Filii, et Spiritus Sancti. Amen."

⁵⁵ In 1997 the Vatican placed certain restrictions on the use of the term "ministry" in any sense other than that which it has in relation to the ordained. See the Instruction, "Some Questions Regarding Collaboration of Nonordained Faithful in Priests' Sacred Ministry," from the Congregation for the Clergy and seven other Vatican offices, dated August 15, 1997, *Origins,* vol. 27, no. 24, 397–409, at 402–03. However, these restrictions do not apply to the sense in which I have interpreted the term here.

⁵⁶ Vatican II's Dogmatic Constitution on the Church *(Lumen gentium)* no. 11, Flannery, 15.

⁵⁷ For this and the immediately following references to Trent see the *Rituale Romanum* of 1614, the 1929 reprint by F. Pustet of Ratisbon, 70–71.

⁵⁸ See RP 18.

⁵⁹ See Trent's Doctrine on the Sacrament of Penance, Dupuis 1633, 1653, and the *Rituale Romanum,* 69, no. 19, which paraphrases the council on this matter.

⁶⁰ See chs. 8 and 9 of Doctrine on the Sacrament of Penance and canons 12–15, Dupuis 1630–34, 1652–55.

⁶¹ Karl Rahner, "Kirchenschatz," LTK 6 (2nd ed.) 257 (references apart from scriptural omitted).

⁶² "Ablass," LTK 1 (3rd ed.: 1993) 51–58, Gerhard Ludwig Müller 51–55, at 54–55.

Chapter Four

# The Rites of Reconciliation

In this chapter we shall be dealing with the four forms of penance offered by RP. The first three are sacramental, and the fourth is non-sacramental. Each sacramental rite is the subject of a separate chapter in RP. Chapter 1 is titled "Rite for Reconciliation of Individual Penitents"; chapter 2 is "Rite for Reconciliation of Several Penitents with Individual Confession and Absolution"; and chapter 3 is "Rite for Reconciliation of Several Penitents with General Confession and Absolution." We shall refer to these rites as the "first," "second," and "third" "rite" (of reconciliation), respectively. I have decided to deal with them not in their numerical, but in their logical order, which is first, third, and second. The logic is clear in that the first is an individual celebration, the third communal, and the second a mixture of individual and communal features. Next, we shall deal with the non-sacramental form of penance, which is the subject of appendix II of RP, titled "Sample Penitential Services." Accordingly, we shall refer to this kind of celebration as a "penitential service." By way of conclusion, some comparisons will be made among the three sacramental forms. In this chapter I shall be referring frequently both to RP itself and to the commentary on it produced by Franco Sottocornola, secretary of the committee that produced it.[1] In order not to overburden the notes, these references will be supplied in the text. Without further ado, then, let us embark on our examination of RP's four forms of reconciliation.

## The First Rite

The component parts of this rite are as follows:[2]

1. Reception of the penitent (RP 41–42):
   • welcoming the penitent (RP 41);
   • sign of the cross (RP 42);
   • invitation to trust in God (RP 42).
2. Reading the word of God (optional) (RP 43).
3. Formula of general confession (optional), personal confession, and acceptance of satisfaction (RP 44).
4. Manifestation of repentance on the part of the penitent (RP 45).
5. Prayer of absolution (RP 46):
   • special prayer;
   • the priest holds his hands (or his right hand) extended over the head of the penitent and at the end makes the sign of the cross;
   • the penitent replies: Amen.
6. Proclamation of the mercy of God (RP 47).
7. Dismissal of the penitent (RP 47).

The introduction to RP, under heading 4, "The Celebration of the Sacrament of Penance," gives descriptive instructions for the celebration of the first rite in RP 15–21. Chapter 1, RP 41–47, then gives the texts and rubrics of this rite. In what follows we shall concentrate on RP 41–47, making reference to RP 15–21 wherever it seems necessary or helpful. RP 15 makes the point that both priest and penitent should prepare themselves for the celebration by prayer.

At the beginning of the sacramental celebration, the first direction which RP (41) gives is as follows: "When the penitent comes to confess his sins, the priest welcomes him warmly and greets him with kindness." Obviously, the purpose of this human touch is to put the penitent at ease at the start of an inevitably demanding exercise. Doubtless, too, it is meant to recall the example of Jesus, of whom his critics complained, "This fellow welcomes sinners and eats with them" (Luke 15:2, NRSV). Next the sign of the cross is made by the penitent, and by the priest too if he wishes. This simple action and prayer has been performed by Christians from very early times as they embark on prayer whether private or public, and indeed as they enter upon any action of consequence. It recalls both the "Trinity God"[3] who reconciles us to himself and the cross of Christ by which this reconciliation was wrought in human history. Then the priest, using either one of the set forms provided or his own words, exhorts the penitent to place their trust in God.

This is a fitting reminder at the start of the ceremony, for the penitents should place themselves in the presence of the loving and forgiving triune God and not rely on their own efforts, however sincere, brought to the sacramental encounter. RP 16 adds that this is the time for the penitents to state how long it has been since their last confession, what their state of life is, that is, whether they are married or single, or whether they happen to be a cleric or a religious, any special difficulties they may experience in leading the Christian life, and indeed any other fact that may help the confessor better contextualize and understand their confession. RP 16 itself mentions that these contextualizing facts should only be given if the penitent is unknown to the priest. Hence if it is a case of open confession and the priest is the penitent's regular confessor, the repetition of these facts would clearly be superfluous.

The second element of the rite is the reading of the word of God from Scripture (see Sottocornola, 115–16). As a pastoral council, the Second Vatican Council worked hard both to reinstate the Bible at the heart of the spiritual lives of Catholics, and to enliven the celebration of the sacraments through a closer integration of the Church's ministry of word with its ministry of sacrament.[4] Hence all the revisions of sacramental rites following the council give prominence to the reading of, and reflection on, the word of God. The sacrament of reconciliation is no exception to this. RP provides a wide selection of readings from both the Old and the New Testaments. Moreover, it is permissible to go beyond this selection by choosing some other biblical text if it be deemed suitable and helpful.

However, in the case of this sacrament the reading from Scripture has been made optional. The reason for this is that it may not always be pastorally advisable to include it. Excusing reasons can be manifold: lack of time; the discerned inability of the penitent, stemming from whatever cause, to benefit from it; unpropitious physical circumstances, such as lack of adequate light, etc. Over time, the result has been that by now this element is scarcely ever performed. This is highly regrettable, because in the long run it deprives penitents of a valuable opportunity to develop their spiritual lives and to derive maximum benefit from the sacrament. It requires on the part of pastors a determined and persevering effort at ongoing education of the faithful and the provision of the physical means whereby it can be carried out in a dignified and efficient way. At least in the United States, given the relatively small number of people now going to the sacrament, lack of time is hardly ever a valid excuse.

Certainly, the reading of Scripture works best in the context of open confession, where it can contribute not only to the ends mentioned above but to the building up of a sure bond of trust and communication between the penitent and the confessor. For the reading should not be left simply as a bare reading: it should be commented on and discussed in a conversation between confessor and penitent, in which the latter is encouraged to express how the reading has affected them, how it applies to their life, and how it inspires them to a deeper sorrow for the sins they are about to confess. This last provides the main reason for having the reading at all. As the word of God, it is meant to elicit from the penitent a response of trusting and loving faith directed to enlivening the work in hand, namely, reconciliation with God, Christ, and the Church through the sacrament. It should also move the confessor to a deeper commitment to the ministry with which he has been entrusted. In this sacrament the conversation of confessor and penitent that takes place at this point replaces and does the work of the homily that would normally follow the reading of the word of God at other liturgical celebrations. Finally, the reading can be chosen and/or read by either the penitent or the confessor. Provided the penitent is willing and able, there are clear advantages in having them do this.

The next element of the rite is the optional general confession, the personal confession, and the acceptance of satisfaction. By "general confession" here is meant the recital of the Confiteor ("I confess to almighty God . . .") or some equivalent formula before proceeding to the specific confession of sins. Older people, in their childhood preparation for the sacrament, were taught to say the Confiteor at this point, and many still do. But most people do not do this, as it was never part of their catechesis or practice, and I am not recommending its reintroduction. RP (44) says only that it takes place "where it is the custom." Sottocornola passes it over in silence (p. 116). Indeed he presumes that the natural course of events is that the conversation which we discussed in the last paragraph should merge imperceptibly into the specific confession of sins. This does indeed seem a desirable progression.

As to the specific confession of sins, I have nothing to add here to what I have already said in the last chapter. At the same point in his own presentation (p. 116), Sottocornola likewise has nothing to say, but I would now like to quote, with approval, something he has said on this subject earlier in his commentary (p. 108):

Confession to the Church has the sense of manifesting interior repentance. Without it there would be a simple psychological introspection, a self-criticism, but not a sacramental action. However, the accusation of one's faults, of one's proper responsibility in the sin of the world, can never be separated from trust in God, hope for his mercy, and his pardon. Therefore the accusation of sins is based on the proclamation of the liberating power of God and on the strength of his merciful love. [My trans.]

There should follow at this point a few words of encouragement and spiritual counsel from the priest, concluded, perhaps, with an assurance that he will remember the penitent in his prayers. Such words are important as they round off the confession, and indicate to the penitent both that their concerns are understood and taken seriously and that their confession has been accepted. RP, at nos. 18 and 44, is somewhat more specific in its directions to the priest, emphasizing the help that should be given to elicit an integral confession, the instruction that may be necessary, and the restitution that should be enjoined for harm done or scandal caused. The priest then gives the "penance," "satisfaction," or penitential work, to which the penitent agrees, assuming it is suitable. RP 18 notes that this work should be adapted to the situation of the penitent, and may suitably assume one of the three traditional forms: prayer, self-denial, or service, which highlight the social dimension of sin and its forgiveness.

The next element of the rite, manifestation of repentance by the penitent, serves the purpose of making explicit what is implicitly conveyed in the confession itself, as Sottocornola has pointed out in the last given quotation. For this reason it is not numbered among the essential parts of the sacrament. Nevertheless it serves a useful pastoral purpose, in that it drives home to the penitent the one indispensable motive required for receiving the sacrament, the force that has impelled them through the various steps that have brought them to this point.

For expressing repentance, RP 45 provides a number of alternative forms, and RP 85–92 some additional ones, from which the penitent may choose. They may also use their own words if they wish, though RP 19 cautions that it is best that the words used be based on Scripture. It is good to see that the "Jesus Prayer" of the Eastern Orthodox Church, "Lord Jesus Christ, Son of God, have mercy on me a sinner," surely one of the staples of Orthodox spirituality, has been included among the options. Under the previous discipline the absurd practice was tolerated that the priest gave absolution at the same time as the penitent said the prayer of penance. This should never happen now. The priest should listen in silence as the penitents make their prayer of repentance, and the penitents should do the same as the priest gives absolution.

The priest then pronounces absolution (RP 46). Sottocornola emphasizes the significance of the priestly gesture approximating to the imposition of hands (p. 116), as I myself did in the last chapter. At the end of the formula, as he mentions the names of the persons of the Trinity, the priest makes the sign of the cross, and the penitent answers "Amen." Sottocornola, presuming open confession, points out that the penitent may sit or kneel, and that the confessor would normally sit (p. 117). However, for the absolution the confessor may stand and the penitent may choose to kneel. The reader is referred to my treatment of this subject in the last chapter. RP 19 asserts that the new ritual of absolution "underlines the ecclesial aspect of the sacrament because reconciliation with God is asked for and given through the ministry of the Church." Though this is correct, the fact remains that in this ritual only the gesture of the approximation to the imposition of hands, unaccompanied by any explanatory words, expresses reconciliation with the Church, a "forgotten truth" about the sacrament of reconciliation reclaimed by the Second Vatican Council.[5]

The next two elements, proclamation of the mercy (RP says "praise") of God and dismissal of the penitent, are combined by RP, in no. 47. The first of these is liturgically significant, as it is nothing other than the *exomologesis* ("confession") that we first encountered in Tertullian, in the early history of the sacrament. The reader will recall that there it had the rich meaning of the confession of one's faith, then of the praise, and especially the mercy (hence Sottocornola's emphasis), of God, and finally of one's sinfulness. This richness is what RP attempts to recapture at this point. The penitent has already confessed their faith in approaching the sacrament, and has just confessed their sins. Now, after absolution has been given, is the appropriate time for confessing the praise and the mercy of God. The fact that this is done in a very brief formula should not blind us to its importance. It gives the correct theological and liturgical emphasis to all that has preceded it in the rite. The formula is divided between priest and penitent. The priest says, "Give thanks to the Lord, for he is good," and the penitent replies, "His mercy endures for ever."

The priest then dismisses the penitent with one of five options offered by RP. The first one and two of the others emphasize peace, the "peace of the Lord" which the world cannot give (see John 14:27), and which is offered to us before Holy Communion at Mass. Sottocornola (pp. 116–17) rightly points out that it was this peace that the risen Christ, in John 20:19-23, bestowed on his disciples when he gave them the mandate to forgive sins. "Peace," continues Sottocornola (p. 117), "is the fullness of the messianic gifts and the most complete fruit of salvation. It is the joy of the full and vigorous life that Christ has revived in the heart of his forgiven brother or sister" (my translation). This is the peace that settles on both confessor and penitent at the conclusion of the celebration of the sacrament. Thus is explained a fact that many will have noticed, namely that the Latin word for peace, *pax,* is engraved on the doors of many confessionals.

Concluding his treatment of the first rite (p. 117), Sottocornola remarks that, in regard to the place for hearing confessions, RP 12 simply refers to the current canon law, which at that time was the 1917 Code. He points out, however, that the sacramental sign, which includes the imposition of hands and the sign of the cross, should of its nature be visible, and that this in turn requires that the confessor and the penitent be able to see each other. Recognizing that future legislation would probably include confessionals with grills—as in fact it did—he nevertheless expresses the opinion that pastoral theology is working toward an eventual abolition of the confessional, at least as it was envisaged in the post-Tridentine reform. In my own treatment of this delicate subject in the last chapter, I emphasized the need to provide both the grill for those who wanted it and the ongoing education of the laity that would lead eventually to its disuse and abandonment. We have not reached that point yet. The grill is required at least as an option by the current legislation, and in fact most penitents continue to avail themselves of it. By the "particular decree" of the Congregation for Divine Worship referred to in the Preface,[6] RP 12 has been modified in line with canon 964 of the 1983 Code of Canon Law, which legislates for the provision of confessionals with grills in churches and oratories, where, "except for a just cause," confessions are to be heard. The grill is to be available as an option for "those who desire it."

## The Third Rite

### *History of General Absolution*

The present Church legislation permits the celebration of the third rite of reconciliation only in cases of "grave necessity." The absolution of a number of penitents together without prior individual confession is not something entirely new in the life of the Church. It was always permitted to absolve a dying person who was unable to confess. General absolution was first permitted in the context of war. At the outbreak of the Second World War, the Holy See, through the Consistorial Congregation, issued faculties empowering priests to give general absolution without previous confession, to soldiers in danger of death from actual or imminent war, and to civilians whose lives were endangered by air raids. These people were to be told that they must be rightly disposed and must subsequently confess any grave sins.[7] A year later the Apostolic Penitentiary responded to the problem that when hostilities were judged to be imminent there might not be time for a priest to give absolution to soldiers, by saying that absolution could be lawfully given as soon as it was judged necessary.[8] Still later in the war an Instruction from the same Apostolic Penitentiary repeated the permissions already given, and in the case of civilians broadened the life-threatening occasions from air raids to situations of war in general.[9]

The Instruction then took a significant step forward by envisaging situations other than war in which general absolution could be justified. It went on to say that if the danger of death was not present, it was not permitted to give general absolution merely on account of the great number of penitents. But if in addition to this there was some "other grave and urgent necessity, proportionate to the gravity of the divine precept of integral confession" (my trans.), then general absolution could be given.[10] The Instruction then offered an example of such a necessity: that people would otherwise be deprived of the grace of the sacrament of penance or of Holy Communion "for a long time" (Latin: *diu*). The proper judge of this necessity, to whom priests were bound to have recourse if possible, was the "local ordinary." (The latter term is defined in canon 134 #2 and #1 of the new Code as covering several diocesan officials among whom the bishop is one [the main one, however].)

We can reasonably inquire as to what principle is operative here. None is enunciated, but I suggest that the quotation just given from the Apostolic Penitentiary provides a clue to its thinking. In other words, as the reason must be in proportion to the gravity of the divine precept of integral confession, it must at least be a *spiritual* reason, and probably also fall under divine precept, that is, be *iure divino*. On both counts the danger of death qualifies as such a reason, for in this danger there is a spiritual need to be fortified by the sacraments. The deprivation of the means of grace for a long time is also clearly such a reason. On the other hand, factors like the large number of penitents and the shortage of priests are physical facts, influential ones certainly, but not on the same plane as a truly spiritual and divinely imposed reason. If, therefore, one or more of these facts provide the immediate impetus for considering giving general absolution, they do not on their own constitute an adequate reason, and they should therefore be combined with a serious reason of the spiritual and divine order. To me this seems the best explanation of the discipline here adopted for the first time but from this point on to become normative.

Over twenty years later, in peacetime, the Congregation for the Doctrine of the Faith issued a similar authorization for Papua New Guinea in the context of its missionary situation.[11] The grounds put forward in the request by the local Bishops' Conference were twofold: the great number of people wanting to receive Holy Communion on major feasts, and the shortage of priests in the region. The Roman Congregation granted the permission, but referred in its reply to the terms of the permission already given by the Apostolic Penitentiary. By this means the Congregation was not only saying that grave sins forgiven in this way had to be confessed subsequently, but it appeared to be saying that the large number of people and the shortage of priests did not constitute sufficient reason on their own. Here too, presumably, an additional, spiritual and divine reason had to be sought, and, presumably again, it was found in the spiritual deprivation that the people would otherwise suffer. If I am correct in this interpretation, we would have in this permission another example of an adequate spiritual reason being required in addition to the physical facts put forward in the request.

Not long before the appearance of RP the Congregation for the Doctrine of the Faith, in reaction to both pre- and post-conciliar liturgical experimentation in France and Holland, issued a document known as "the Pastoral Norms," which regulated the use of general absolution, at the same time expanding the possibilities for, and setting out the restrictions on, its use.[12] General absolution could be justified only by a serious need, and this was constituted not just by insufficient confessors but also by the fact that otherwise people would be deprived of the grace of the sacrament or of Holy Communion for a long time (norm 3). Note that spiritual deprivation was here elevated from being an example of an adequate spiritual reason, to being the one required on all occasions. It was for the local ordinary to decide if the necessary conditions were fulfilled, but if a priest did not have time to consult him, he (the priest) could make the decision on his own, but he must inform the ordinary as soon as possible about both his decision and the grounds on which it was based (norm 5). Those thus absolved of grave sins had to confess them in the usual way before again receiving general absolution, and in any case within one year (norm 7). The Pastoral Norms remain important for the influence they exerted both on RP, being invoked by it no fewer than nine times,[13] and on the 1983 Code of Canon Law.

## Requirements for the Third Rite

What is essentially new about the third rite is that in it the Church has provided for the first time a specific liturgy of general absolution. RP 31–34, headed "The Discipline of General Absolution," is devoted to laying down the circumstances under which the celebration of the third rite is lawful, and the responsibilities of both confessors and penitents in regard to it. As this section of RP has now been superseded by canons 960–964 of the Code of Canon Law,[14] in this matter it will be more appropriate to comment on the canons than on RP. This, therefore, I shall now do, after which I shall briefly visit RP 31–34. The changes mentioned above are now incorporated in new printings of the text of RP by order of the "particular decree" of September 12, 1983, of the Congregation for Divine Worship, to which attention has already been drawn.

Canon 961 adopts a negative approach from the outset: "General absolution . . . *cannot* be given . . . *unless* [my emphases] . . ." Two justifying reasons for general absolution are given. The first is the danger of death combined with insufficient time to hear the individual confessions. The second is the situation of "grave necessity" arising from the combination of insufficient confessors to hear the individual confessions within an appropriate time, and the spiritual detriment that people would suffer through denial of absolution, that is, deprivation of the grace of reconciliation or Holy Communion for a long time. The canon goes on to say that a large number of penitents, as on the occasions of major feasts or pilgrimages, is not a justifying reason on its own. The judge of the necessity is the bishop of the diocese, who shall take into account the agreed criteria of the episcopal conference to which he belongs.

Canon 962 stresses the importance of the penitents' being properly disposed and the necessity of confessing grave sins subsequently. The faithful are to be instructed as to these obligations, both in general and on each occasion of general absolution if possible. Penitents are to be exhorted to make an act of contrition before receiving general absolution, even in danger of death if time allows. Canon 963 reinforces the provision of canon 989, namely that people with grave sins are bound to confess them at least once a year. However, continues canon 963, grave sins forgiven in general absolution must be confessed at the earliest opportunity before receiving another general absolution unless a just reason intervenes (note that a "just" or "good" reason is not as great as a "grave" or "serious" reason).

Canon 989 makes no reference to canon 920, the canon that prescribes annual Holy Communion in "paschal time," which time, for this particular purpose, is extended, by special permission for the United States, to embrace the period between the first Sunday of Lent and Trinity Sunday.[15] Therefore the confession to which canon 989 refers is one that occurs not longer than a year since that person's last confession of grave sins, and is not necessarily tied to the Easter Communion. The obligation of individual confession of which the canon speaks applies only to those with grave sins, and even for them it applies only once a year, in the sense that no longer than a year is to intervene between their successive confessions of grave sins. However, if a person with grave sin is in the situation of having to make their Easter Communion, obviously they must first have their sins absolved, and this could mean for them having to go again to confession, that is, during or shortly before paschal time. But perhaps, instead, they receive the third rite. In this case they do not need to go to individual confession before their Easter Communion, as there is no canon or theological reason that absolutely requires it. However, as intimated above, they must still confess within a year of their last confession of grave sins.[16]

The sense of canon 963 now emerges more clearly. Allow me to give a literal translation of the Latin: "Without prejudice to the obligation laid down in canon 989, a person whose grave sins are remitted by general absolution must go to individual confession as soon as possible, when the occasion presents itself, before receiving another general absolution, unless a just reason intervenes."[17] From this we see, in the light of our discussion, that in regard to any grave sins forgiven in general absolution (as well as any others committed subsequently but not yet remitted), this person is obliged to confess them in individual confession (a) within a year of their last confession of grave sins, and perhaps even sooner, that is, in connection with their next Easter Communion if otherwise they would be unable to fulfill this obligation, and (b) "as soon as there is an opportunity to do so before receiving another general absolution unless a just cause intervenes" (as the commentary on the Code of Canon Law commissioned by the Canon Law Society of America translates this part of the canon).[18]

The apparent conflict between (a) and (b) is resolved by the consideration that each envisages a different kind of situation. The first, having to do with the grave obligations of both annual confession of grave sins and Easter Communion, deals with the length of time that may be allowed to pass without going to confession before the obligation to do so becomes grave. In the case of grave sins subsequent confession is and remains an essential part of the sacrament, which cries out for completion and forbids its needless postponement. The second has to do with completing one celebration of the sacrament before embarking on another of the same kind. People, therefore, who, having without good reason passed up opportunities to complete the sacrament, find themselves in the situation of initiating another reception of it according to the third rite, would be at fault in the eyes of God, as they lack the respect due to the sacrament. However, the obligation that they have neglected cannot be termed grave, since it requires only a "just" or "good" reason, as distinct from a "grave" or "serious" one, to excuse from it. The canon, therefore, is saying that while there is a grave obligation to confess within a certain time, there is a further obligation, even if not grave, to do so at the first opportunity, especially if there is a likelihood that they may again want to receive general absolution according to the third rite.

What should a priest say when explaining these requirements to the people? From the pulpit he cannot give the full explanation that I have offered here. In terms of practicality, I would suggest that he cannot say much more than the following. Anyone having grave sins absolved in the third rite should take the first opportunity to complete the sacrament by individual confession; in any case they should do so before embarking on another celebration of the third rite; and they *must* confess these sins within a year of their last confession of grave sins, or perhaps even sooner, that is, if otherwise they would be unable to make their Easter Communion.

For the sake of clarity three points now need to be made, and in the course of doing this we shall refer to the provisions of RP 31–34 as promised. The first point is the meaning of the expression "for a long time" *(diu),* the period for which deprivation of the grace of the sacraments constitutes a justifying reason for general absolution. The reader will have noticed that this expression was introduced in the Roman Instruction of 1944 and has been repeated from then on. How long is "a long time"? Here we have to consult the canonists. The Canon Law Society commentary states that a period of one day could constitute the "long time" of which the canon speaks.[19] Readers may be surprised at this. But if a week is a long time in politics, apparently a day is enough for this in canon law! The commentator writes cryptically that the term is to be understood "relatively." By this he means, presumably, that for a devout Catholic it would be a heavy burden to have to wait a day to receive the grace of the sacraments; and apparently it is the devout who set the standard here.

The second point is that the appropriate judge for approving, in general terms, the conditions permitting general absolution is said in both canon 961 #2 and RP 32 to be the bishop of the diocese, whereas Pastoral Norm no. 5 had in this role the "local ordinary," a term which embraces other diocesan officials in addition to the bishop. In this respect, therefore, RP and the canon law represent a tightening of the discipline.

The third point is that, according to RP 32 and Pastoral Norm no. 5, if a priest is convinced that in the area for which he is responsible there exists a particular need for general absolution apart from the ones established by the bishop, he needs to have recourse in each instance to the local ordinary, and if this is not possible, he must inform him as soon as possible afterwards both of the need and of the fact that he gave absolution. However, canon 961 is silent about what action if any a priest might take if the bishop cannot be contacted; and the provision of RP 40c that in this case responsibility for the decision devolves on the priest has been omitted from the 1983 "particular decree" of the Congregation for Divine Worship to which reference has already been made. This, however, does not mean that the priest is left powerless to act. According to the Canon Law Society commentary, itself based on a response of the Pontifical Commission for the Interpretation of the Code of Canon Law, he may put into effect the principles of moral theology for the appropriate course of action when recourse to proper authority is impossible.[20] It can further be argued that, in the absence of positive guidance from the canon law, the provision of RP 32 and 40c and of Pastoral Norm no. 5, referred to above, would be that course of action.

There is only one provision of RP 31–34 not covered already in our treatment above. This is the statement of RP 31 that "individual, integral confession and absolution remains the only ordinary way for the faithful to reconcile themselves with God and the Church, unless physical or moral impossibility excuses from this kind of confession." This assertion is echoed by canon 960. (The provision of RP 33 concerning the necessity of right dispositions in the penitent has already been dealt with in our discussion of canon 962, which repeats the contents of this paragraph.) RP 31's insistence on individual confession as the sole ordinary means of reconciliation has been taken up by Pope John Paul II as a recurrent theme of his pontificate. Between the Middle Ages and Vatican II it was the sole form in which the sacrament existed; in the conciliar reform it provided the point of departure from which the two new rites were fashioned; and in the present postconciliar period it remains their point of reference. The first rite simply embodies it, the second preserves it intact, and the third remains dependent on it in the sense that grave sins therein absolved must eventually be submitted to it. The statement of RP 31 and canon 960 needs to be interpreted in this light. It by no means constitutes a disparagement of rites two and three.

## *Structure of the Third Rite*

We turn now to the structure of the rite itself. As with the first rite, the introduction to RP gives descriptive instructions for the third rite, in RP 35. However, as these are repeated in chapter 3, RP 60–66, which is devoted to this rite, we need make no further reference to it here. As the third rite has some parts in common with the second (reconciliation of several penitents with individual confession and absolution), for these RP is content to refer the reader to that rite. I now list the various parts of the third rite with references to RP including these second rite references.

The component parts of the third rite are as follows:

1. Introductory rites, including a hymn (optional) (RP 48), greeting, instruction on "the importance and purpose of the celebration and the order of the service" (RP 49), and opening prayer (RP 50).
2. The celebration of the word of God (RP 51), including a homily (RP 52).
3. The specific instruction (either in the course of the homily or after it) on the requisite conditions (as already discussed), and the giving of a penance (RP 60).
4. Examination of conscience (RP 53).
5. General confession. Those wishing to receive absolution are asked to give a sign of penance, for example kneeling or bowing the head (RP 61). The penitents then recite a formula of general confession, such as "I confess to almighty God, etc." This may be

followed by a litany or suitable hymn. RP offers options at nos. 54 and 202–05. The Lord's Prayer is then recited (RP 61).

6. General absolution, given by the presiding priest with hands extended over the penitents (RP 62). Sottocornola adds that other priests present may likewise extend their hands with him (p. 121).

7. A concluding hymn of praise and thanksgiving; blessing and dismissal (RP 63).

We shall now comment on these parts, concentrating on those proper to the third rite. As to the introductory rites, the greeting, in the case of this and the second rite, obviously cannot be personal as in the first rite. RP 49 offers five options of short liturgical greetings for the priest to choose from. The brief instruction on the significance of the celebration and the order of service can be given either by the priest or by another minister. On the significance of the celebration, what is said would differ according as it was the second or the third rite that was being celebrated. In the case of the third rite the significance is that the sacrament is being celebrated in a fully communal way, while in the second rite it would be that communal and personal elements are combined. (In the first rite the significance is that the personal dimension is emphasized, though the communal is still affirmed, through the presence and ministry of the priest, who is the representative of the community.) RP 50 offers six options for the opening prayer, which is preceded by a short period of silence that gives the congregation an opportunity for personal prayer.

The celebration of the word of God, including a homily, is a very important component of the sacrament, as we stressed when treating the first rite (where, however, a discussion replaces the homily). RP offers many options, in nos. 51 and 101–201. There may be three readings, ideally one from the Old Testament, one from the letters of the New Testament, and one from a gospel, the first being followed by a responsorial psalm, and the gospel being preceded by an acclamation. Or there may be two readings, or even just one, in which case it is preferable that it be from a gospel. The homily, as always, should be a reflection arising from the readings, and it should be focused on repentance and conversion in the hearts of the hearers.

If the specific instruction has not been given already in the homily, it should be given immediately after it. For the third rite RP, in no. 60, concentrates on the formation of the necessary dispositions in the penitents. By this is meant that they should be exhorted to repent sincerely of their sins and to be resolved with the help of God's grace both to avoid sin in the future and to repair whatever scandal or harm they may have caused. Without these dispositions the third rite is of no use or benefit to a person. Further, they should be urged to resolve to confess individually within the proper time any grave sins they may have on their conscience. The priest is to explain the rules for this in the instruction. Sottocornola points out (p. 122) that a person who has no intention of confessing their grave sins subsequently demonstrates thereby that they lack the requisite dispositions for the sacrament. On the other hand, he continues, if they intend to confess them when they receive the sacrament but later change their mind, their sins would certainly be forgiven on the first occasion, but they would commit a new sin on the second. And the earlier sins would still have to be confessed. RP 60 ends by saying that following the instruction the priest proposes "some form of satisfaction to be done by all" (my translation), to which individual penitents may add if, and according as, they wish. Clearly, under the circumstances this is the most that the priest can do, and it reveals an inherent limitation of the rite itself. The satisfaction, or "penance" as it is usually called, will normally belong to one of the traditional categories of which RP 18 speaks, "prayer, self-denial, and especially service of one's neighbor and works of mercy." If the sins are subsequently confessed in individual confession, as they must be if they are grave, the priest may then impose a more suitable penance if he judges it opportune to do so.

There follows the examination of conscience (RP 53). It is important that an adequate period of silence (or soft music) be allowed for this, though in addition to the silence the priest or other minister may help by making brief statements (which can be put in question form if desired), or by leading the congregation in a kind of litany focused on the moral and spiritual life and on repentance. Whatever the priest or minister says should be practical, that is, ordered to the particular state of life of the penitents. The examination of conscience is not an exercise in self-laceration; rather it is a sober review of life in the light of God's merciful love and it should lead to renewed repentance and trust in God and ultimately to his praise and glory.

Next comes the general confession (RP 61). This part of the ceremony is well named, as the name stresses the fact that even in the third rite there is a sense in which confession precedes absolution, though the confession is not complete or integral (and hence is called general). The same term is also used for another kind of confession, which people can make if they wish at a turning point in their lives, for example, before marriage, final religious profession, or ordination to the priesthood. In this kind of confession the penitent confesses not just the sins committed since their last confession but in a general way the sins of their whole life. After receiving the sacrament of reconciliation, one always makes a new start in life, but this sense is heightened on the occasion of a general confession, and this explains its relevance to such turning points. These two senses of "general confession" should not be confused. In the context of the third rite it does not denote an individual confession at all. Here its elements consist of the giving of a sign of repentance, about which I shall speak in the next two paragraphs, a communally recited formula such as "I confess to almighty God, etc.," which can be followed by a suitable hymn or a litany, and finally, the common recitation of the Lord's prayer. The suitability of the latter shines forth on even the briefest review of its contents: the focus on the completion of the kingdom of God, on doing God's will, on divine forgiveness and our own readiness to forgive, and on God's help in the future.

We comment now on the sign of repentance. As mentioned in the schema, RP suggests either kneeling or bowing the head. To these Sottocornola adds standing (p. 121), which, however, does not seem appropriate in the context of the United States. James Dallen suggests that the penitents approach the presiding priest and receive from him the imposition of hands, adding that the presider can be helped in this task by other priests taking part.[21] He justifies this participation of other priests by saying, "This is not the rite of reconciliation." But an approximation to the imposition of hands *is* part of the rite of reconciliation. Hence involving other priests in an imposition of hands could create confusion in the minds of the people as to who the actual minister is.

If there is only one priest but many penitents, imposing hands on all of them could take an inordinate amount of time. If there are few penitents, the question arises as to why the priest does not hear their individual confessions. Hence Dallen's suggestion does not seem appropriate. The purpose of giving the sign is to distinguish the penitents clearly from the rest of the congregation. In the light of this, one of the signs suggested by RP, bowing the head, does not seem so suitable, as it is not a particularly clear sign. If I am correct in this, kneeling finishes up as the best option. The penitents continue giving this sign until the absolution is completed. RP, in nos. 35b and 61, mentions that the episcopal conference can determine the sign or a range of choice of signs, but in the United States no such determination has been made, and presiding priests are left free to decide for themselves.

The giving of a sign of repentance is an important action which fulfills two functions. First, distinguishing the penitents in this way indicates that the priest is not absolving the whole world or even, necessarily, the whole congregation; he is absolving only those who wish to be absolved and who have translated this wish into the communal and social, and hence sacramental, forum by giving a clear external sign. The second function of the sign is that those in the congregation who do not wish to receive the sacrament and hence do *not* give the sign thereby represent visibly, with the priest their leader, the community to which the penitents are in the first instance reconciled. They represent the Church, which always, but especially at the celebration of reconciliation, "by charity, by example and by prayer labors for their conversion."[22] With the priest they constitute "the reconciling community" (as Dallen so aptly named his book). However, if everyone in the congregation gives the sign and receives the sacrament, the reconciling community is still represented by the priest, though not as clearly as when a significant portion of the congregation associates itself with him in this. In our brief history of the sacrament in chapter 2 one can see that in the ancient Church the reconciling community was represented by layfolk as well as the bishop and that they exercised this role consciously. The priest would do well to explain this second significance of the sign, as both penitents and the rest of the congregation benefit greatly from an appreciation that those receiving the sacrament are being reconciled not only to the reconciling God, but also to, and by, the reconciling community, in an exercise that represents a function of the coordination of the ordained and the common priesthood.[23]

We now come to the absolution (RP 62). As we have already treated this subject at length in chapter 3, here we shall confine ourselves to an observation about the absolution specific to the third rite, namely general absolution. The penitents are absolved as a group and not individually, and they are addressed as a group. This is not clear in the English, as the same pronoun, "you," can serve as either a singular or a plural; but it is perfectly clear in the Latin, which has distinct pronouns and here uses only the plural, *vos*.[24] Yet each penitent is absolved not from a form of social sin that they might have in common, but from their individual sins, which are unique to each person. In this there appears an anomaly inseparable from the rite.

We shall now make a comparison between what takes place in the third rite and what happens in the offering of the sacrifice of the Mass. This latter issue we considered to some extent already in chapter 2. Here we restrict the discussion to the forgiveness of grave sin. In the offering of the Mass, which we here consider in distinction from the reception of Holy Communion, the grace of reconciliation is available *ex opere operato*, by virtue of the "sacramental sacrifice," to all present, which ultimately means to each person individually, though they are not addressed, either as a group or as individuals. This grace will be effective only for those who allow it to dispose them aright, namely, those who attain perfect contrition, but when it is effective, it operates indirectly, that is, through the penitent's dispositions, that is, *ex opere operantis*.[25]

Here we have a unique feature of this unique sacrament: its grace is offered to all *ex opere operato*, but when it operates in a particular person it does so *ex opere operantis*. This is because in regard to reconciliation it is carried through directly, *ex opere operato*, not by virtue of itself, for in itself it gives no one a personal assurance of forgiveness, but only by virtue of one of its "derivative" sacraments, namely reconciliation, which does give this assurance, and which, therefore, it never supplants. This means that there is no guarantee that in the eucharistic sacrifice reconciliation takes place in any particular instance. Nor, as canon 916 enjoins, are those who believe themselves forgiven in the Eucharist free to receive Holy Communion, unless they have a grave reason to do so. In effect they are in the same situation as those restored to the life of grace through an act of perfect contrition *outside* the celebration of Mass. Under normal circumstances they need to receive absolution before receiving Holy Communion.

Let us now consider what happens in the third rite of reconciliation. Here the grace of reconciliation is not available to the whole congregation as such, nor to every individual in it, but only to those who have designated themselves recipients of the sacrament by giving the sign of repentance. Though the word of forgiveness is addressed to them as a group, each member is thereby absolved of their personal sins, and has an assurance that this is so, since they belong to the group that has been specifically assured by this word. However, the word is effective only for those who are rightly disposed, that is, those with at least imperfect contrition or attrition. (It is presumed that this will be the case with all of them.) As their dispositions have not been able to be adjudicated by the priest, the word of assurance cannot be as strong for them as it is for those who make individual confession. Its effectiveness depends on their really having the dispositions that they claim to have. Of course, it is possible also in individual confession for a person lacking the right dispositions to receive absolution, which in this case too would be ineffective. This means that the assurance of forgiveness can never be iron-clad, but when it is given, it is sure enough for us to be able to rely and act on it. Provided we have done our best (which will always be with the help of God's grace), we can and undoubtedly should have this confidence, leaving it to God to make up for whatever human deficiencies we may have. Hence, unlike those who believe themselves forgiven at Mass, those absolved of grave sin in the third rite are free to approach Holy Communion, though, as we have said many times, they remain obliged to confess their sins in due course.

The final element of the rite is the concluding hymn of praise and thanksgiving and the blessing and dismissal (RP 63, with reference to RP 58 and 59). Not much needs to be said about this. We have here the climax toward which the whole rite has been moving from its inception, the confession of the praise of God on the part of the whole congregation, the *exomologesis* of the Church that provides the ultimate rationale of the rite from start to finish. It sets all that has preceded it in the correct liturgical context of the worship of God. The congregation needs to be reminded of this, so that no one departs before the end of the ceremony unless they have good reason to do so. For reason or reasons that remain unexplained, RP, in nos. 35d and 63, says that the concluding prayer of thanksgiving by the priest, which is prescribed for the second rite in RP 30 and 57, is omitted in the third rite.

## *Reflections on the Third Rite*

We conclude with some reflections on the third rite as a whole. We have already encountered two anomalies exhibited by the rite, the fact that, despite their differing situations, all the penitents are assigned the same work of penance, and the fact that, though each is absolved of their own individual sins, it is the group as such rather than each person individually that is addressed by the word of forgiveness. These anomalies stem in turn from a more basic one, namely that in the third rite it is impossible for the minister to exercise the discretionary judgment enjoined on him in John 20:23.

It cannot be objected here that this text is more likely to be dealing with the decision of admission to, or refusal of, baptism rather than that of the remission or nonremission of postbaptismal sin. We saw in chapter 2 that the invocation of this text by the Council of Trent in relation to penance is accepted by Catholic scholars, even granted the objection just expressed. That is to say, interpreting John 20:23 in regard to penance is admitted as a legitimate application of this text. The reason for this is that as the responsible custodians of the sacraments, the Church's ministers must exercise discretion as to whose sins they remit through their ministry. If at the birth of Christianity this discretion was seen as exercised only at baptism, it did not take long—indeed it occurred within the New Testament period—for the realization to dawn that sin would be an ongoing problem and that therefore the same discretion was called for in dealing with postbaptismal sin as well.

This does not mean that ministers have arbitrary power to decide who shall, and who shall not, receive the sacrament of reconciliation. As I pointed out in chapter 3, the judgment to be exercised here is not arbitrary, nor is it a judgment of approval or condemnation, but rather, out of a pastoral spirit of respect for the sacrament and of concern for the good of the penitent, it is basically a judgment of determining whether the penitent is properly disposed or not. This judgment is still exercised in the case of baptism: adults are not baptized until they prove themselves instructed and committed, nor are infants unless there exists a credible guarantee that they will be raised as members of the Church.

The same judgment must also be exercised in the case of reconciliation, the "second plank after baptism." In the third rite, however, it is not exercised at all. Instead, the penitents' assurance that they are properly disposed, conveyed by their sign of repentance, is accepted without question. It is not surprising that the Church requires a grave necessity to legitimize this procedure. It goes without saying that in the case of grave sin this discretion and judgment will be exercised later, when penitents who had grave sins make their individual confession. If they then show themselves not to have been properly disposed, their earlier absolution according to the third rite will stand revealed as having been of no benefit to them. But nothing can detract from the fact that in this rite the priest absolved them not on the condition that they were properly disposed, but absolutely. We conclude that to absolve without the exercise of discretion is clearly an anomaly inherent in the rite itself, permissible only on account of a proportionately grave reason.

We have been reflecting on certain drawbacks of the third rite. However, the rite also possesses undeniable advantages, and to these we now turn. First, as we saw in chapter 2, as a totally communal experience of reconciliation it embodies, more effectively than the other two rites, the wish of Vatican II that as a result of the prescribed reform the "social and ecclesial character" of the sacrament should be made more evident. This is achieved not just through the suppression of all private elements, but through the fact that the giving of the sign of repentance and the general absolution enable a sense of a "reconciling community" to emerge with a clarity that is simply not possible in the case of a purely private absolution.

Sottocornola mentions another advantage, namely that the postponement of confession until after absolution emphasizes both that confession is not, and that repentance is, the paramount "element" of the sacrament (p. 113). I would like to revise this statement in the following way: the postponement of confession brings home the fact that repentance is more important than confession. (This is how Sottocornola himself puts it when he comes at the subject a second time, on p. 128.) And the same must be said about satisfaction as a result of *its* postponement. These postponements exemplify the statement of RP 6a that "the most important act of the penitent is contrition."

This revision opens the way for observing that the most important element of the sacrament is not one of the acts of the penitent at all, but rather the act of God whereby he extends the grace of forgiveness through the ministry of the priest, namely absolution. It is this grace, which comes to its highest expression in absolution, that has already moved the penitent to repentance in the first place, and that continues to move them through confession and satisfaction. Here, then, we have a further advantage of the third rite: in postponing confession (as well as satisfaction) until after absolution, it reveals the primacy of God's grace over all human acts, including those by which a penitent returns to God in reconciliation. This truth is most evident in the parable of the prodigal son, in Luke 15:11-24. The prodigal, having come to his senses, sets out on the long journey home, composing as he goes the confession he will make on meeting his father. But the father does not wait upon any confession. Seeing his son still a long way off, he hastens to meet him and begins immediately to embrace and kiss him. The son has not had a chance to utter a single word of his carefully rehearsed confession. At the first opportunity he does begin this confession, but he does not get far before the father interrupts him with urgent commands to the servants, "Bring quickly the best robe, and put it on him; and put a ring on his hand, and shoes on his feet; and bring the fatted calf and kill it, and let us eat and make merry; for this my son was dead, and is alive again; he was lost and is found" (vv. 22b-24a).

Here, then, there may well be an additional advantage of the third rite: in extending absolution before confession, far from causing confession to be neglected, it may in some cases actually facilitate it. It has been frequently reported by pastors that people who have been away from the sacrament for a long time and who would like to return to it often cannot face the prospect of going to confession. But, so it is said, an experience of the third rite gives them precisely this confidence. Secure in the knowledge of forgiveness received, and buoyed up by the support extended by the reconciling community in this rite, they no longer find confession the obstacle it had previously appeared to be.[26]

We conclude this treatment of the third rite with the observation that it presents some highly positive and desirable features and at the same time some anomalies that render its celebration legitimate only under conditions of necessity. This is certainly a curious and unusual state of affairs, arising perhaps from a clash of personal and institutional interests.

## The Second Rite

Below we give the component parts of the second rite, following Sottocornola (p. 118) with some modifications. Apart from one reference to the introduction and another to chapter 4 (optional texts), they come from chapter 2 of RP, nos. 48 to 59, "Rite for Reconciliation of Several Penitents with Individual Confession and Absolution."

1. Introductory rites, including, according to circumstances, a hymn, greeting, and introductory prayer (RP 23, 48–50).
2. The celebration of the word of God (RP 51), including a homily (RP 52).
3. Examination of conscience (RP 53).
4. Rite of reconciliation (RP 54–57):
   • general confession of sins (RP 54, see also RP 202–205): the penitents recite a formula of general confession, such as "I confess to almighty God, . . ." which may be followed by a litany or suitable hymn; the Lord's Prayer is then recited;
   • individual confession and absolution (RP 55);
   • proclamation of praise for God's mercy (RP 56).
5. Concluding rite (RP 58–59):
   • blessing (RP 58);
   • dismissal (RP 59).

As with the other two rites, the introduction to RP, in nos. 22 to 30, gives descriptive instructions for the conduct of this rite. From this section I wish to draw attention to three points. First, in no. 22, it is said that "after each person has confessed his sins and received absolution, all praise God together for his wonderful deeds on behalf of the people he has gained for himself through the blood of his Son." In the light of the history of the rite since its introduction, this is a point that needs to be stressed. One of the weaknesses and disappointments of the rite is that when it is carried out in a normal parish congregation, it is well nigh impossible to persuade the people to remain to the end. Our treatment of *exomologesis* (the confession of the praise of the mercy of God) in this book has stressed the fact that it is an important element of the sacrament, providing the ultimate purpose and context for celebrating it at all. If this element is important even in a private, individual celebration, it is much more so in a communal one. But in this rite it is undeniable that when the time comes for the individual confessions, and confessors and penitents gravitate for this purpose to different stations around the church, the momentum of the ceremony quickly ebbs away to zero.

People will stay to make their confession and pray their penance, but then they leave. They cannot face the prospect of remaining in the church with nothing to do (but pray!) for an indeterminate period until all the confessions have been heard. No matter how much the pastor may implore them, they will not stay. The result is that by now the unequal struggle has largely been given up and victory ceded to the people. In most places, to my knowledge, the pastor does not even ask them to stay. He conducts the first part of the service (up to the confessions) according to the rubrics, but at that point he gives up, and the people depart unchallenged after making their confessions. This means that *exomologesis* as an important liturgical element is lost and the ceremony is experienced as truncated in an inappropriate and individualized way.

I am not sure that there is any remedy for this, as it appears to be a weakness inherent in the very concept of a communal service with individual confessions in a parish setting. As we shall see, it can be a different matter if the setting is other than this. My conclusion is that while the second rite may well be the most suitable one for certain other kinds of congregation, it is not well adapted for normal parish use.

The second point comes from RP 24, which provides useful criteria for the selection of the Scripture readings. The following are the kinds of text that this article recommends:

1. those that emphasize conversion;
2. those that speak of reconciliation through the death and resurrection of Christ and the gift of the Holy Spirit;

3. and those that, as a help to the examination of conscience, emphasize God's judgment on good and evil in our lives.

The third point, contained in RP 26, is that, if it be judged suitable, the examination of conscience can replace the homily, provided the former is clearly based on the Scripture passages just read. The fact that RP offers this as a second choice implies that as a general rule a homily will be preferable. However, there may well be occasions when the other possibility is judged more likely to be effective. There is a logical connection between the readings, the homily, and the examination of conscience. Hence to proceed straight from the readings to the examination of conscience is to "streamline." While there will be occasions for this, most congregations will be best served by preserving the integrity of this part of the celebration. Though this is not an argument against doing it, priests will probably find composing an examination of conscience on the basis of determined Scripture readings more challenging and time-consuming than preparing a homily.

The individual parts of the rite as outlined in chapter 2 of RP do not require comment, as they have all been sufficiently expounded already in connection with our treatments of rites one and three. The single exception is the individual confession and absolution described in RP 55. This article has the priest offering "suitable counsel," assigning a penance, and giving absolution in the usual way. But that is all. The reason for this is that anything else he might say, by way of proclamation of praise and dismissal of the penitent, is attended to in the concluding rite when the congregation reassembles. This leads me to add something in this context to what I said on confession and absolution when dealing with the first rite. It is as follows.

If the presiding priest has decided to end the communal celebration at this point, there is normally no great pressure on the confessors and penitents to get through the individual confessions as quickly as possible. This means that abuses are far less likely to occur. But when in the parochial setting, and in the presence of a large congregation and relatively few confessors, the pastor decides to preserve the rite in its integrity and so to reassemble the congregation for the concluding ceremonies, the above-mentioned pressure emerges and is felt by all. In these circumstances the danger is that the integrity of confession is likely to be the victim. The anxiety of the pastor often comes to expression in an admonition to the penitents that they be brief and to the point in their confessions, and in an exhortation to the confessors, beforehand, to give only the most summary of counsel. This already prepares the way for damage to the integrity of the sacrament. But sometimes an outright abuse is enjoined on the penitents, namely, that each is to confess only one sin. We have to say that there is simply no excuse for this: it is nothing less than a serious abuse. But even if nothing is done directly to harm the integrity of confession, the imposition of the need for haste can effectively destroy the serenity that is essential in both penitent and confessor for a fruitful reception of the sacrament by the former.

In the face of such dangers, experienced particularly on occasions such as pilgrimages or major feasts, Sottocornola offers the following advice (remember, this was in 1974):

> On these occasions there are too often few priests available. One must therefore be satisfied with a hurried individual celebration that leaves insufficient time for a serious encounter. It would certainly be more helpful to have a reading of, and a communal meditation on, the word of God in view of a celebration of the sacrament with collective absolution (my trans., p. 124).

And again:

> It should be noted that, speaking of the possibility or necessity of a collective absolution, the Pastoral Norms and the new Rite of Penance always presuppose that it is not possible to have well made individual confessions (RP 31). It is therefore not enough to say, "But still, everyone can go to a confessor and accuse themselves and receive individual absolution; so why not keep to this form?" One should have the concrete possibility of *doing this well*, with the requisite time and peace of mind, and it is precisely this that is absent when penitents in serried file impatiently await their turn (my trans., p. 124).

But this reasoning, which seemed obvious to Sottocornola, the secretary of the commission responsible for RP, has not prevailed.

Restrictive interventions in the meantime by the Roman Curia in regard to the practice of the third rite in various places around the world led James Dallen to observe in 1986, "The Roman reaction seems to indicate the curial view that despite theological consensus and existing regulations [RP and canon law] only physical impossibility excuses from observance of the Tridentine requirement."[27] There existed, however, another factor in the Roman thinking not taken into account in this statement. This we shall explore when we take up the question again toward the end of the chapter. Dallen is correct, however, in seeing the Curia as insisting on a strict observance of its requirements for use of the third rite. It continues today undeviating in the same policy. The official position seems to imply that a hurried celebration of individual confession and absolution such as is criticized by Sottocornola is preferable to a celebration according to the third rite. It would be interesting to know how Rome would react to the now commonplace practice of abbreviating the second rite as described above. Would it insist on the celebration of the rite in its entirety, thereby restoring pressure, however unintentionally, on the quality of the confessions, or would it tolerate the present widespread abbreviation of the rite in the interests of a more fruitful reception of the sacrament by penitents? In the context of large parochial celebrations it seems very difficult adequately to secure both values, that is, the integrity of the liturgy and the quality of confessions, in this rite at the same time.

My own view, therefore, is that the second rite has proved not well suited to the conditions prevailing in the large, understaffed parishes that are rapidly becoming the norm in the Western world. As the number of the clergy continues to decline and more and more parish communities are amalgamated, this situation can only deteriorate further. However, there are other communities in which the second rite not only works well but appears to be ideal. These are religious houses, seminaries, retreat centers, and other places of this kind. In such institutions, in contrast to the usual bustle of a parish church, an atmosphere of peace and recollection prevails, presenting in advance a favorable ambiance for the celebration of this rite. The participants can be involved in the planning of the celebration. There is usually no problem in gathering a sufficient number of confessors, and this ensures that the ceremony does not get bogged down at the point of the individual confessions. Plenty of space is available, if not in the chapel, at least nearby, for confessions to be heard in ideal settings of reverence and privacy. Nor is it necessary for the congregation to remain in the chapel while confessions are being heard. Some will leave it in any case, to go to confession. People will be free to stroll around, go to their rooms, or stay in the chapel, as they wish. The presiding priest will be able, in view of the number of penitents and confessors, to assign a determined time for the congregation to reassemble for the concluding rite. Finally, the congregation will not be tempted to desert the ceremony, as they will be well motivated to return, and would not have anywhere else to go in any case. The sense of frustration that marks the celebration of the second rite in large parishes is replaced in this situation by exhilaration and satisfaction at a communal experience of repentance and forgiveness that has gone well.

While I believe this view of the feasibility of the second rite in large parishes to be widely shared and soundly based, there are, unfortunately, no available statistics to which appeal can be made for a more objective judgment. If there are still some regions where a suitable ratio of confessors to penitents can be secured, so that the ceremony can be conducted in its entirety within a reasonable time in a liturgically correct way, my concerns about it would disappear, and I would be as enthusiastic about it as about its celebration with the special groups discussed above, provided, that is, that it succeeded in drawing significant numbers of parishioners (and not just the stalwart few who support every parish venture). One positive feature that such celebrations would exhibit over the first and third rites is that in bringing together priests from neighboring parishes, they would convey to parishioners a sense of the wider Church beyond the confines of their own parish.

## Penitential Services

RP deals with penitential services in two places, in the introduction, RP 36–37, under the heading "Penitential Celebrations," and in (and as) appendix 2, "Sample Penitential Services."[28] Let us deal with the introduction first. The first two sentences of RP 36 constitute a descriptive definition of penitential services: "Penitential celebrations are gatherings of the people of God to hear the proclamation of God's word. This invites them to conversion and renewal of life and announces our freedom from sin through the death and resurrection of Christ." There are two points that need to be made immediately: first, that penitential services are nonsacramental, that is, they are not simply a new form of the third rite; and second, that they fulfill a different objective from the three sacramental rites, an objective, moreover, that is valid and important in itself. Let us take these points in turn.

When we say that penitential services are nonsacramental, we are denying them the status accruing to the seven sacraments of the Church, and specifically to the sacrament of reconciliation. We do not deny, indeed we affirm, that they are sacramental in a broad sense of the term, in that they mediate grace through ritual. But in this sense every ceremony of the Church—let us say, for example, Benediction of the Blessed Sacrament—is sacramental. The distinction here intended is expressed technically through the expressions *ex opere operato* and *ex opere operantis,* which have already been explained in this chapter. Penitential services function *ex opere operantis,* that is, through the dispositions of those taking part, while the sacrament of reconciliation, in each of its three forms, functions *ex opere operato,* that is, by virtue of the sacramental action itself (we are not hereby suggesting that the dispositions of the participants are irrelevant in a sacramental celebration).

The point needs to be spelled out because, as we shall soon see, some theologians have defended, or at least not ruled out as a possibility, the proposition that penitential services are sacramental *ex opere operato.* In my opinion, RP as it stands is clear enough on this matter, but it must be conceded that it is not as definite as it might have been. Echoing Pastoral Norm no. 10, it simply says, in art. 37, that "care should be taken that the faithful do not confuse these celebrations with the celebration of the sacrament of penance." Moreover, ten years later the report of the International Theological Commission was no more precise when it said, "They [penitential services] must not be placed on the same level as the sacrament of penance, much less replace it."[29] While these statements might suffice for most people, they fail to satisfy some theologians. To do this they would at least have to say explicitly that penitential services are nonsacramental (in my sense of the term), and precisely this they have not done. The reasons for my position will emerge as we deal with this matter.

The second point is that penitential services fulfill a different objective from the three sacramental rites. The latter, while embracing all four parts of the sacrament, focus on the act of reconciliation itself, which takes place in priestly absolution. The former, as the definition of RP 36 makes plain, concerns itself with repentance, without which there can be no reconciliation: the word of God there proclaimed "invites them [those participating] to conversion and renewal of life." Contrition, as RP 6a tells us, is "the most important act of the penitent" in the reception of the sacrament. One purpose, therefore, of penitential services is to prepare people for the subsequent celebration of the sacrament. But in addition to this they have an importance that, while not independent of this purpose, is related to it more remotely, in as much as they inculcate a penitential spirit as an essential element of the Christian life. At a time of crisis not only for the sacrament but even for an awareness of sin, it is fitting that the Church offer liturgical services that help people attain a deeply felt conviction of the reality of sin and of the need for penance in their daily lives. There can be little hope for a recovery of the sacrament without a prior recovery of this profoundly countercultural conviction and practice.

RP 37 lists five purposes of penitential services. The first is the last mentioned one above, namely "to foster the spirit of penance within the Christian community." The second is the one first mentioned above, preparation for subsequent reception of the sacrament. The third is "to help children gradually to form their conscience about sin in human life and about freedom from sin through Christ." This should be seen both catechetically, as a help to the children concerned, and strategically, as an essential step in the realization of the first purpose. In other words, if the virtue of penance is to have its rightful place in the life of the Christian community, a start must be made with children. The fourth purpose, analogous to this, is "to help catechumens during their conversion." It is understood that often, though not necessarily always, the person presiding at these services will be a priest.

The fifth purpose, however, makes no such assumption. Awarded a paragraph of its own, it deals with the ever more common phenomenon of priestless parishes and communities. Where the sacrament cannot be celebrated for lack of a priest, penitential services presided over by religious or laypersons become the most effective available means of preserving the penitential spirit, which, we emphasize, is an essential element of Christian faith.[30]

Let us turn now to the sample penitential services of RP in appendix 2. There is no need for us here to list the various components of these services, as we did for the three sacramental rites, for RP itself does not do this. It is content to say, in paragraph 4, that penitential services follow the same order of service as the second rite, except, of course, that there is no individual confession or absolution. What RP proceeds to do is offer examples of penitential services suited to particular seasons, themes, and classes of people.

We now list the various sorts of sample provided: celebrations for Lent and for Advent; celebrations focusing on sin and conversion, the son returning to the father, and the beatitudes; and celebrations for children, young people, and the sick. In the case of children, these celebrations will be found most helpful during their time of preparation for first confession and Holy Communion, and thereafter they can play a continuing role in fostering a sound moral and spiritual development in the growing child. In the case particularly of children and young people, it will often be desirable that the presider be a religious or lay-person more intimately involved in their day to day lives than a pastor can be. It should be understood, however, that penitential services, like all else that transpires in the parish, should be under the pastor's general supervision.

It is obvious that a good deal of flexibility is allowed in penitential services. Indeed paragraph 2 of the appendix stresses the importance of matching the celebration to the needs of the particular congregation, so that it really will be for each person present an occasion of both enlightenment and repentance. In the same paragraph liturgical commissions (of bishops' conferences[31]) and even individual communities are encouraged to create their own penitential services with this objective in view.

## The Issue of the Sacramentality of Penitential Services

We come now to the question of whether penitential services are sacramental, that is, in the strict sense. Our dialogue partner will be Karl Rahner, in an article published in 1972, the title of which, translated, is "Penitential Services and Individual Confession: Observations on the Roman Decree on the Sacrament of Penance."[32] In this article Rahner argued in favor of sacramentality for penitential services, at least in the sense that it should not be ruled out in advance. The Roman decree referred to in the title was the Pastoral Norms, issued by the Congregation for the Doctrine of the Faith on June 16, 1972. I have two reasons for engaging with this particular article of Rahner: first, to my knowledge it represents the most complete statement of the argument for sacramentality; second, it is referred to frequently in the literature on reconciliation.

In reading Rahner on this matter, however, we should bear in mind that the situation that he was addressing was very different from any that obtains today. His article was an immediate response to the Pastoral Norms, and it was written before the publication of RP. The time at which he wrote was one of widespread liturgical experimentation in regard to reconciliation. The situation was very fluid, lacking the determination eventually brought about by the appearance of RP in 1974. The third rite as we know it did not then exist, though the Pastoral Norms permitted a very restricted celebration of general absolution. There was also no shortage of penitential services, some of which may have been sacramental. James Dallen presents a useful summary account of the events of that time, in which Rahner participated not only as a theologian but as a member of the first committee entrusted with the preparation of RP.[33] However, by the time he wrote the article, this committee had been disbanded and replaced by another, which succeeded in carrying the task through to completion.[34] When, therefore, Rahner spoke about penitential services, we cannot assume that he understood by this term precisely what we today, in dependence on RP, understand. From what he wrote it seems that he had in mind a very particular kind of penitential service, one presided over by a priest, and incorporating a definitive word of forgiveness, which, however, was not couched in the traditional terms of the absolution formula.

How else are we to understand the following statement from the article, which conveys Rahner's principal argument for sacramentality?

> Now when a priest, on the occasion of a penitential service of the repentant community (in the case that we are considering), and in the exercise of his ecclesial-spiritual function in regard to this community, expressly announces in all seriousness the forgiveness of God, which in any case transpires in the depths of the conscience, and when he really intends his words as seriously as they are uttered and as they in any case manifest the certainly vouchsafed grace-event in the public forum of the Church, can he at all prevent his words from being sacramental? I mean, in so far as one said that his words lacked sacramental character because he did not intend, nor was entitled, to utter words that were sacramentally effective, one would, in the concrete situation in which they are nevertheless uttered, rob these words of any serious meaning in a human or Christian sense.[35]

The introduction of RP in 1974 made an enormous difference to the Church's situation in regard to the sacrament of reconciliation, bringing the period of experimentation to an end. Not only did it inaugurate general absolution as a liturgical rite, fixing the formula of absolution (offering a choice of only two of these), but it clearly presented penitential services as nonsacramental and ordered to a different end. In other words, it clarified the distinction, hitherto hazy, between general absolution and a penitential service, though the Pastoral Norms had prepared the way for this.

That penitential services in the sense of RP are nonsacramental can be shown by two arguments. First, the sample services which it provides contain no text capable of interpretation as sacramental. Anyone holding today the view for sacramentality has the onus of pointing out which obligatory text in RP's penitential services expresses the engagement of the Church's ministry of forgiveness. This cannot be done, because there is no such text. This is not to deny that sins are forgiven *in* penitential services. However, they are not forgiven through the service, but through the dispositions of the participants. Penitential services mediate grace not *ex opere operato,* but *ex opere operantis.* The exercise of the ministry of reconciliation, that is, actually to forgive sins in the name of Christ, the Church, and ultimately God, is not the same as an exhortation to repentance or even a prayer for forgiveness.

The second argument is that the penitential services of RP have been so devised as to be able to be administered by a nonordained person. A sacrament effects only what it signifies, and if what it signifies has been so determined that it can be appropriately executed by a layperson, that is, by a person with no claim to act "in the person of Christ" *(in persona Christi)* or "in the person of the Church" *(in persona ecclesiae),* then that rite cannot express the authority to forgive sins. In other words, it cannot be sacramental in the strict sense.

### Further Interaction with Rahner

Thus we have finished with the question of the sacramentality of penitential services after RP. But as interacting with additional statements of Rahner in his article can help us, indirectly (because directly relating to penitential services), toward a deeper appreciation of the sacrament, I propose to devote the remaining pages of this section to engaging in just such an interaction. The first statement of Rahner that I wish to take up in this connection is his observation that penitential services, though adjudged nonsacramental at present, could eventually be recognized as sacramental, as there have been precedents for this sort of thing in the history of the Church.[36] He points to the episcopate, which in the Middle Ages was wrongly thought not to be sacramental, but is now held to be sacramental. However, he says, no harm was suffered in medieval episcopal consecrations (at least on this score), because the Church has never required its ministers to intend to administer precisely a sacrament when performing such rites.

The reader is reminded of my observation in the last section, that by "penitential service" Rahner intended something other than what is meant by that expression today. However, his point is still worth pursuing, because it could also be made by present-day defenders of the proposition that penitential services are sacramental in the strict sense. Rahner's general point is correct here. A minister does not have to intend what the Church *intends;* he only has to intend to *do* what the Church *does.*[37] Thus, in conferring the episcopate, an ordaining bishop does not have to intend to confer the *sacrament* of the episcopate (even though it *is* a sacrament); it suffices that he intend to confer the *office* of the episcopate. In the Middle Ages such a bishop would only need to have had the same intention, though he probably would have *thought* that the episcopate was not a sacrament. In conferring the office, he would in fact have been conferring the sacrament without knowing it. But I would argue that since RP (and hence I am not engaging with Rahner at this point) the case of penitential services is essentially different from this. The argument against the sacramentality of these services is as I have presented it: there is nothing in them to support the idea that the Church's ministry of the forgiveness of sins is there engaged at all. I agree with Rahner that the primary question is not whether penitential services are sacramental. It is whether they express the Church's ministry of forgiveness. But as in RP it is clear enough that they do not, the question of their sacramentality should not now arise.

Another point that Rahner makes is that sacramentality cannot be ruled out for penitential services on the grounds that they embrace the whole congregation. Otherwise, he says, general absolution also would be nonsacramental. Rahner was not to know that RP was about to introduce the requirement that those wishing to be absolved in a ceremony of general absolution should give a prior and public sign of repentance. Hence not all the congregation would be involved, at least in the sense of receiving absolution. This point of Rahner is therefore robbed of its validity. But mentioning it gives me the opportunity to stress the difference between general absolution before RP and general absolution, the third rite, in and after RP. In the history of general absolution given earlier in this chapter, there was never any mention, prior to RP, of the need for those receiving absolution to give a special sign of repentance. This was because (a) general absolution was not at this stage a regular liturgical rite, (b) it was given only at times of the most urgent necessity, whence it could be presumed that (c) all present desired to receive it. Once general absolution became a recognized and regular rite of the Church, however, even though it still required a grave need to legitimize it, the need did not have to be as great as formerly, and the presumption no longer held that all present desired absolution. It therefore became essential to designate those who wished to receive the sacrament. This explains the origin of the sign of repentance.

After RP the situation prevailed, as it still does, that in a celebration of the third rite, those who give the sign receive the sacrament, and those who do not do not receive it. Here, then, is a major difference between penitential services after RP and the third rite: the former embrace the entire congregation, the latter does not (unless everyone in the congregation happens to give the sign of repentance).

Rahner also states that both those who defend and those who criticize the sacramentality of penitential services set out from a flawed conception of sacramentality.[38] His recommendation is that the presider say nothing about the matter. To understand his point here, we need to recall the distinction, made and explained in chapter 2, between the *sacramentum,* the sign, that is, the sacramental rite, *and* the *res,* or *res sacramenti,* or *res tantum,* that which the rite ultimately signifies and effects, which in the sacrament of penance is the grace of reconciliation with God, *and* finally the *res et sacramentum,* situated between the two and called in English the "symbolic reality," which in this case is reconciliation with the Church. Rahner states that defenders and critics alike attach too much importance to the *sacramentum,* at the expense of the *res,* because, as he says, the latter can be realized even without the former.

This is rather a strange point for Rahner to have made. First, it hoists him, as a defender of sacramentality, on his own petard. Second, it is difficult to see how it would be possible to attach too much importance to the *sacramentum* at the expense of the *res* in any case. Because sacraments effect only what they signify, it is entirely reasonable to pay close attention to the *sacramentum,* the signification. The fact that the *res,* grace and forgiveness, is brought about in any case is irrelevant, as it occurs *ex opere operantis.* Without a grave reason, a person thus freed from grave sin would not be free to receive Holy Communion without prior reception of the sacrament, and since there is no sacrament here, they do not receive the *res et sacramentum,* reconciliation with the Church.

With Rahner, I have no desire to underrate the granting of what is in fact the primary effect of the sacrament, grace and forgiveness, when this occurs in a penitential service, but this does not render the question of the sacramentality, or lack thereof, of penitential services unimportant. We should therefore reject as unfounded Rahner's imputation of a flawed or narrow conception of sacramentality to anyone even engaging in a discussion on the sacramentality of the pre-RP penitential services.

In connection with this, Rahner makes the point that the distinction between perfect and imperfect contrition, "contrition" and "attrition," is irrelevant, because in fact attrition will involve the love of God. We met with Rahner's view of this matter in chapter 3, where we dealt with a statement of it published in 1974.[39] Here we have a formulation that dates from two years earlier. This is what it says:

> The distinction, often made in regard to this question in scholastic theology and heard also in the council of Trent, between "perfect" and "imperfect" contrition is basically of no consequence for the question of the certainty of forgiveness, since, when imperfect contrition is truly present, existentially there is no longer any problem about perfect contrition, which supervenes of itself. The reason is that the difficulty about perfect contrition is [precisely] imperfect contrition. Without the latter, no forgiveness at all is possible.[40]

Like the later statement, this could be clearer. So let me offer an interpretation. With attrition, the sinner does not, by virtue of the meaning of this word, therefore "formally," adhere to God by love, but at least they have now, with the help of grace, detached themselves from their sin. But no person lives in a spiritual vacuum. We all live in the positive atmosphere of the constant offer of God's grace. The main challenge to grace is to detach the sinner from their sin. Once that is done, in actual life, that is, "existentially," they are drawn by grace to give themselves to God in love. If I may offer an analogy, the sinner is like a boat in a swiftly flowing stream, but tethered to a mooring (the mooring representing sin). Once freed from the mooring, the boat will not remain stationary in the stream, but will inevitably be drawn by the current toward the sea (God), which exercises a constant attraction on it through the current. In fact, therefore "materially," the sinner detached from sin through attrition will adhere to God in love above all else, that is, in contrition. Materially, the difference between attrition and contrition is purely one of conscious motivation. At the more profound, ontological level they are identical: each presupposes the state of justification and the virtue of charity.

I emphasize that for Rahner the difference between attrition and contrition is *purely* one of conscious motivation. This is clear from his assertion in the 1974 statement that we can be said to have attrition or contrition according as "one or the other may emerge more strongly in our consciousness at a particular time."[41] This must mean that underlying the possibly varying conscious motivations must be a constant *un*conscious motivation common to all variants if in fact they are to represent a single ontological state, namely that of justification. And this latter motivation, if it is to correspond to that state, must in fact be charity.

Allow me now to recall something I said in chapter 3, namely that "we need to bear in mind that the presence of charity is not known through the intensity of emotion felt or avowals uttered (though these are admirable and not to be despised), but through the calm and lived decision to place God and his service at the center of our lives, and even then it can only be prayerfully discerned (as distinct from known directly)." I wish here to endorse these words, though I might have added that charity is not verified by the motivation uppermost in one's conscious mind either. The key word is "discerned": the presence of charity is gleaned from a person's basic attitude and from how they actually live their life. As Jesus said in St. John's Gospel (14:15), "If you love me, you will keep my commandments." I would merely add that in the light of a theology of fundamental option that can perdure in the face of a contrary "imposed necessity" (see ch. 1), this gospel saying is to be interpreted today more in the light of a person's seriousness and perseverance than in that of their statistical success in observing moral precepts. The love of which it speaks is on the unconscious and lived, rather than the conscious, level.

On reflection, I have to say that I find Rahner's account more convincing than that of Aquinas, who had attrition being changed to contrition in the sacrament itself. Aquinas, of course, was considering the matter metaphysically rather than psychologically. Indeed he appears to have discounted the psychological dimension altogether. Had he been thinking psychologically, he would, in the case of a person with attrition only, have been attributing a magical effect to the sacrament, that is, a change in psychological motivation brought about directly by the sacrament. In any case his position is undermined by Rahner's more penetrating and realistic analysis. One thing Aquinas was doing, however, was guaranteeing that, at least in the case of a person with attrition, their sins were forgiven through the sacrament *(ex opere operato)*. For him, a person with perfect contrition was forgiven *(ex opere operantis) before* reception of the sacrament. This raises the question of what, for him, the sacrament actually achieved in the case of such a person. Here we should recall that, unlike his contemporaries, Aquinas did not lose sight of the fact that only the sacrament reconciled the sinner to the Church.

Rahner, however, allows *less* to the sacrament than did Aquinas. He maintains the idea that sin can be forgiven before the sacrament. And since he has attrition as ontologically identical with contrition, for him sins would *in all cases* be forgiven before the sacrament. This is a defect in his theology of which, apparently, he was unaware. It arises, as I have already suggested, from a rationalistic Western preoccupation with pinpointing the exact moment in time when a spiritual event takes place, the prime example of this being the mania (if this is not too strong a word) for determining the very instant of consecration in the Mass. It is far better to view these matters in a theological and human, rather than a naturalistic perspective, and to say that for a Catholic who has committed grave sin, the forgiving grace of God reaches them as a sinner, turns them round by conversion, leads them to confession in the sacrament, is formalized in absolution, and is completed in satisfaction. In this way divine forgiveness is established in the person's life as a whole, in their relationship to self, God, and the neighbor. In this way Rahner's theory of the nature of the relation of attrition and contrition is vindicated in the face of the objection that it presupposes that sin is *always* forgiven prior to the reception of the sacrament, and hence that it *never* allows the sacrament to bestow divine forgiveness *ex opere operato*.

There is, however, another objection against Rahner's theory to which we must attend, namely that it makes excessive demands on the penitent by way of the dispositions to be brought to the sacrament. One way of indicating the *ex opere operato* character of a sacrament is to stress the minimal nature of the contribution that the *subject* makes toward its effectiveness. Thus the Council of Trent required nothing more of the recipient of a sacrament than that they "place no obstacle" in the way of its working.[42] To have demanded anything more would have been to detract from the sacrament itself, and to add what had been subtracted to the dispositions of the recipient, thus rendering its effects at best a mixture of *ex opere operato* and *ex opere operantis*. Reconciliation, however, according to the logic of the council, is an exception to this general law, in that in its case the acts of the penitent enter into the essence of the sacrament. Hence penitents are required, in addition to not placing an obstacle, positively to bring attrition, which in Rahner's theology is ontologically the same as contrition. However, another way of looking at this is to say that the council required nothing more of the recipient in the case of penance than it did in the case of any other sacrament, as remaining attached to one's sin is an obstacle to forgiveness, and attrition is the minimum disposition by which this attachment is undone. Without attrition, therefore, the penitent would be placing an obstacle to the working of the grace of the sacrament.

In one sense, therefore, Rahner demands no more by way of dispositions than did Trent, but in another sense he does demand more: he requires justification, forgiveness, the very object that the sacrament is meant to bring about. This means that in his theology (though I emphasize, he did not appreciate this incongruity himself) the effect of divine forgiveness always takes place prior to the sacrament, hence *ex opere operantis*. The inevitable result of this is to reduce the *ex opere operato* effect of the sacrament simply to reconciliation with the Church. This serious problem is overcome only by adopting, as I have suggested, a theological approach as distinct from a naturalistic one, to the question of "sacramental time."

This opens the way for us to see that the sacrament works *ex opere operato*, a fact evident in any case from the authoritative, "performative" character of the formula of absolution. Hence the terminology of *ex opere operato* remains fully meaningful and relevant in the case of this sacrament as well. Its *ex opere operato* working is verified in the copresence of the three factors listed below. In the absence of any of them, a person's sins may still be forgiven, but this will be *ex opere operantis*, and the sinner will not thereby be reconciled with the Church.

1. The word of forgiveness is an authoritative word. It is neither a wish, nor an exhortation, nor even a prayer for forgiveness. In its structure and content it is a word that claims to forgive sins, and actually does so.
2. This word is uttered by a person who has the authority from God, Christ, and the Church to do so, namely an ordained priest with the faculty to absolve.
3. This word is addressed not to the world or the Church at large, nor even to a particular congregation as such, but ultimately to designated persons who have shown themselves both repentant and desirous of receiving it.

## Conclusion

To conclude, we shall make some comparisons among the three official forms of the sacrament of reconciliation, depending heavily on Sottocornola. Canon 960 states:

> Individual and integral confession and absolution constitute the sole
> ordinary means by which a member of the faithful who is conscious

of grave sin is reconciled with God and with the Church. Physical or moral impossibility alone excuses from such confession, in which case reconciliation may be attained by other means also.[43]

The content of the first sentence of this canon had been officially stated many times before the publication of the Code in 1983, and has been restated many times since. We need to bear it in mind when making comparisons among the three existing rites of the sacrament and when trying to make suggestions conducive to the latter's recovery from its present malaise. Grounded in the Council of Trent, individual confession is a principle firmly established in the first two of the aforesaid rites, and it constitutes the point of reference for the third, in the sense that anyone whose grave sins are forgiven in this way must have recourse to it. This is not to say that the first two rites are inherently superior to the third. Since every celebration of the sacrament of reconciliation takes place in a particular context, it is the context that will decide in each case which is the best form of celebration.

Each rite has its advantages and disadvantages. The first incorporates individual confession and is free of external pressure for haste, but it is weak in its communal dimension, the community being represented only by the priest, its leader. The second also has individual confession, and at the same time is a community celebration. It works well in certain special situations, but in the most important situation of all, namely, that of a large parish community, it is hardly satisfactory, as there its two dimensions, individual and communal, prove extremely difficult to harmonize. In this setting it is also exposed to abuses resulting from the pressure to get through many confessions in a limited time. As a community celebration, the third is ideal, but it suffers from the defect that, lacking individual confession, it does not allow the priest to exercise the discretion required by the gospel (John 20:23). Further, as already stated, a person whose grave sins have been forgiven in this rite is not finished with the process, but is obliged to return for individual confession within a reasonable time.

The "other means of reconciliation" (in the Latin *aliis modis,* which is plural) mentioned in the second sentence of the canon probably refers principally to perfect contrition, which will include at least the implicit desire for the sacrament, and which brings about reconciliation with God, though not with the Church. Secondarily it would refer to the third rite, or to the first or second rite with a less than integral confession (when integrity is impossible). These means effect reconciliation with both God and the Church. Reconciliation with the Church can only be accomplished in an action in which the Church itself is officially involved and, in a sense, takes the initiative, in other words in a sacrament. The fruitful administration of any sacrament of the Church, but especially the Eucharist (as Holy Communion), must at least implicitly signify, and therefore also accomplish, reconciliation with the Church before it can bestow its other benefits. This will presume that the recipient is already reconciled with God through contrition, is impeded from the sacrament of reconciliation, and is in grave need of receiving this other sacrament, whichever one it be. However, the reconciliation with the Church brought about through some other sacrament is incomplete, since it awaits completion in precisely the sacrament of reconciliation, which is never simply supplanted by another, even the Eucharist.

Three times in the course of his article (pp. 101, 114, 128), Sottocornola emphasizes that the two ways, individual and communal, in which reconciliation is offered in the three rites, that is, respectively, individual, individual and communal combined, and communal, should be regarded not as *strictly* alternative to each other, but as alternative only in the sense of complementary. Here is how he puts it in his first statement of this theme (p. 101):

> The presence of two alternative forms of reconciliation (individual and communal) should not be understood as an offer, on the part of the Church, of two entirely equal ways between which one can choose indifferently. Rather, it has to do with two complementary forms, which place the accent respectively on the personal and the communal aspect. It will be the task of a wise pastoral theology to educate the faithful to take advantage of each of these two ways (my trans.).

This means that he regards it as desirable that each of the faithful should discover and experience in their own spiritual life the right balance, for them, of the individual and the communal in their celebration of reconciliation. In this he was most likely reflecting the intentions and wishes of the committee responsible for RP, of which he was the secretary.

However, things did not work out as planned. Individual confession according to the first rite is now greatly neglected, and has in fact been explicitly rejected by many people in the local churches of Europe, North America, and Australia. The second rite, initially welcomed in the parishes, has fallen off in popularity and frequency, and, as mentioned earlier, is rarely celebrated in the complete manner laid down by RP, that is, with the congregation reassembling after the individual confessions. However, it still proves a success with special groups. The third rite, hugely popular wherever and whenever it is celebrated, operates under such severe restrictions from the Holy See that it is now scarcely to be found at all. We shall comment on this state of affairs when it comes time for prognostications for the future in chapter 5.

Sottocornola's formulation of the respective merits of the three rites is of particular interest, especially in regard to the third rite (p. 128):

1. The first [rite] better favors personal conversion, a sense of responsibility in the life of the individual and the community, and a deepening of the spiritual life through dialogue with the priest.
2. The second permits the development of a critical conscience in the community as such, a communal engagement; it favors more a sense of reconciliation among the members, which is a condition of reconciliation with God; it better establishes the balance between personal and communal factors.
3. The third permits a more frequent reception of the sacrament than would otherwise be possible, that is to say, because of the necessity of prior confession people would be inclined not to attend or to attend less often (my trans.).

We endorse without qualification what Sottocornola has here written about the first rite. What he says about the second is also true, provided the celebration works well, which, it must be admitted, it often does not. His statements about the third rite will come as a surprise. The rite that now (because of official restrictions) is scarcely celebrated at all was perceived in 1974 as the one that would be celebrated most often! It is likely that here too Sottocornola echoes the intentions and wishes of the committee responsible for RP. The attitude is to be explained by the balance, referred to earlier, that he desired to see struck by each individual person between the personal and the communal elements of reconciliation.

At a time when the number of clergy was already dwindling, and when, as a result of the reform, personal confession had become more demanding than it had been before, it was envisaged that the majority of people would settle for the third rite as their normal way of receiving the sacrament, with the first received occasionally according to spiritual desire or need and preceded by a more intense period of preparation. The second rite would also be celebrated occasionally, on retreats or in special groups, and in parishes on those comparatively rare occasions when the pastor succeeded in recruiting a sufficient number of confessors from the already overburdened pastors of the neighborhood.

The frequency which Sottocornola anticipated for the celebration of the third rite in the average parish was once a month (see p. 123). He even characterized the history of the sacrament as consisting of three successive stages: the era of penance, the era of confession, and the era of reconciliation (pp. 111–13). The first consisted of the early centuries, when the accent was placed on the period of expiating penance preceding official reconciliation; the second was that introduced by the Irish monks and terminated by the Second Vatican Council, in which personal confession was emphasized; and the third was that inaugurated through the reforms of the council. By postponing the confession of grave sins to a later time, it placed the emphasis firmly on the most important element of the sacrament, that is, on reconciliation with God and the Church. Sottocornola drew attention to the particular significance of the name by which the sacrament was known in each of these eras, "penance" in the first, "confession" in the second, and "reconciliation" in the third (see p. 112).

Sottocornola's analysis of the advantages and disadvantages of each of the rites appears very sound, both theologically and pastorally. From it emerges with logical rigor his principle of complementarity: each of the faithful should be able to find for themselves the right balance in the use of the different rites in their personal experience of the celebration of the sacrament. However, the Church in the West and in some mission countries faces an unprecedented crisis of its ordained priesthood. We may soon be in a situation where the possibility of choice among the rites no longer exists in these places. The first and second rites will become a luxury hardly ever to be enjoyed, and the third will be the only option remaining.

## Notes, Chapter 4

[1] Franco Sottocornola, "Les nouveaux rites de la pénitence," *Questions liturgiques* 55 (1974) 89–136. For this commentary the references will be simple page references.

[2] The way in which the parts are listed here is influenced in some degree by Sottocornola, 114–15.

[3] *Deus Trinitas,* the title by which St. Augustine invokes God in prayer in the concluding sentence of his great work, *De trinitate.*

[4] See Vatican II, Constitution on the Sacred Liturgy *(Sacrosanctum concilium)* nos. 24 and 35 (1), Flannery, 127, 130, and Dogmatic Constitution on Divine Revelation *(Dei verbum)* no. 21, Flannery, 111–12.

[5] See Vatican II, Dogmatic Constitution on the Church *(Lumen gentium)* no. 11, Flannery, 15.

[6] "Decretum quo Variationes in novas editiones Librorum liturgicorum, ad normam Codicis iuris canonici nuper promulgati, introducendae statuuntur," in Xaverius Ochoa, ed., *Leges Ecclesiae post Codicem iuris canonici editae,* vol. 6, Leges annis 1979–1985 editae (Rome: Ediurcla, 1987) n. 4997, cols. 8669–76, at VIII: In Ordinem Paenitentiae, cols. 8673–74.

[7] See the Index of Faculties of the Sacred Consistorial Congregation of December 8, 1939, AAS 31 (1939) 711–12, no. 14.

[8] See the *Dubium* (doubt) solved by the Apostolic Penitentiary in its response of December 10, 1940, in AAS 32 (1940) 571.

[9] See the Instruction of the Apostolic Penitentiary of March 25, 1944, in AAS 36 (1944) 155–56.

[10] Note the comma after the word "necessity" in this quotation. It is present in the original Latin, and is very important, as it indicates that the first "grave and urgent necessity," namely the large number of penitents, is *not* proportionate to the gravity of the divine precept of integrity. The significance of this will soon emerge in the text above.

[11] See C. van der Geest, "Die Generalabsolution in Papua–New Guinea," *Liturgisches Jahrbuch* 21 (1971) 174–76. Van der Geest refers to a response from the Sacred Congregation for the Doctrine of the Faith dated June 17, 1966 (Prot. N. 673/66).

[12] "Normae pastorales circa absolutionem sacramentalem generali modo impertiendam," AAS 64 (1972) 510–14; available in English in Thomas C. O'Brien, trans. and ed., *Documents on the Liturgy* (Collegeville: The Liturgical Press, 1982) 948–51, nos. 3038–51.

[13] See James Dallen, *The Reconciling Community: The Rite of Penance* (New York: Pueblo Publishing Company, 1986) 243, n. 43.

[14] See Canon Law Society of Great Britain and Ireland, *The Code of Canon Law* (London: Collins, 1983) 174–75.

[15] See James A. Coriden, Thomas J. Green, and Donald E. Heintschel, eds., *The Code of Canon Law: A Text and Commentary* (New York: Paulist Press, 1985) 655, col. 2.

[16] This is the sense also of RP 34, though it is not clear from the English translation, which omits the vital word "for" *(enim)* at the beginning of the paragraph's last sentence. Only the inclusion of this word allows the phrase "within a year," which concludes the preceding sentence, to be specific, that is, to answer the question, "Within a year of what?"

[17] "Firma manente obligatione de qua in can. 989, is cui generali absolutione gravia peccata remittuntur, ad confessionem individualem quam primum, occasione

data, accedat, antequam aliam recipiat absolutionem generalem, nisi iusta causa interveniat." See Codex Iuris Canonici (Rome: Libreria Editrice Vaticana, 1983) 172.

[18] See *The Code of Canon Law: A Text and Commentary,* 680, col. 1.

[19] See ibid., 679, col. 1.

[20] See ibid., 678, col. 2; and Pontificia Commissio Codici Iuris Canonici Recognoscendo, *Relatio complectens synthesim animadversionum ab Em. mis. atque Exc. mis. Patribus Commissionis ad ultimum schema Codicis Iuris Canonici Exhibitarum, cum responsionibus a Secretaria et Consultoribus datis* (Rome: Typis Polyglottis Vaticanis, 1981) 228.

[21] See Dallen, *The Reconciling Community,* 340.

[22] Vatican II's Dogmatic Constitution on the Church *(Lumen gentium)* no. 11, Flannery, 15.

[23] See David Coffey, "The Common and the Ordained Priesthood," *Theological Studies* 58 (1997) 209–36.

[24] See *Ordo Paenitentiae,* no. 62.

[25] This expression is the opposite of *ex opere operato,* and denotes an effectiveness resulting not from the "work done," that is, by the sacrament itself, but from grace working through the dispositions of the recipient. As is pointed out in the text, in the case of the sacrament of reconciliation the *ex opere operato* effect also requires positive dispositions (as distinct from a mere negative non-placing of an obstacle, which is all that is required in other sacraments), but this is because in reconciliation the acts of the penitent enter into the essence of the sacrament. Even here, however, the effectiveness comes directly from the sacramental action and not from the dispositions, which still only fulfill the function of conditions (though in this case positive ones), not that of a cause.

[26] This is the finding of C. van der Geest, in "Die Generalabsolution in Papua–New Guinea," 176.

[27] Dallen, *The Reconciling Community,* 246, n. 55.

[28] RP is inconsistent in its terminology here, using "penitential celebrations" in the introduction and "penitential services" in appendix 2. That the two expressions are meant to be synonymous is evident from a comparison with the original Latin, which has the same word, *celebratio* ("celebration"), in both places.

[29] Report of the International Theological Commission, "Penance and Reconciliation," *Origins* 13 (1984) 513–24, at 522, C. II. 3.

[30] Sottocornola states (p. 131) that "when it is impossible to receive the sacrament [in a priestless community], the effect of these celebrations can be equal to that of the sacrament itself: one can therefore obtain God's pardon and be reconciled with him and the Church" (my trans.). I agree that in regard to obtaining God's pardon the effect *can* be the same, but I can see no justification for the unsubstantiated claim that reconciliation takes place with the Church. On the contrary, only a sacrament of the Church can have this effect.

Sottocornola says that those whose grave sins are forgiven in a penitential service under the conditions he stipulates are free to receive Holy Communion. My comment on this is that, in accordance with canon 916, such persons are free to receive Communion only if they have a grave reason to do so. Their mere presence at Mass or a Communion service does not constitute such a reason. I refer the reader to the place in ch. 2 where I rejected Sottocornola's view that a person with grave sin moved to repentance at Mass is *thereby* rendered eligible to receive Communion on that and on subsequent occasions.

[31] See Vatican II's Constitution on the Sacred Liturgy *(Sacrosanctum concilium)* nos. 39 and 22 #2, Flannery, 132 and 126–27.

[32] Karl Rahner, "Bußandacht und Einzelbeichte: Anmerkungen zum römischen Erlass über das Bußsakrament," in *Stimmen der Zeit* 190 (1972) 363–72, at 369–72.

[33] See Dallen, *The Reconciling Community*, 190–93.

[34] For information about the activities of these committees, see ibid., 209–15.

[35] Rahner, "Bußandacht und Einzelbeichte," 370–71; my trans.

[36] See ibid., 370.

[37] See the Council of Trent, Decree on the Sacraments, Dupuis 1321.

[38] See Rahner, "Bußandacht und Einzelbeichte," 370.

[39] Our reference was to his booklet, *Allow Yourself To Be Forgiven: Penance Today*, an English trans. published in 1975. The German original, however, appeared in 1974, as stated above.

[40] Rahner, "Bußandacht und Einzelbeichte," 369; my trans.

[41] Quoted in ch. 3.

[42] See the Council of Trent, Decree on the Sacraments, Dupuis 1316.

[43] *The Code of Canon Law*, 174.

# Chapter Five

# Prognostications

T hus we have arrived at the final topic of this book, prognostications for the future of the sacrament of reconciliation. The question arises: Could Franco Sottocornola's vision, presented in the last chapter, eventually prove right? My opinion is yes, it could. But this opinion must now be argued in detail. One thing we have been able to observe in relation to the development of the third rite out of the previous practice of general absolution is the way that the Roman congregations proceed in the formation of policy and legislation. A response is formulated in regard to some problematic situation, a particular form of words is adopted, and this becomes the norm, the precedent, for related responses in the future. Minute changes are gradually introduced by way of new responses to an ever changing situation. Through this process a continuous line of development is traceable.

General absolution began its history in a setting of emergency and urgency, an association that it retained, even if in mitigated form, when it passed into a regular rite of the Church. Thus, to justify its celebration there needed to be a grave necessity arising from there being too few confessors to hear the confessions of the penitents in a proper manner, coupled with the spiritual harm that they would suffer if deprived of the sacrament for a long time. Once the canonists had informed us that in this context "a long time" meant only one day, many observers were puzzled at Rome's continued refusal to permit the third rite for communal celebrations at Easter and Christmas, when the legal requirements appeared to be amply fulfilled. I have already pointed out that while the aspect of emergency and urgency might have begun to fade at the regularization of the rite, the aspect of requiring a grave need to justify it did not, as there was a *theological* reason for it, namely that the rite did not permit, on the part of the priest, the exercise of the discretion required by the Gospel itself (John 20:23). This discretion could only be exercised on the basis of an integral confession.

The 1944 Instruction of the Apostolic Penitentiary broke important ground in permitting general absolution in situations of grave need outside that of the danger of death (in war). The Pastoral Norms of the Congregation for the Doctrine of the Faith in 1972, and specifically norm 3, carried this further by formulating for the first time the double requirement of too many penitents and not enough confessors on the occasion of a penitential celebration *and* the spiritual harm that would be suffered by the penitents through deprivation of the sacraments for a long time. It is this double requirement that we find in RP, in 1974, and the Code of Canon Law, in 1983.

However, between RP and the Code there were two further important documents from the Faith Congregation, both being responses to the situation in the diocese of Memphis, whose bishop at the time was Carroll T. Dozier. These were a Letter commenting on the Pastoral Norms, dated January 14, 1977, and a Reply to a query on general absolution, dated January 20, 1978.[1] The Letter, commenting on Pastoral Norm no. 3, says, in point no. 2, that "in ordinary circumstances the faithful would be able to provide for their proper reception of the sacrament of penance in the normal way if not during, then before or after the large gatherings mentioned." This was the ground on which the Congregation ruled against Bishop Dozier's permission of the third rite in his diocese. In the judgment of the Congregation, the grave need required by the law was simply not verified in Bishop Dozier's situation, as there was no need for people to be absolved specifically on the occasions of the large gatherings mentioned. In addition to the large number of penitents, in itself a mere fact, there existed no spiritual reason to justify use of the third rite. The people could just as easily have gone to confession beforehand or afterwards. If there was a shortage of priests in Memphis, it was not serious enough to constitute an obstacle to the general availability of the sacrament in the diocese. It appears that the Congregation would not be impressed with the canonical opinion that one day was enough to constitute a "long time."

The Congregation's principle was spelled out further in the Reply of a year later. In point no. 1 the following is said: "The case described does not offer any reason why the faithful could not find other opportunities for confession and holy communion, which are normally offered on a regular basis in their parishes; a reason might be present, for example, where a priest could visit a remote mission station only infrequently." Nothing could be clearer than this. It is also clear that the Congregation would reject, as I myself rejected in chapter 2, the claim of Sottocornola that mere presence at the Eucharist coupled with sincere repentance, on the part of a person in grave sin, constitutes the grave need required to justify reception of Holy Communion.

Against this I argued that the need had to arise from some situation external to the celebration rather than from the celebration itself. The same reasoning is present in this argument as in the Reply of the Congregation. The required deprivation of sacramental grace for a long time arises in situations of an objective shortage of clergy in the region rather than from the subjective situation of the penitent, who in a normal parish might have to wait a few days before being able conveniently to go to confession. I submit that these documents from 1977 and 1978 explain the continued refusal of the Faith Congregation, and of the other Roman congregations, to condone a more general celebration of the third rite. I suggest that it explains the Roman intervention in the Church of Australia in 1998, by which celebration of the third rite was to be reined in,[2] as well as the refusal, in 1999, to allow the Episcopal Conferences of Scotland, Ireland, and England and Wales (three conferences in all) to authorize celebrations of the third rite throughout the United Kingdom and Ireland to mark the advent of the millennium.[3]

Of course, it must be pointed out that once the shortage of clergy reached the point where the presumption on the part of the Congregation of the ready availability of confession in the normal parish no longer held, then its refusal to condone the third rite could no longer be maintained. Perhaps that point has been reached already in certain places in Europe, North America, and Australia. However, it would not be very satisfactory if the third rite became more generally available on these grounds alone, for they are negative. It would be much better for a liturgical development to take place, if it were to take place at all, on the basis of positive grounds, even if negative ones coexisted with them.

Can any positive grounds be envisaged? As we have pointed out many times, the basic theological problem with the third rite is that it prevents the exercise of discretion by the minister of the sacrament. However, if both clergy and people are properly instructed, and if Church legislation is faithfully observed, discretion does come to be exercised in those cases that demand it, namely those of grave sin, when the penitent goes to confession at a later time. This answer goes some way toward solving the problem, but it does not do so completely, since it does not cover the case of the penitent who needs to go later to confession but never has any intention of doing so, even though he or she is well aware of their duty. In such a case the sacrament would be invalid. Not only would it bring no benefit to the penitent, but it would add the sin of sacrilege to the sins they already had.

In permitting a more general practice of the third rite, the Church would take the risk of exposing the sacrament to the danger of invalidity. Should, or may, the Church take such a risk? In reply it has to be acknowledged that even in the case of individual confession it is possible for a penitent lacking the requisite dispositions to be given absolution. This can happen if the priest, with or without his own fault, fails to discern the true condition of the penitent, or if the penitent through some obscure motivation succeeds in deceiving the priest into judging that they are properly disposed. In other words, the Church can only do its human best, and in the end there is no watertight guarantee that the administration of the sacrament will be valid on all occasions, that is, in the first and second rites as well as the third.

The sacraments are for human beings, and human beings are fallible, weak, and, at times, malicious. Some invalid absolutions will inevitably occur. But this is no reason for not dispensing the sacrament. Admittedly, the risk is greater with the third rite than with the first or second, but it could still be a risk worth taking. Just as after the Carolingian compromise the Church learned to trust penitents to supply the prescribed penitential work (another essential part of the sacrament) after absolution, so now perhaps it could learn, in the context of the third rite, to trust those who need to go to confession to do so.

What, then, are the positive values to be secured by taking the risk of making the third rite more readily available? First, it would offer penitents a truly communal experience of the sacrament. Each of the three rites is an official liturgy of the Church, but Vatican II reminds us that "liturgical services are not private functions but are celebrations of the church which is 'the sacrament of unity,' namely, the holy people united and organized under their bishops."[4] The third rite, better and more successfully than the others, brings out this essential property of the liturgy. To the objection that the second rite also does this, it must be answered that this rite is a compromise, and one that succeeds only in particular circumstances, which are not those of the normal Catholic parish.

Second, a more general availability of the third rite would be more likely to promote rather than impede the practice of individual confession. More and more evidence is accumulating that people, especially those who have been away from the sacraments for a long time (I emphasize that I am not using this expression in the canonical sense), and for whom the prospect of confession presents a seemingly insuperable psychological barrier, find that this difficulty melts away once they have been assured, through a celebration of the third rite, that they have been forgiven. For them the confession of sins is readily transformed into *exomologesis*, which includes a joyful confession of the praise of God.

This was the strategy behind the British and Irish plan, vetoed by Rome, to hold nation-wide celebrations of the third rite for the millennium. These were to have taken place on Palm Sunday, and were to have been followed by individual confessions on the Monday, Tuesday, and Wednesday of Holy Week.[5] One thinks again of the parable of the Prodigal Son (Luke 15:11-24), who was forgiven by his loving father before he could express his well rehearsed confession. Third—and here we take up Sottocornola's point—an increased availability of the third rite would emphasize, correctly, that repentance and reconciliation, not confession and satisfaction, are the most important elements of the sacrament. The meaning of the sacrament's new name, reconciliation, would shine forth for all to see. These are the reasons, or some of them, that can be brought forward to justify the claim that the positives outweigh the negatives, that is, that the pastoral advantage to be gained outweighs the risk of occasional invalidity to be suffered if the authorities were to permit a more general availability of the third rite. They may well constitute a spiritual reason, "proportionate to the gravity of the divine precept of integral confession," that would justify this kind of availability.

The fear is sometimes expressed that a more general availability would only inflict further damage on the first two rites, each of which entails individual confession. This seems to be the sentiment behind the statement of Pope John Paul II that "the exceptional use of the third form of celebration must never lead to a lesser regard for, still less an abandonment of, the ordinary forms. . . ."[6] This is a worry that needs to be faced, and which no doubt would be justified in some cases. However, as already pointed out, there now exists a widespread observation on the part of pastors that the opposite more commonly happens, that is, that an increased availability of the third rite actually increases respect for, and practice of, individual confession. As far as many, perhaps most, laypeople are concerned, at least in the anglophone countries, it is not a question of a choice between the first two rites on the one hand and the third rite on the other. Rather, it has become a question of either an increased availability of the third rite or no participation in the sacrament at all.

In my view (and in that of others as well), at the heart of this problem is an inadequate theology of sin. I refer the reader to my comments on this in chapter 1. Here, for the sake of brevity, I wish to quote the article of Gerald Gleeson referred to earlier (in which he acknowledges a debt to my work in this respect). I am convinced that Gleeson here describes the present pastoral situation accurately. Whether he (and I) are correct or not, it is true that no progress can be expected unless official policy take the actual pastoral situation as its point of departure. Gleeson writes:

> A third point of theological tension concerns the theology of sin itself. Magisterial teaching (as reflected in the *Catechism of the Catholic Church*) has been slow to embrace the transition from an act-centred to a person-centred understanding of sin. It is not that individual acts don't matter, they do—precisely because it is in and through one's actions that one's moral character is both formed and expressed. Still, the true significance of one's actions in relation to God is grounded in a variety of *antecedent factors* which determine one's responsibility and guilt because they impact on one's true freedom, even in cases where people may consciously suppose themselves to have "full knowledge and consent."[7]

A little later he continues:

> Most older Catholics today don't believe the teaching about mortal sin they received as children, and rightly so. The tragedy is that neither they, nor younger Catholics, have been introduced to a more mature, and theologically more adequate, understanding of sin and sinfulness. This more adequate theology calls for both a renewed appreciation of the subject matter of sin and a deeper discernment of one's personal guilt and responsibility. This is why the recent experience of many priests and people in Australia is so significant: they have found that a break with ingrained, and immature, patterns of individual confession, along with the educative potential of communal celebrations of reconciliation, are helping to bring about a renewed understanding of sin. . . . For these reasons many believe that the current rejection of sacramental reconciliation in the form of individual confession constitutes a "grave reason" for using the "extraordinary" form of the sacrament which Vatican II has made available to us.[8]

Allow me to make three comments on this. First, the reader will see that Gleeson and I are at one on the theological question. Here I wish to take one step further and say that, while the inadequacy of the current magisterial teaching on sin is not the only problem for the sacrament today, until this teaching undergoes the *aggiornamento* that it can receive at the hands of philosophy, psychology, Scripture, and systematic and moral theology, a recovery from the present malaise cannot be expected. A renewed teaching on sin would have to be followed up with a massive program of reeducation of both clergy and laity, a supreme effort that in order to succeed would need to be based on an accurate assessment of where both groups stand on this matter at present. The second comment is that in my view it is a sounder procedure to argue for a greater availability of the third rite on the basis of positive grounds, as I have done here, than to do so on negative grounds such as are selected by Gleeson. To me his argument, based as it is on the rejection of individual confession, is at best subsidiary. Third, once a person-centered view of sin is adopted, grave sin, though always remaining both a possibility and a fact, will be perceived as far less frequent than hitherto thought.[9] This in itself should help smooth the way toward a greater availability of the third rite.

As we approach our conclusion, I still have a few points to make. First, the fact that RP erected general absolution into an official liturgy of the Church is a fact that hitherto has not exercised the impact that it potentially contains. It means that eventually the third rite could lose the exceptional character that it inherited from the aura of emergency surrounding general absolution. The third rite is not exactly the same as the old general absolution; it is something more and new and different: it is official church liturgy, and as such acquires an air of regularity and normality. To embrace this perspective would require a fundamental change of approach on the part of the Roman Curia or perhaps of a future ecumenical council. Still requiring justification, the third rite may find it in the actual pastoral situation of the Church. Secondly, the tradition of the Church dictates that individual confession must remain the point of reference of whatever other forms exist. This truth must never be lost sight of. Third, if the third rite is to be given a new prominence in the life of the Church, a very important way of preserving individual confession will be to emphasize the benefits of devotional confession. This practice, which has had its critics in the past, is firmly established in the tradition of the Church, can be of enormous help to people desiring advancement in the spiritual life, and in the projected future will retain an important place in the spectrum of penitential practices available and commended in the Church. And fourthly—and lastly—the vision of Sottocornola for the postconciliar renewal of the sacrament of reconciliation might be realized after all!

The future of the sacrament of reconciliation will be decided by the church authorities, the pope and bishops of the world. This future, whatever it may be, will hopefully involve a positive development from the present situation. The possibility that here presents itself is a different and greater role for the third rite. This will at least require that it be made more generally available. But this point itself is contentious at present. Favoring a greater availability we find: the great majority of the people, who are voting with their feet, as they have done before in the history of this sacrament, many theologians, priests and bishops, and now entire national hierarchies. On the other side, standing for the status quo on this issue, is the Roman Curia, with some layfolk, theologians, priests, and bishops. Both sides have legitimate concerns, and it is to be hoped that a negotiated solution will be able to be embraced by both. Eventually pope and bishops will make a decision securing the future, as has been done many times before in the history of the Church. But time presses, for while the Church waits, it witnesses an ever hastening decline of the sacrament. In the meantime theologians should not shrink from saying what they really think. Any honest, informed expression of opinion should be valued by both sides as a contribution to the eventual discernment that, though it will finally be concluded by the pope and bishops alone, will necessarily be a process involving the whole Church, with each member contributing according to his or her lights, lights, let it be remembered, that have been kindled by sacraments other than reconciliation, those, namely, of baptism and confirmation.

## Notes, Chapter 5

[1] These are to be found in Thomas C. O'Brien, trans. and ed., *Documents on the Liturgy* (Collegeville: The Liturgical Press, 1982) 978–79 and 980–81, documents no. 375 and 377, respectively.

² For which see Gerald Gleeson, "The Future of the 'Third Rite' of Reconciliation," *The Australasian Catholic Record* 77 (2000) 20–31. My attention has been drawn to the recent Circular Letter concerning the Integrity of the Sacrament of Penance from Cardinal Jorge Medina Estévez, Prefect of the Congregation for Divine Worship, dated March 20, 2000 (Prot. N. 700/00/L), and at my time of writing not yet officially published. As the Letter acknowledges in its introduction, it was occasioned by this intervention. It does not need to be considered here, as it is professedly nothing more than a restatement of the official position, which has been presented already in these pages.

³ For which see the interview with Archbishop Keith O'Brien of St. Andrews and Edinburgh in *The Tablet* 253 (October 30, 1999) 1481–82.

⁴ The Second Vatican Council's Constitution on the Sacred Liturgy *(Sacrosanctum concilium)* no. 26, Flannery, 128.

⁵ See the interview with Archbishop O'Brien, 1482.

⁶ Pope John Paul II, post-synodal apostolic exhortation Reconciliation and Penance *(Reconciliatio et Paenitentia)* (Washington, D.C.: United States Catholic Conference, 1985) 133. The Pope continues in the same sentence: ". . . nor must it lead to this form being considered an alternative to the other two forms." The Pope is here speaking within the context of the present ecclesiastical legislation. The question being asked today, and being dealt with in this book, is whether a further development is possible, a development that would entail changes to the present legislation.

⁷ Gleeson, "The Future of the Third Rite," 24–25.

⁸ Ibid., 25.

⁹ Rahner argues similarly on p. 368 of "Bußandacht und Einzelbeichte," where he writes, "Guilt, considered grave from a completely human and communal standpoint, but which, in and for itself, at least in its subjective imputability alone, after serious reflection is judged *not* to exclude from the Kingdom of God, is the proper subject of a penitential service, a common confession and a promise of forgiveness on the part of the Church's representative" (my trans.). All the more, then, is the third rite, when also without obligation of later confession, suitable for this purpose. Sottocornola makes a similar point. Without exploring the theology of sin, he remarks that the obligation of subsequent confession will be "occasional and exceptional" ("Les nouveaux rites de la pénitence," p. 113), a statement that could hardly be made on the basis of the present official understanding of grave sin.

# Index